D1001860

MENUS *and* MEMORIES
from PUNJAB

THE HIPPOCRENE COOKBOOK LIBRARY

MENUS *and* MEMORIES
from PUNJAB

New Providence Memorial Library
377 Elkwood Avenue
New Providence, NJ 07974

MEALS TO NOURISH BODY AND SOUL

Veronica "Rani" Sidhu

Hippocrene Books, Inc.
New York

Copyright © 2009 Veronica Sidhu.

All rights reserved.

Book and jacket design by Wanda España/Wee Design Group.

For more information, address:
HIPPOCRENE BOOKS, INC.
171 Madison Avenue
New York, NY 10016
www.hippocrenebooks.com

B+T 29.95 6/10

Library of Congress Cataloging-in-Publication Data

Sidhu, Veronica.
  Menus and memories from Punjab : meals to nourish body and soul / Veronica "Rani" Sidhu.
    p. cm.
  ISBN 978-0-7818-1220-7 (alk. paper)
  ISBN 10: 0-7818-1220-8
  1. Cookery, Indic. 2. Cookery--India--Punjab. I. Title.
  TX724.5.I4S46 2009
  641.5954'552--dc22
                                        2009014764

Printed in the United States of America.

CONTENTS

The Menus

> **Legend**
>
> (VG)   vegan—no dairy, eggs or meat/fish
> (E)   eggs
> (F)   fish or shellfish
> (M)   meat
> (D)   dairy or *ghee*
>
> Note: *The recipe for a dish listed in [brackets] in the menu*
>   *may be found in another menu section of the book.*

Dedication

This book is dedicated to my teachers, courageous women and men who have come from several generations and many professions, cultures, and religions.

Now I look to the next generations of wonderful men and women—my daughters, sons, granddaughters, and grandsons, both spiritual and physical, whom I have been privileged to know, to love, and to teach. From them I continue to learn the true meaning of courage.

"Truth is the highest virtue, but higher still is truthful living."
—Guru Nanak Devji

Three of my culinary masters enjoying their pupil's handiwork—Bebeji, me, cousin Raj, and Auntie Avtar.

ACKNOWLEDGMENTS

I bow in deep gratitude to God and all of my spiritual teachers.

It takes a whole village to raise a child, or as it turns out, to complete this book! Parmpal, my husband, guide, and *"Pattee Parmeshwar,"* deserves credit for being the patient "guinea pig" for all my culinary experiments. Luckily for him I've had some very good teachers, especially his mother, *Bebeji* Jagdish Kaur, who allowed me to observe her for the thirty years that we worked side by side in the kitchen. My husband also soldiered through the past year, taking the beautiful food photographs that add so much to this book. I am very grateful for his support.

Many ladies have taught me in the *gurudwaras* and in their homes, but I will mention only a few. Auntie Surindera K. Dhaliwal has been most helpful and patient as I learned from her so much of the Punjabi culture and cooking. Baldev K. Dhaliwal taught me to make many sweets over the years. Hardarshen Kaur bought the first Sikh history books and translations of prayers that were to become so important to my life and the lives of so many children.

Seven years ago I began to raise money for the Bennett Singh Brand Memorial Playground, and more recently for academic programs for gifted, deserving students, by teaching Indian cooking in my home. The response has been wonderful. Special thanks to the McGinn School parents, to the members of the Jewish Community Center of Scotch Plains, to the Dunellen High secretaries and to many relatives and friends—standouts were Baljeet Sanghera, Kiran Dhaliwal, Judy Steinberg, Gurpreet K. Singh, Carolynn Bridge, Doli K.Sodhi, Elaine Coupe, and our daughters, Raji and her husband David, and Sheila and her husband Jonathan, and our son Paul and his wife Nancy—all scheduled classes for their friends and helped me in the kitchen. And then I began to give the menus titles that sparked memories of stories related to the titles. I also asked women to help me by sending recipes. Several generously did, and I've acknowledged them in the recipe headings.

In addition, the following people were helpful in testing my recipes in their own kitchens: Daljeet K. Sandhu, Ellen Johnson, Melissa Keenan, Surindra K. Dhaliwal, Adina Ziegler, Jaswinder K. Mangat, Karam Singh Kalouria, and our daughter Sheila.

Carolynn Bridge of Bridge Kitchenware now of New Jersey, a professional food stylist and recipe consultant whom I met at one of the fundraisers, was instrumental in providing the encouragement to complete this book and also taught me some basics of foodstyling and photography. She sent me a brochure from the New School in New York City to take a course with Andrew F. Smith, the prolific cookbook editor and teacher. He put me in touch with Hippocrene Books. Wow! What a guy! Thanks, Andy!

The unofficial, but expert editor of my first query letter and proposal, Julie Saltman, also propelled me forward with her suggestions. Arjit Mahal, Tonia and Jasbir Kalouria, Marybeth Connolly, Marilyn Nayar, and Shalinder Singh read some of the vignettes and were kind to comment and give great suggestions.

Thanks also to the "geniuses" at the Mac Store—especially Tom, Danny Vasquez, and Nick Saleeba for helping my husband and me not only to take better photos, but also to learn to edit them. The talented Meghan K. Dhaliwal, a high school student at the time, took some of the first, most beautiful photos.

And to the folks at Hippocrene Books, especially Priti Chitnis Gress, Barbara Keane-Pigeon, and designer Wanda España. Thanks for having faith in me and seeing this project through. It was great fun and my gratitude is profound.

Now, to you, dear readers and cooks, my husband and I thank you in advance for your support of this book, since the author's proceeds will be used to further enhance community projects here and in India. Find out more at http://www.ranisrecipes.com.

FOREWORD

A song in the Rodgers & Hammerstein musical *The King and I* proclaims: "If you become a teacher, by your students you'll be taught." This cookbook is proof of this couplet. Veronica Sidhu attended my class at the New School University in Manhattan on how to publish a cookbook. Within six months, she had written and submitted a proposal, negotiated a contract, completed the manuscript, developed a marketing plan, and finished the work for publication. I don't know if this is a world record for the speed with which a cookbook has been completed, but it is amazing.

And it wasn't just the speed of mastering the mechanics and art of publishing a cookbook that was surprising. Just as astonishing was the content of the cookbook. Of the tens of thousands of recipes that are published each year in the United States, the vast majority are derivative—meaning they are borrowed with minor changes from previously published cookbooks and are usually presented without attribution. In the case of this book, borrowing from published sources would have been difficult, simply because there has never been a cookbook published on Punjabi food in the United States—and only a couple have been published in England and India. For this work, Mrs. Sidhu has dipped into her family's and friend's recipes, and in so doing, she has opened the door to rich and fascinating culinary traditions.

This is not to say that non-Punjabis will be surprised by all the recipes in this cookbook. Punjabis have been immigrating to America for sixty years and many have opened restaurants. Many traditional foods served in Indian restaurants, such as tandoori chicken, naan, roti, daal, and curried vegetables, are also part of Punjabi culinary traditions.

For those who don't know history, the Punjab was once one of British-controlled India's largest and most productive provinces. It extended from the Himalayan Mountains in the north and east to much of what is western Pakistan today. Punjab's capital was Lahore, but the province included the Golden Temple at Amritsar, the center of the Sikh religion, and extended to Delhi, India's capital. With independence in 1947, the Punjab was partitioned based upon religion. The western part, which was mainly Muslim, ended up in the new nation of Pakistan, while the eastern portion, which was mainly Hindu and Sikh, became part of the new nation of India. The Indian portion of the Punjab was subsequently divided into four parts, one of which is the Indian state of the Punjab.

India's Punjab is home to many religious groups, including Jains, Christians, Muslims, and Buddhists, but the majority of the population are Sikhs. This cookbook draws largely on Sikh culinary traditions, although it includes many recipes common to all Punjabis. Mrs. Sidhu has dipped into—and helped preserve—a rich culinary tradition that extends back hundreds of years. My congratulations to her and to Hippocrene Books for helping save these culinary treasures and making them available for all to sample and savor.

Enjoy!

Andrew F. Smith

Food writer and historian, Editor of *The Oxford Companion to American Food and Drink*

PREFACE

With a Little Personal and Community History

Bebeji surrounded by admirers, including nephew Balvinder giving her a hug.

Your life is busy! Making tasty and wholesome food for a family is challenging and it means a commitment. Some would say it is a sacred duty.

Everyone should have a good mentor in the kitchen, and I was extremely lucky to have many, especially my mother-in-law, Jagdish Kaur, who was from the north Indian state of Punjab. We cooked side-by-side, a collaboration that would continue for thirty years. We called her *Bebeji* (mother), as did the entire congregation that formed around her. An unusually strong woman, deeply spiritual, she went from being veiled from head-to-toe, rarely leaving her husband's compound, to traveling alone across continents. She was so revered that hundreds came from all over the country to pay their respects at her funeral. My wish is to pass *Bebeji's* knowledge on to you. She truly loved all as her sons and daughters, no matter of what country, color, or religion. The stories we shared are the basis for the memories that I hope will entertain you as you peruse the book. This book is our gift to you!

My mother-in-law and I managed to prepare a fresh vegetable, lentil, and bread every day for the family. It was simple food for the most part. In the early days we had very few spices to choose from, yet the food was delicious and Punjabi. Neither did we have the more exotic (to Americans) vegetables. Now, with so many Asian markets in the U.S., especially in the metro areas, it is easier to find most ingredients. Luckily for the cook today there are a variety of foods and spices, including commercially prepared products in the supermarket in all seasons. Also Web sites have made it so much easier to find unusual ingredients—even if you live in a rural area. At the end of this book, you will find a section on how to obtain what you need.

Dishes made from scratch do take extra planning and time, but they are more delicious and healthful. If you love Indian food and want to prepare an entire meal for a party of family and friends, this is the book. Over 150 recipes have been tested in home kitchens and are organized around twenty-two menus. They are clearly written and use a mix of modern and traditional techniques. As a former Girl Scout and Girl Scout leader, I know how empowering it is to "Be Prepared!" and have included a section in each menu to help "newbies" and those of you with busy schedules organize successfully. Follow along confidently. You will produce delicious and satisfying Punjabi-style meals. Or simply choose to make a single recipe. As a working mother myself, I found that when going to the trouble of cooking from scratch, I enjoyed having some leftovers to serve on another, even busier, day; so each recipe usually provides eight servings.

Our grandson, Bennett Singh, on the playground he loved.

Life takes many twists and turns and our lives were no exception. This cookbook was born from tragedy. In 2002, our grandson Bennett Singh, who was not quite five, died suddenly from what we would later discover to be a rare immune disorder, CGD. A friend suggested to my daughter that a new playground where our kids went to elementary school would be a fine memorial to him. We thought so too, and threw ourselves into it at the same time that we all went into grief counseling.

Raising funds by teaching Indian cooking would be a good discipline for me. I desperately needed some glue to hold my body and mind together while my soul tried not to fall into the ever-present pit of grief. I had not written down any recipes in thirty years of cooking, so I began to standardize them for a class of six plus my husband and myself. It took me several months to get five menus together with recipes and then I taught all five consecutively in one week in my own kitchen. (How do chefs do it!?)

Looking back, however, you could say cooking was in my blood. I always managed to be in charge of the meals wherever I was—except in the convent of the missionary sisters Servants of the Holy Spirit that I joined at age fourteen. The food was hearty German and Dutch fare, made from ingredients grown on the farm right there in Techny outside of Chicago, and cooked by the nuns themselves. It was usually delicious, but I did dread the boiled eggs made by the novices because they were usually raw inside. We were expected to eat them anyway. I hoped I would do better when it was my turn.

A back injury sustained in a dive before I joined the convent eventually sidelined me from the formal religious life, but there was much work in store for me in another religion. We were one of only a handful of families who held religious gatherings in our homes and in the Knights of Columbus hall around the corner from us. These families would organize the first Sikh community in New Jersey and the first *gurudwara* (temple). During the subsequent thirty years, I not only learned the Punjabi language, but also was taught a variety of dishes from other Punjabi women while we prepared food in large quantities for the free community meal almost every Sunday. I also learned to cook meals quickly and efficiently for the hundreds of guests we would entertain over the years.

Educating children was dear to my heart as Director of Counseling for a public high school and a teacher of a course for twenty years in our Sikh temple. I called it *Living Sikh Religion and History* and it was developed from books and from reading the wonderful Sikh scriptures. With Mrs. Surinder Kaur Puar teaching Punjabi and Shabad Kirtan (sacred music) and Auntie Surindera Kaur Dhaliwal teaching the smallest children, we founded the first Sikh children's program in New Jersey.

Harbhajan Singh Nayar with Uncle Gurmit Singh Dhaliwal chose the land and first building for the Gurudwara Bridgewater. It was a private home that had been converted into a Unitarian Church and now would be a Sikh temple. My husband volunteered on the working committees and with Arjit Singh Mahal and Harbhajan Singh Braich in the lead with the other dedicated members, drafted the first historic constitution. Raising funds for the first *gurudwara* (Sikh temple) building was a huge job, and because the congregation was so small, it was a distinct leap of faith. My husband was honored to be elected president when the first hall was built. It was a very busy life, even during the summer when we worked on the first camps for Sikh children in New Jersey. Over the years many wonderful volunteers joined us—Bhupinder Singh Sran, Tejinder Singh Jassal, and later, Gurparkash Singh, and Navjot Kaur. Many more *sewadars* stand out in my mind for their service. It was a privilege to serve with them.

Food brings people together, whether in the home or the temple. Use this book as a magnet to lure your family and friends into the heart of your kitchen where they will feel the love you pour into the food you serve. Our home, wherever we made it, was filled to the brim. Hospitality was in our blood and we enjoyed serving our guests who came from all over the world—India, Japan, Mexico, Canada, and South America. We had great and glorious times together! It is my fondest hope that your friends and family will gather around you. May you have great success and I would love to hear from you. Please contact me through my Web site at http://www.ranisrecipes.com to learn new recipes and the progress of this fundraising project. All of the author's profits will be donated.

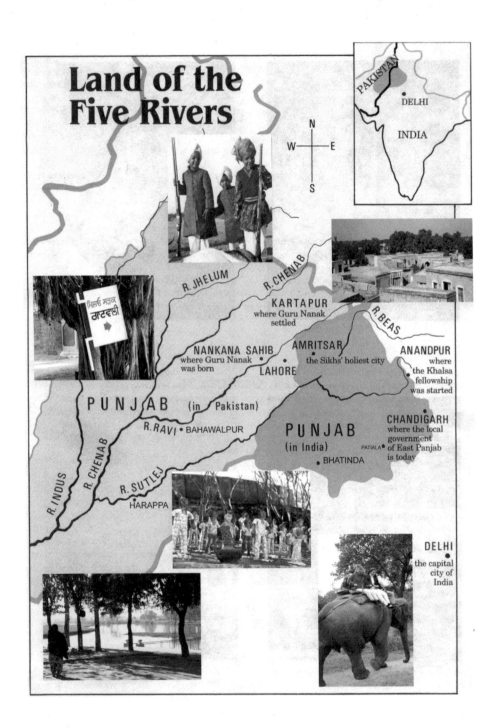

Land of the Five Rivers

N W E S

PAKISTAN
DELHI
INDIA

R. JHELUM

R. CHENAB

KARTAPUR
where Guru Nanak
settled

R. BEAS

NANKANA SAHIB
where Guru Nanak
was born

AMRITSAR
the Sikhs' holiest city

ANANDPUR
where
the Khalsa
fellowship
was started

LAHORE

PUNJAB (in Pakistan)

R. RAVI • BAHAWALPUR

CHANDIGARH
where the local
government
of East Panjab
is today

PUNJAB
(in India)

PATIALA •

• BHATINDA

R. INDUS

R. CHENAB

R. SUTLEJ
• HARAPPA

DELHI
•
the capital
city of
India

INTRODUCTION

A Little about Punjab, Punjabi Cuisine, and the Punjabi Language

Whole wheat, legumes, greens, and milk products are the four sturdy legs of the Punjabi table. Add the fabulous tandoori specialties and it is no wonder that Punjabi food is a favorite around the world. Isn't it exciting to know that you will now produce those wonderful dishes you have tasted in grandma *Naniji's* kitchen, or in your favorite Indian restaurant? Those restaurant dishes most likely had their origin in the north Indian state of Punjab. They have been imitated all over the world because, quite frankly, Punjab has one of the great cuisines of the world. This is not by accident. Punjab was the crossroads and melting pot of many cultures and cuisines for thousands of years. Scythians, Greeks, Turks, and Moghuls, all left their culinary footprints. The best of the best have survived.

Historically Punjab is a large area that straddles both India and Pakistan with a civilization that dates back 5,000 years to the Harrapans. Several principalities in India encompassed much of the plains of the five rivers that enrich the fertile soil from the Himalayan foothills bordering Jammu and Kashmir to the Khyber Pass in the west. The Land of Five Rivers was divided several times, the first in 1947 during the horrors of the Partition of India, the greatest forced migration of human beings on the planet. On the Indian side, Punjab was again divided when part was designated the state of Haryana in the south to Delhi, and part in the hills of the northeast was turned into the state of Himachal Pradesh. Today, approximately 25 percent of Pakistanis are Punjabis, while under about 3 percent of the total Indian population remain technically Punjabi.

Learning the art of cooking Punjabi food and creating memorable meals, like learning most great cuisines, may take years. Learning to balance and enhance a rainbow of colors, tastes, and textures while using a variety of cooking techniques—wet (curry/*thurry*), dry (stir-fry, *bhuna*), baked/steamed (*dum puhkt*), and the famously grilled (*tandoor*)—could be a long process if left on your own. Additionally, a successful, memorable Punjabi meal has several "textures"—wet, dry, creamy, and crunchy. But with this book, you no longer will have to guess about how to reproduce the taste of Punjabi foods you love or how to combine them. In these menus you will find tried-and-true hits of both *desi* (native) Punjabis and Americans. With this book, you will begin to cook like a *Desi Punjaban*!

The spellings of Punjabi dishes one finds on restaurant menus are only approximations. There is no standard spelling for Punjabi words in English, nor even a single alphabet. *Gurmukhi* is the script of Punjabi, developed by the Sikh teachers to help the people learn to read and write their spoken language. But Punjabi may also be written in the Arabic script like *Urdu*, or in *Devangari*, the script of Hindi. When one of my American friends pronounced the popular milk drink like the name of the famous movie dog because it is usually spelled *lassi* on menus, I knew I had to use knowledge gained from a linguistics course to give English speakers a better grasp of the sounds. For example, in my friend's case, she said "*lassie*," when it is really pronounced "*lussee*" with a short U sound. So in this book I will spell the recipe names the way the words sound in English—approximately!

Why approximately? Because there are sounds in Punjabi that do not occur in English and vice versa. For example, there are four different "t" sounds and four different "d" sounds, **none** of which match the "t" and "d" spoken in English. There is also a letter in Punjabi that is not found in English but whose sound approximates the English "rd" sound. Most transliterations, however, write this sound as plain "r." Unrefined sugar is usually written "*gur*" in transliterations. But that is **not** the "r" of English. The sound in Punjabi is rolled on the tongue and is more akin to the English "rd" so that is how I have written it.

Hindi terms are given in the glossary for some items that are labeled that way in most markets. For example, *gurd* is also known as *jaggery* in Hindi. In addition, there are variations in the manner of speaking from the urban or sophisticated and schooled populations to the rustic villagers. And each region has its own typical dialect and vocabulary! The Punjabi language I have used in this book was learned from my mother-in-law who was raised in a village in the Bhatinda District. Please pardon me if I sound rustic (some people think it is charming).

Social standing, wealth, and the difference among villagers, city dwellers, and residents of the palaces determine the sophistication of the palate and even the manner in which meals are served. The typical Punjabi meal (with no British influence) is served all at once on a brass tray called a *thali*. Small dishes called *cowlees* hold the wet preparations, like a *thurree* of lentils. The bread, rice, sweet, or fried tidbit is place directly on the tray. Kids of any age could eat dessert first, no one would mind! In this book, however, with few exceptions, I have divided the meal into American-style courses—an appetizer, the main dish with sides, and the dessert. The appetizer may also be served with tea in the afternoon as it would be in the Punjab. If a fresh salad is not part of the menu you are planning, I would suggest doing what the Punjabis do and cut up some fresh tomatoes and onions with a few slices of lemon. But in the end, it is your choice when and how you make and serve these recipes and meals.

How do you eat like a Punjabi? Well that again depends on how much European influence is in your family. In the village, one ate from the *cowlees* by tearing off a piece of bread with the right hand, making a little scoop of it, and then using it to pick up a small amount of vegetable, meat, or lentils. A fresh, hot bread would be served as soon as the prior one finished until all the *cowlees* were empty. Dishes are rarely, if ever, mixed together on the *thali*.

For a quick meal, try practicing with the following recipe. Buy some pita bread or *naan* and serve plain yogurt in a separate *cowlee*. After this basic recipe are some other recipes you will be referring to again and again.

Learning Basic Punjabi Cooking—A Recipe

The Punjabi trinity of aromatics with dried lentil balls and red chiles in the foreground.

To give any meat or vegetable that Punjabi flavor, you need to learn the basic technique used in most Punjabi recipes and six ingredients:

- The *tardka* or tempering technique
- The trio of aromatics—*Onions, Garlic, and Ginger*
- The trio of spices—*Turmeric, Cumin, and Coriander Seeds*

By cooking and stirring (sautéing) the aromatics and the spices in some oil until they are golden brown, you bring out their flavors. Sometimes chopped tomato or a chile pepper is added to this *tardka* or "tempering" before it is poured over lentils or before vegetables and/or meat are added.

The *tardka* is sometimes made at the beginning of a dish and then the meat or vegetables are added using the *bhuna* or stir-fry method. Most often no water is added. Sometimes the wok, or *kardhai* in Punjabi, will be covered for a short time to bring some moisture and so that larger pieces will finish cooking.

Or in the case of beans and lentils, for example, the food is boiled or simmered in water—stewed, so to speak. And then the *tardka* is added at the end of a dish so that there is a concentrated taste, almost a layered effect, as when the *tardka* is poured over a *thurree*, also pronounced "curry." This is a preparation to which water is added to make a dish with some sauce.

Traditional kitchen utensils, several of which are used for grinding spices and grains.

A Basic Punjabi Recipe for Four

3 tablespoons canola oil

1 medium onion, chopped

1 large clove garlic, minced

1-inch piece ginger, minced or grated

$^{1}/_{2}$ teaspoon ground turmeric

$^{1}/_{2}$ teaspoon whole or crushed cumin seeds

$^{1}/_{2}$ teaspoon crushed or ground coriander seeds

Any combination of fresh or frozen vegetables and/or cubed or ground fresh meat*

$^{1}/_{2}$ to 1 teaspoon salt, or to taste

To make *tardka:* Heat a sauté pan or wok and then add the oil. When hot, add the onion and sauté until translucent. Add the minced garlic and then the ginger. When they are starting to brown add the turmeric, stir for about 10 seconds. Add the cumin seeds and coriander seeds. Stir for 10 seconds.

Add any vegetables or meat and salt. To cook wet, add a little water to make a sauce and cover the pot. Simmer over low heat until cooked. Or for a dry dish, cut the pieces of vegetables or meat uniformly and stir-fry them uncovered. Good job!

*You need about 3 cups cubed or ground meat; 5 cups zucchini; or 6 to 8 cups packed fresh, watery vegetables like spinach that reduce when cooked.

PUNJABI FINISHING SPICE MIXTURE

Garam Masala   *vegan*

This Punjabi-style spice mixture is most often used sprinkled on a dish after it is cooked to add aroma. I used a commercial, pre-ground brand until my friend Baldev bought me a spice grinder and I realized how much better fresh, toasted, then ground spices could taste. The Indian market carries prepackaged cellophane bags of this mixture of whole spices (in somewhat different proportions) that may also be toasted and ground.

YIELD: APPROXIMATELY ½ CUP

¼ cup black cardamom pods (*buddi ilaichi*)

2 tablespoons whole coriander seeds

¼ teaspoon whole cloves

2½ teaspoons whole cumin seeds*

⅛ of a whole nutmeg

1 cinnamon stick, broken up

2½ teaspoons green cardamom seeds, removed from pod**

4 teaspoons whole black peppercorns

2 bay or cassia leaves

It is optional to separate the seeds of the black cardamoms from the pods: fold the pods into a clean towel and smash them with a rolling pin. Open the pods, one at a time, over a small bowl. Save only the black seeds and discard any that are gray along with the pods. You should have about 1½ tablespoons of seeds.**

Heat all the ingredients in a dry skillet over medium heat for about 3 minutes or until fragrant and lightly toasted. Keep tossing/stirring them so they do not burn! Cool and then grind together. Store in a tightly covered jar away from heat and light.

The whole spices used in garam masala.

* Use black cumin called *shah zeera* if you have it, but ordinary white will do. If using black, toast it separately, it is much more delicate and more likely to burn than the other ingredients.

**Green cardamom seeds can be found in the Indian market without the husks, but not the black.

4

PUNJABI SPICE MIXTURE FOR SALADS AND KEBABS

vegan   Chaat Masala

Sprinkle this addictive mixture on any kebab, raita, or even fried potatoes, chips, or corn on the cob. It is a blend of sweet, sour, salty, and slightly funky (from the black salt) that adds a fresh flavor to almost everything. Adjust the proportion of cayenne pepper in this recipe according to your family's preference for heat.

Toast the cumin seeds and peppercorns lightly in a small dry skillet and grind in a spice or coffee grinder. Mix with remaining ingredients and store in a tightly closed container.

YIELD: APPROXIMATELY 15 TEASPOONS

4 teaspoons whole cumin seeds

1 teaspoon black peppercorns

2 tablespoons green mango powder

½ teaspoon cayenne pepper

¾ teaspoon ground black salt

1 teaspoon salt

1 tablespoon dried mint, crushed (*optional*)

HUNG YOGURT

Gardee Dehin   *dairy*

Thick or Greek-style yogurt is easy to prepare and is much better than regular yogurt for making marinades because it clings to the preparation rather than running off into the bowl.

YIELD: 2 CUPS

4 cups (32 ounces) plain yogurt

Line a colander with a clean, thin cotton cloth or several layers of cheesecloth. Dump the yogurt into the cloth and drain over a bowl for 3 to 4 hours to catch the two cups of whey. (The whey adds protein if used as the liquid in lentil or vegetable preparations.) Refrigerate the drained yogurt and use in any recipe calling for hung or thick yogurt. Or add orange marmalade or honey and use as a dip for fruit.

Girls of our village on their way to the fields with breads and yogurt for the workers.

CLARIFIED BUTTER

dairy

*"There are a hundred uncles, but only one father.
There are a hundred medicines, but only one ghee!"*

— *Punjabi rhyme*

Quick method: Microwave 1 pound of unsalted butter in a deep dish for 3 to 5 minutes at 30 power. Remove the foam from the top and carefully pour as much of the clear *ghee* as possible into a container minus the milky residue that remains at the bottom. Strain the remainder through a fine mesh or towel into another bowl several times before adding to the container of clear *ghee*. (Use the milky residue for vegetables or on *rotees*, or discard.)

Slow method: In a small saucepan, heat 1 pound of unsalted butter at a very low temperature for 45 minutes, until milk solids are slightly brown. Strain through a fine mesh or towel. This truly clarified butter need not be refrigerated.

Note: European-style butter has fewer milk solids and water than American-style. Although it costs more, it makes superior *ghee*. A butter from Canada, Desi Mukkhan®, has almost no milk solids either.

YIELD: ONE POUND OF UNSALTED BUTTER YIELDS 1 CUP OR MORE OF *GHEE*.

FIRST THINGS FIRST!

Five Basic Principles for Success

Before you begin, it is important to understand the following five basic principles for success:

1. **Practice makes it easy.** In the preparation of Indian food, several techniques are used with many ingredients, but they are straightforward and easy to master. With very little practice, the basics will be learned quickly and you will be making your favorite dishes without using a recipe. Try the Basic Punjabi recipe (page 3) if you are new to Indian food or just want to learn how to make your own variations.

2. **Follow your own taste.** In Punjab, if you were to dine at a neighbor's house, you may find the same dish you ate last night in your home looking and tasting very differently because of the emphasis your neighbor put on another spice, the amount of liquid, or the size of the pieces. Also the "heat" of the dish may change drastically with the addition or subtraction of cayenne pepper, black pepper, or ginger, and with the heat of the variety of chile peppers used in the dish. **The recipes in this book are mild to only moderately spicy. But you may add more spice or heat, if you like.**

    Salt and sugar are ingredients that are used at the discretion of the cook. It is better to use less to prevent high blood pressure/diabetes. Add more only after tasting your dish and then make it the way you and your family enjoy it. I follow my mother-in-law's way of spicing, salting, and sweetening. No one spice dominates.

    If you like more *ghee*, add it. Chop or grind the onions for a different consistency. Add more or less water, some yogurt perhaps. Are you getting the picture?

3. **You don't have to make the entire meal. Nor do you have to follow the organizational plan—it is only a guide!** In fact, it is better to practice one or two recipes at a time, especially if you are new to flatbreads. Use the index at the back of this book to choose individual recipes from the categories listed. The recipes usually produce eight half-cup servings unless otherwise noted. But most of the recipes can easily be halved.

    If you do make a single recipe, please note that the yield for the recipes is based loosely on a dietician's recommended serving size. Some people may eat more than one serving. On the other hand, remember that if you are making the entire menu, people who normally take two helpings at a simple meal, may take only one serving of everything when there are six dishes.

4. **Share the work. Share the fun. Share the expense.** Form a group of cooks who would like to learn to cook Indian food. Buy your spices in the larger and much less expensive packages in the Indian store and save money by dividing them—and the cost.

    Good planning and enlisting the help of family and friends is another key to success. Ask your friends or family members to each make one of the dishes at home. And if all of you have the same cookbook, it becomes easy and fun to plan the menu over the phone. It becomes a relaxed party when all pitch in to cut the salad while someone else rolls out the breads and another sets the table. Everyone can help clean up!

5. Be Safe. "*Huth dho lo*" ("Wash your hands") was one of the first phrases I learned in Punjabi from my mother-in-law. Wash your hands with soap and water before beginning and frequently throughout the prep period—and have your helpers do the same. This is especially true when handling raw meat. Don't forget to wash cutting boards and knives frequently during the prep as well. Certainly don't use the board you used to cut meat for anything else unless washed with hot, soapy water and a good brush. It is safer to use one board for meat and another for everything else. Don't use the same plate for the cooked food that you used for raw food, a common mistake when grilling that can cause a gastric disaster!

Keep hot foods hot and cold foods cold. Let's face it: Indian food just takes more time to cook. This can be to your advantage as you leave a dish on low heat (180-200 degrees) on the stovetop, oven, or slow cooker. Do not leave anything on the counter for more than two hours. Although many meat and vegetable preparations use some natural antibacterial ingredients—lemon juice, salt, garlic, and spices—it is better to cool dishes to 38 degrees and warm them again, rather than leave them out.

Wash vegetables, lentils, rice, and fruits before using them. Soak leafy vegetables in plenty of cold water and shake them so that sand and grit will sink to the bottom. Then give them another thorough rinse under the tap. Both lentils and rice need to be picked over to remove stones or other debris and then rinsed thoroughly until the water runs clear. Soaking them cuts down on cooking time.

Be sensitive to the food preferences, taboos, or allergies of your guests. I try to ask my guests if there are foods they prefer not to eat or if they are allergic to any food before I prepare the meal. Nuts are a common but sometimes deadly allergy, so I try to garnish the dish with the whole or sliced nuts used to alert the guest to what is inside.

Timesavers

- Read the recipe(s) <u>from beginning to end</u> well before you plan to make it (them). At the same time make your grocery lists. I divide mine into items I have to purchase from the Indian market, those staples I will purchase from the regular supermarket, and the meat/fish. Also check ahead to see what equipment you will need, such as a spice grinder (highly recommended), rolling pin, large wok, griddle, etc.

- Even though you are not expecting guests, make the entire recipe or even double it and freeze the rest in the size portions you will be most likely to use. Or make several recipes at once with similar preps. Wrap your food well as keeping the air out will prevent freezer burn.

- "Fresh" herbs and some vegetables vary in quality. Some are to be purchased no more than a few days in advance, unless you freeze them. Blanch pieces of larger, "exotic" veggies in boiling water for a few seconds before plunging in cold water, draining, and then freezing in a single layer. Gather in a plastic freezer bag (push all air out) once they have frozen solid.

- Some people peel and chop garlic, ginger, and herbs, portion them in ice cube trays, freeze, and then save the cubes in plastic bags to be used when needed.

- Line up the ingredients you will be using (especially spices) for multiple recipes and measure as you go along. When making multiple recipes using onions, garlic, and ginger, it makes sense to peel, chop, and measure for each recipe at the same time to save on cleanup. Once you have experience, you will no longer need to measure.

- If you are making multiple dishes, it makes sense to toast the spices and grind them ahead of time. The same goes for chopping nuts. You save lots of time on multiple clean ups this way.

- Make enough dough for *phulkas* or other breads for several days at the same time and store in the refrigerator. Take out only as much as you need for that meal and leave the rest.

- Although fresh tastes best, you could make a large batch of *tardka* (see page 3) and keep refrigerated or frozen in portions. I did this when we took our RV across the country. Use a nonstick pan to make the *tardka* in order for it to brown properly and more quickly.

- To hasten cooking time, start making the sauce or *tardka* while partially or wholly cooking the vegetables (but not meat) in the microwave and then combine.

Additional Tips Before Starting

- Unless otherwise noted, the yogurt referred to in recipes is regular, homemade plain or the regular, plain yogurt found in the dairy case of your supermarket. You may choose the fat content, depending on your taste and health concerns.

- Ginger, onions, and carrots are always peeled. This instruction will not be mentioned again in the recipes.

- Scrape, rather than peel ginger with the edge of a spoon. If grating ginger, do not cut off the piece first, but notch the amount needed and then, by holding a much larger piece, you can grate only the amount specified without harming your knuckles. A microplane is great if you want more juice than pulp.

- Start with the basic spices—turmeric, cumin, and coriander seed. Curry powder is an invention of the West. Indian cooks choose from an array of many spices, freshly ground, to make each dish taste a little different. If you must use it, toast it in a dry pan or fry it in a little oil for a few seconds. If using commercial spice mixture, please check the date of manufacture for freshness. But soon you will be making your own garam masala (finishing spice/see page 4) or *chaat masala* (kebab and salad spices/see page 5).

- Store nuts in the freezer or refrigerator to keep them from going rancid.

- Cut your vegetables and meat in uniform pieces; they will cook more evenly.

- Check your oven temperature (center) with a good oven thermometer. You will be surprised that even the most expensive oven takes longer to heat up than the signal indicates. My oven takes at least 20 minutes to heat to 350 degrees and half an hour to 450 degrees, yet my signal says it's always ready after 10 minutes.

- If not using a machine with a dough hook, grease your hand with oil before mixing or kneading—or use a disposable latex glove. And if the dough does not roll out as thin as you would like, roll out the dough as far as it will go and then let it rest for a few minutes, covered with a clean towel, as you partially roll out the rest of the breads. When you go back to the first one, it will roll out to the proper size.

- If cutting thin slices of meat for kebabs, etc., half freeze (or thaw) the meat and it can be more easily sliced.

- My mother, Margaret, taught me to clean up as I go. When cooking Indian food, keeping order in the kitchen becomes even more important! Keep your counter clean and neat. Wash pots and pans as they are used. Put your spices away.

- Last but not least, don't forget, "*Chardee Kalaa*!" Lift up your spirits with healthful food and fun!

THE MENUS

THE WAY TO A MAN'S HEART

I meet my future husband

In the fall of the year we met.

ARE WE PREDESTINED TO DO what we do, or do we have free will? That was the toothsome problem I would mull over in adolescence and that drew me into the spiritual life. What does draw us, attract us? Is it molecular, like hydrogen and oxygen? Fate? Destiny? Paprikash?

On a scorching day in June in a little town in Michigan, I realized I was out of stamps and the post office had already closed. I had just finished collecting the medical certificate and completing a new application to rejoin the convent of the Missionary Sisters Servants of the Holy Spirit where I had spent four years. A recurring back problem caused by a diving accident when I was only eleven kept me from being accepted permanently but now I had the "proof" I needed for re-admittance. With lots of exercise and by sleeping on a board, the injury had been corrected.

It was so hot that afternoon! My little brother Eddie and I changed into our swimsuits at home. My sister Catherine drove us to the beach at Baw Beese Lake. We immediately swam out to the dock. I dove into the water, but instead of diving like a swan, I dropped like a rock! The noise must have echoed in the surrounding hills, because as I surfaced, almost everyone on the beach was wading toward me. The first one to reach me was (pardon the cliché) a tall, dark, and handsome guy. "Are you okay?" he asked. I must have stammered some answer because he didn't seem to think anything was amiss. If he had known that I had actually heard a voice in my head saying clearly and urgently, "You must marry this man!" what would his reaction have been?

With my mind racing, I managed to ask him where he was from and what religion he was. When he answered, "Sikh," this young Catholic girl wondered what God was getting her into. He asked me to play tennis the next day and I said yes, though I had never before played in my life. I hadn't even asked his name.

My sister was astonished when I asked her to drive me to the library—in a wet bathing suit! The S encyclopedia flew off the shelf. "Hmm." They believe in one God. All men, and even women and children, were equal and could lead the congregation. "Okay." They pray daily and repudiate ritual and dogma. They are known to fight for justice (in WWII for Britain and for Independence in '47)

13

and some are baptized as soldier-saints. They give 10 percent of their earnings to charity. "Pretty good, actually. Guess I could live with that." I memorized the Sikh greeting as best as I could without having heard it before, and recited it for my astonished new friend. "*Wahe Guru ji ka Khalsa! Wahe Guru ji ki fateh!*" (How great are God's pure ones! Victory belongs to them!)

That weekend was my parents' anniversary and I invited my new friend for the dinner I was making—chicken paprikash and cucumber salad with onions and sour cream. Classic Hungarian. The man never looked up from his plate. Between mouthfuls we heard, "How did you know?" Of course, at that time, I didn't. He thought I had made chicken curry and cucumber raita.

Was it fate, or grace, or paprikash that brought us together?

The "Way to a Man's Heart" Menu

You, too, will fall in love—with Punjabi food—when you try this menu. The recipes I've chosen are what my future husband thought I had made at our first meal together—the Punjabi versions of chicken paprikash and of wilted cucumbers in sour cream. Cucumber raita is far and away the most popular one in Punjab. Peppers are the signature of Hungarian cuisine but in this recipe they are lightly filled with a sweet-sour-savory mixture that is pure India. Chocolate fudge was the first recipe I ever learned to make—from my father. It seemed to take hours to make to a kid. But the chocolate burfee recipe here is finished in minutes.

It is not unusual for Punjabi men to prepare the meat dishes for the family. It's analogous to American men donning aprons to barbecue. Uncle Kuldip Singh, my mother-in-law's middle brother, made this version of chicken curry for us when he visited one summer. It was memorable for the light sauce sweetened with raisins and sparked with lemon juice. Dive in and try it all!

Appetizer:	MIRCH MASALADAR Stuffed Poblano Peppers
	PAPARD Lentil Crisps
Main Course:	MURGA DOE PAYAZA Double Onion Chicken Curry
	ALOO GOBEE DUM PUHKT Oven-Baked Potatoes and Cauliflower
	PARAUNTHA Layered Whole-Wheat Flat Breads
	KHEERA RAITA Yogurt with Cucumber Salad
Dessert:	CHOCOLATE BURFEE Chocolate-Almond-Cherry Fudge
Next-Day Brunch:	ALOO/SUBZE PARAUNTHA Layered Vegetable-Stuffed Flat Breads
	LAL MIRCH TE GAJJER ACHAR Punjabi Red Pepper and Carrot Pickle
	ACHAR MASALA Spice Mixture for Fish, Grilled Vegetables, and Pickles

- **Three to Four Months Prior:** Beautiful peppers come into our farmers' markets in late July. I like to buy them then to make a pickle for the rest of the year.

- **Three Days Prior:** Read the recipes from start to finish. Prepare your grocery lists. Buy the cream, chocolate, dried cherries, yogurt, poblano peppers, onions, cauliflower, potatoes, and chicken from the supermarket. Buy the spices, *papard*, tamarind, chapatti flour, coconut, nuts, and whole milk powder from the Indian market.

- **Two Days Prior:** Make the chocolate fudge, cut, wrap, and refrigerate. Make the *paraunthas*, cool completely and then place a layer of waxed paper between them. Wrap tightly in foil and refrigerate.

- **One-Day Prior:** Peel the onions and garlic. Wash the cauliflower and cut up into florets and store in a plastic bag in the refrigerator. Wash, slit, and seed the peppers. Make the chicken curry (except for the garnish) and store in a heatproof serving dish in the refrigerator.

- **The Day of:**
  AM: Turn on the exhaust fan and make the cauliflower and potatoes and the peppers.
  PM: Make and refrigerate the *raita*. Cut the garnishes. Clean up.

- **An hour before serving time:** Begin heating the chicken curry over low heat. Heat the *papard* and warm the peppers and serve with drinks. Make the breads. Garnish the dishes.

STUFFED POBLANO PEPPERS

vegan   Mirch Masaladar

These peppers are not filled completely like the stuffed peppers of Hungarian cuisine. It's surprising that peppers were brought to Hungary and to India from the Americas, hence the use of poblanos. I saw a recipe like this in a magazine on the way back from Australia. The world has really shrunk, hasn't it?

Wash and carefully dry the peppers with a paper towel. It is your choice to cut off the caps or leave them on. Slit along one side of the pepper to remove the seeds and white pith. Heat the oil and fry the peppers until the skin lightly blisters but the flesh is tender crisp, about one minute per side. Remove to a plate lined with paper towels. (Alternatively, you may heat the peppers under a broiler until the skin is blistered on both sides.)

Add the onions to the oil and fry until golden.

Meanwhile toast the coconut and fenugreek, sesame, cumin, and coriander seeds by tossing in a hot, dry pan, being careful not to burn them. Grind to a paste in a coffee or spice grinder.

Put the garlic and ginger in a food processor and grind until smooth. Add the fried onions and grind again.

Drain all but 1 tablespoon of the oil left in the pan and add the turmeric. Fry for a few seconds and then add the seed paste and onion paste. Fry for a minute and then add the tamarind, salt, and 3 tablespoons water. Mix and cook for 2 or 3 minutes over low heat. Add the cilantro and whole curry leaves. Remove from heat.

You may wish to wipe the blistered skin from the peppers with a paper towel. Spread approximately 1 tablespoon of filling along the inside of each pepper. Before serving, rewarm if needed. Sprinkle with sea or kosher salt, and place the peppers on a plate. Cut into small diagonal slices so you can scoop them with pieces of grilled, fried, or microwaved *papard*.

YIELD: 8 TO 10 SERVINGS

8 to 10 poblano peppers

¼ cup canola oil

4 cups sliced red onions (about 4 medium)

1 tablespoon unsweetened grated coconut, dried or frozen

¼ teaspoon whole fenugreek seeds

1 tablespoon sesame seeds

2 teaspoons whole cumin seeds

2 teaspoons whole coriander seeds

1 large clove garlic, sliced

1-inch piece ginger, sliced

¼ teaspoon ground turmeric

1 tablespoon tamarind concentrate

½ teaspoon sea salt

1 cup finely sliced cilantro leaves

5 fresh *kari* (curry) leaves (*optional*)

LENTIL CRISPS

Papard (*Pappadum* in Hindi/*Pappad* on most menus) *vegan*

Buy this variation on bread—more like a large chip made of lentil flour—at an Indian market. You will find them in packages of 8 to 12 of plain, peppered (red or black), with cumin seed, or with garlic. They are great for snacking, or as a first course with chutney, or in this case with stuffed peppers. My friend Micky taught me to heat them in the microwave.

Newlyweds.

Gingerly press the *papard* down in spots on a hot griddle with a clean tea towel (folded to avoid the flame) until the color and texture change from slightly translucent to opaque and crisp. Or fry them one at a time and drain on paper towels. My favorite method, however, is to microwave them two or three at a time—no fat! Experiment with the time it takes in your microwave prior to your party. They are best served warm.

DOUBLE ONION CHICKEN CURRY

Murga Doe Payaza

Uncle Kuldip Singh, my mother-in-law's brother, in youthful sartorial splendor.

Uncle Kuldip Singh's famous recipe—a symphony of flavors! Don't have a complete array of Indian spices in your pantry? Simplify this recipe by substituting the spices (turmeric through fenugreek) with a commercial chicken curry masala mix or paste. But when you do make the investment in spices, it is well worth it.

Trim the extra fat from the chicken with kitchen scissors and cut through the bones into 3½-inch pieces. Soak the chicken pieces in cold, salted water for five minutes, until ready to cook. Drain and rinse.

Finely chop two of the onions and slice one onion in thin half moons. In a large, heavy-bottomed pot, sauté the chopped onions in the hot oil until transparent. Add the garlic and ginger and sauté until onions begin to brown. Add the spices (turmeric through fenugreek) and sauté for 1 minute. Add the sliced onion to the pot along with the tomatoes, chile pepper, raisins, and salt, sauté for 2 minutes and then simmer for 10 minutes.

Add the chicken pieces and stir thoroughly. Cover tightly and simmer for 30 to 45 minutes. Do not boil and do not add water, the gravy will be made naturally. Stir again and then cover and simmer until the meat is tender (30 to 40 minutes).

Stir in the lemon juice and garam masala. This dish improves if cooled and then stored overnight in the fridge and reheated. Sprinkle with cilantro before serving.

YIELD: 10 SERVINGS

5½ to 6 pounds skinless chicken thighs and breasts (with bones)

3 medium to large onions

¼ cup canola oil

3 cloves garlic, minced

2 tablespoons minced ginger

2 teaspoons ground turmeric

1 tablespoon ground coriander seeds

2 bay leaves

1½ teaspoons cumin seeds

1 cinnamon stick

2 black cardamom pods or 4 green cardamom pods

½ teaspoon cayenne pepper (*optional*)

½ teaspoon whole or ground fennel seeds (*optional*)

½ teaspoon ground fenugreek seeds (*optional*)

1 cup chopped tomatoes or 2 tablespoons tomato paste

1 chile pepper, seeded and chopped

½ cup golden raisins

2½ teaspoons salt, or to taste

Juice of 1 lemon

1 teaspoon garam masala

½ cup sliced cilantro leaves

OVEN-BAKED POTATOES AND CAULIFLOWER

Aloo Gobee Dum Puhkt   *vegan*

This most popular Punjabi vegetarian dish can be prepared several ways. I like to use the oven when I have other preparations on the stove. Cousin Birinder Kaur adds tomato paste to her recipe. Auntie Surindra uses chaat masala. *Sweetness or tang? I take both today!*

YIELD: 8 SERVINGS

1 large head (1½ to 2 pounds) cauliflower

3 large potatoes (about 2 pounds), peeled

1 long green chile pepper, seeded and minced

2 large onions, cut into crescent slices ½-inch thick

2 to 3 teaspoons salt, or to taste

1 tablespoon garam masala

1 teaspoon ground cumin seeds

2 teaspoons ground turmeric

½ cup canola oil

1½-inch-piece ginger, minced

3 large cloves garlic, minced

2 tablespoons tomato paste mixed with 2 tablespoons water

2 tablespoons *chaat masala* (page 5)

½ cup sliced cilantro leaves

Heat the oven to 450°F. Rinse the cauliflower; trim any brown or gray areas and discolored leaves and discard. Slice any nice green leaves and set aside. Cut out the stem and dice. Break the head into florets and cut the larger ones in half.

Cut the potatoes in half lengthwise, and then into medium wedges, about 10 per potato. Put the potatoes, cauliflower florets and leaves, chile pepper, and onions into a large bowl.

Mix the salt, garam masala, cumin seeds, and turmeric together in a separate small bowl with the oil. Add the ginger and garlic. Stir in the tomato paste mixture and *chaat masala*. Drop spoonfuls in dollops on the vegetables in the bowl. Cover your hands with latex gloves. Mix thoroughly with your hands, coating the vegetables as evenly as possible.

Spray or grease a roaster pan. Spread out the vegetables evenly in the pan. Cover tightly with foil. Put into the preheated oven for 20 minutes. Uncover, stir, and then turn down the heat to 400°F. Bake for about 30 more minutes, turning with a spatula at 10-minute intervals until the largest piece of potato can be easily pierced with a fork and there are some brown spots on the vegetables. Sprinkle with cilantro before serving.

LAYERED WHOLE-WHEAT FLAT BREADS

vegan Parauntha

This bread is quite substantial, and easy to make successfully even the first time. When paired with the Aloo Gobee Dum Puhkt *(page 18), it becomes a simple and delicious supper.*

Combine the flour and salt. Gradually mix in the water until it adheres in a ball and then knead the dough until it is no longer sticky. Refrigerate, covered, for at least half an hour or overnight.

Put the oil or *ghee* in a small bowl. Lightly flour a board and rolling pin and keep some *chapatti* flour handy. Divide the dough into eight equal balls and flatten each in the loose flour. Roll out each ball into a disk about 5½ inches in diameter. Brush a disk with some oil and fold into thirds like a burrito. Brush again with oil and fold into thirds the other way until you have a square. Repeat with the remaining disks.

Preheat the griddle. (A drop of water will dance on the surface when ready.) Press a square with your hand and then using the rolling pin, roll into a square approximately 5½ to 6 inches. Pick up with a spatula and flip onto the hot griddle. Heat for about 45 seconds and turn over. Brush with oil and cook for less than a minute. Turn and brush with oil. Heat for 10 seconds, and then flip again. Check for any uncooked edges or spots and press with the spatula until they are cooked. (The breads will puff slightly with steam.) Remove from the heat and repeat procedure with the remaining dough squares. This bread is best served immediately.

To freeze: Cool, put waxed paper between the breads and wrap tightly in foil and then in a freezer bag, with all the air pressed out.

YIELD: 8 BREADS

2½ cups *chapatti* flour or
   1¼ cups whole-wheat flour and
   1¼ cups white flour

1 teaspoon salt

1 to 1⅓ cups lukewarm water

¼ cup canola oil or melted *ghee*

YOGURT WITH CUCUMBER SALAD

Kheera Raita   *dairy*

This raita is so refreshing, especially on a hot summer day. It's a favorite in our house and will be in yours. Use your own homemade yogurt (page 127) or any of the popular brands found in the supermarket. Ground cumin is less strongly flavored than the whole toasted seeds.

YIELD: 8 ½-CUP SERVINGS

4 cups (32-ounces) plain yogurt

¾ cup seeded and grated cucumber

1 medium tomato, seeded and chopped

¼ cup seeded and minced green chile or bell pepper

½ cup minced red onion

1 teaspoon toasted whole or ground cumin seeds

1½ teaspoons salt, or to taste

Pinch cayenne pepper (*optional*)

½ cup sliced cilantro leaves

In a medium bowl, beat the yogurt, adding a few spoonfuls of milk or water, if desired. Stir in the rest of the ingredients, reserving a tablespoon of cilantro for the garnish.

CHOCOLATE-ALMOND-CHERRY FUDGE

What food is more associated with love than chocolate? I was inspired to try my hand at chocolate burfee when I found out that it is the only kind our nephew Parmeeth will eat. However, I was tired of stirring and burning ricotta cheese on the stove (my old method) and decided to try making burfee in the microwave. Voila! Instead of hours, it takes minutes. Just make sure to line up all ingredients before you begin. The cherries are our daughter Raji's idea. Pure delight!

Spray or grease an 8-inch square glass baking pan and set aside. If using cherries, reserve six for the garnish and chop the rest.

Place the chocolate, sugar, almond paste, and cream in a 2-quart microwavable (preferably glass) casserole or bowl. Melt in the microwave on HIGH for a total of five minutes, stirring halfway through and breaking up any chunks with a wooden spoon.

Stir in the *ghee* and chopped cherries and heat again for another minute on 50 power. Add the vanilla and then gradually, while the mixture is very hot, stir in the milk powder. Keep folding and cutting it in, making sure it is very thoroughly mixed.

Turn the mixture into the greased baking pan, and with a damp hand, pat it smooth. Press on the sliced nuts, if using. Cool in the refrigerator for at least two hours. Cut into squares. Wrap well before storing in the refrigerator or freezer.

YIELD: 36 2-INCH SQUARES

1 cup dried cherries (*optional*)

2 squares (2 ounces) unsweetened chocolate

¾ cup sugar, or more to taste

½ tube or 4 ounces of canned almond paste, crumbled

1 cup plus 2 tablespoons heavy cream

3 tablespoons *ghee*

1 teaspoon vanilla extract

4 cups whole milk powder*

¼ cup sliced almonds (*optional*)

*Whole milk powder (*mava*) is usually packaged in clear cellophane bags in the Indian market. In a pinch you may use the nonfat variety dry milk powder found in the supermarket, but it does not taste as great.

NEXT-DAY BRUNCH

LAYERED VEGETABLE-STUFFED FLAT BREADS

vegan   Aloo/Subze Parauntha

This is the same bread as the recipe on page 19, only stuffed with goodness from leftover aloo gobee *or potatoes. It is my all-time favorite for breakfast with plain yogurt, pickle, and a pat of butter on top. (Not very vegan, but very Punjabi of me!)*

Mix the flour, salt, and water and knead the dough until smooth and elastic, about 5 minutes. Cover the dough and allow to rest in the refrigerator for at least a half hour.

(If using leftover potatoes and cauliflower, mash them, and skip to the next paragraph as they are already seasoned.) Boil the potatoes, allow to cool, and coarsely mash. Add the ginger, onion, chile pepper, cilantro, cumin seeds, coriander seeds, garam masala, and pomegranate seeds and mix thoroughly.

Divide the potato mixture into 12 equal portions. Heat a griddle until a drop of water sizzles. Put the oil into a small bowl.

Divide the dough into 12 equal portions. Roll one portion out to a 5-inch disk and spread it with oil (a pastry brush works well for this job). Put a ball of the potato mixture on the disk and pat it flat but not to the edge. Pick up the dough at the edges and twist it around the potato "patty" to make a sack or purse and then press it down. Place it on some dry flour and with gentle pressure roll it out in a 4- to 5-inch circle. Turn it over and roll it in the other direction to about 7 inches. Flip it onto your palm and flip it onto the griddle on med/high heat. Cook on one side for 45 seconds to 1 minute. Flip and spread oil on that side. Cook for 1 more minute, flip again and oil the other side. Cook for 1 more minute. Flip and cook for 30 more seconds. Remove from heat and repeat process with remaining dough and potato mixture. Serve immediately with or without butter and Indian-style pickle.

YIELD: 12 BREADS

2½ cups *chapatti* flour or
   1¼ cups whole-wheat flour
   and 1¼ cups white flour

2 teaspoons salt

1 to 1⅓ cups lukewarm water

2 large potatoes, or 2 cups leftover
   potatoes and cauliflower
   (page 18 or page 148)

1 tablespoon minced ginger

1 small red onion, finely chopped

1½ tablespoons minced green
   chile pepper

½ cup sliced cilantro leaves

1½ teaspoons toasted cumin seeds

1 teaspoon ground coriander
   seeds

1 scant teaspoon garam masala

1½ teaspoons dried ground
   pomegranate seeds *(optional)*

⅓ cup canola oil or *ghee*

Flour for dusting

PUNJABI RED PEPPER AND CARROT PICKLE

Lal Mirch Te Gajjer Achar   *vegan*

Three years ago I saw beautiful red cherry peppers in the farmer's market and decided to stuff them like the famous Punjabi Mirch Achar found in cans in most Indian markets. I had several cups of the spice mixture left over and used it on broiled cod and grilled vegetables when my friend Micky and her husband came to dinner. They loved the mixture so much that they asked for a jar. So keep the extra spice mixture in this recipe in a separate container "for sprinkling."

YIELD: 2 QUARTS PICKLE PLUS ³/₄ CUP SPICE MIXTURE

2 pounds cherry peppers or small banana peppers

1 pound baby carrots

¹/₂ cup **edible** mustard oil or mustard-flavored oil*

2¹/₂ cups or more canola oil

Achar Masala (spice mixture for fish, grilled vegetables, and pickles):

¹/₂ cup whole coriander seeds

2¹/₂ tablespoons whole black mustard seeds

2¹/₂ tablespoons whole fennel seeds

4 teaspoons whole cumin seeds

2 teaspoons whole carom seeds (*ajwain*)

2 teaspoons whole fenugreek seeds (*methi*)

2 teaspoons whole onion seeds (*kolonji*)

²/₃ cup dried ground green mango powder (*amchoor*)

¹/₂ cup kosher salt

¹/₂ teaspoon black salt

¹/₂ teaspoon ground turmeric

Thoroughly wash (sterilize in boiling water, if possible) and then thoroughly dry an attractive 2 quart jar with a wide mouth.

Wash and dry the cherry peppers. Carefully cut out the stem end, pith, and seeds. Sprinkle lightly with regular salt and turn over on paper towels. Rinse the carrots and thoroughly dry with paper towels.

Heat a dry frying pan and toast the coriander seeds until fragrant but not burned. Finely grind in a coffee/spice grinder. Toast the rest of the whole seeds, grind, and add to the coriander seed. Mix in the mango powder, kosher salt, black salt, turmeric, ¹/₄ cup of the mustard oil, and ¹/₄ cup of the canola oil.

In a large wok, heat the remainder of the mustard and canola oils. Add the carrots and fry for two minutes. Remove with a slotted spoon to a bowl. Reserve the hot oil.

Fill a few peppers with some of the spice mixture and carefully place them in the prepared jar in one layer. Fill around them with a few carrots being mindful of the way the outside of the jar looks (if clear glass). Sprinkle the first layer with a little spice and continue, stuffing the second layer as full as possible. Pour in the reserved oil, just to cover, and see if you can fill in any more spots with either carrots or peppers before filling more layers.

Begin the next layer, placing the stuffed peppers and carrots in the nooks and crannies. Finish with a layer of spice. Reheat the oil and carefully pour into the jar. If the oil does not reach the top after a minute, reheat more canola oil and pour in until it reaches the top. Add a little more spice. If using a metal lid, put a layer of plastic wrap on top first and close tightly. Leave the jar in the sun, if possible, and do not open for at least three months. While you are waiting, you have a decorative piece for your kitchen.

* **Note:** Do not use mustard oil labeled "for external use only" or "for massage only."

SIGNATURE FARE

Punjab, the Breadbasket of India

New Providence Memorial Library
377 Elkwood Avenue
New Providence, NJ 07974

A wheat grinding stone from our village.

BREAD—THE MOST BASIC OF western foods is also the signature food of the Punjab, the breadbasket of India. My husband never felt he had eaten unless he had his *rotee*, the generic name for all types of bread, and there are many. The *phulka*, the light and tender whole-wheat round is the daily bread of the gentry and the *rotee*, larger and heavier, is the bread of the peasant.

It was when I saw wheat waving and glinting, golden in the sun on those flat plains, that I really felt the romance of that nourishing grain. The soil is especially fertile in Punjab, which literally translates into a land of five (*punj*) rivers (*ab*). Two and sometimes three crops can be grown in a year. My husband's family owned a large farm in a village that was situated at the very end of the open canal which ran from the Sutlej River, over one hundred miles away. As a consequence their land was very dry—until the Bhakra Dam was completed in 1963. Miraculously the water table rose and the land became fertile. It was only a few years later when we passed men working the wheatfields, crouching with one hand holding the ripe wheat while the other hand cut it with a sickle. It was brutal work in the blazing sun.

Making the circle of life complete, some ladies of the family were in the process of preparing the bread that fed the *seerees* who did the heavy labor in the field. It was an amazing sight to see women working together in a rhythm that could rival any orchestra. Seated on *peedees* (very low, woven-jute stools), or even just crouched on their haunches, each woman had a specific task. Some kneaded ten pounds of dough at a time in three-foot wide bronze trays called *praants*. Some rolled countless *paydas*, small balls of dough, in their palms. Using only their hands, patting back and forth and stretching the dough, some flattened the breads into perfect circles. At least two women worked in tandem over the hot *loh*, a huge, slightly convex cast-iron griddle set over open coals or dried cow-dung fueled fires. One woman slapped the bread onto the blisteringly hot surface while the other turned it over with long steel tongs and moved it to a slightly cooler spot to make room for the next *rotee*. Sometimes six large breads would be baking at once. All of this fabulous, rhythmic production was taking place while the women socialized—sharing stories, gossiping, trying to ignore the intense heat of the sun and the fires.

The women would then take the breads wrapped in a cloth out to the field along with an earthenware vessel filled with *lussee* (salted buttermilk) and a pail of lentils. Another person, usually a child, would put an onion smashed with salt and red pepper on top of a short stack of breads for each worker.

This is the only job Uncle Gurmit remembers having occasionally done during his breaks from school. Otherwise, like my husband, he was a *kakaji*, the landowner's son, who never had to get himself a glass of water. Of course things changed very quickly when they arrived in the U.S.!

What did not change was their love of *rotee*, with plenty of raw onions, please!

The "Signature Fare" Menu

This menu features dishes familiar to most people who eat at Indian restaurants. You will rarely go out again after you have tasted these versions that do not need lots of practice to produce. They will become favorites of your whole family. Additionally, beginners may find the spice mixtures and other ingredients like the chutneys and toasted vermicelli in the Indian market, so that the full menu may be made quickly, until you become an expert Punjabi cook and make everything yourself from scratch.

Appetizer:	*ALOO PAPARDEE CHAAT* Crunchy Street Snack
Main Course:	*MURGH MUKHANEE* Butter Chicken (*Tikka Masala*)
	BHEY SUBZE Roasted Lotus Roots, Carrots, and Potatoes
	PHULKA Whole-Wheat Flat Breads
Dessert:	*SEVIAN* Toasted Vermicelli Pudding

- **Three Days Prior:** Read the recipes from beginning to end. Make your grocery lists. Purchase what you need from the Indian market—lotus root, *masalas, papardees, chapatti* flour, toasted *vermicelli, kewrda*, and pistachios. If using either the syrupy ginger or tamarind chutney buy the ingredients and make it, or buy the prepared chutney. Buy the cilantro and mint if you cannot find them in your supermarket, and wrap in damp paper towels to store in a plastic bag in the refrigerator. Purchase what you need from your supermarket—the chicken, yogurt, chickpeas, large carrots, long potatoes, tomatoes, tomato products, milk, and cream.

- **Two Days Prior:** Make the dough for the breads. Make the *sevian* dessert. Refrigerate both the *sevian* and the dough.

- **One-Day Prior:** Make the sauce for the chicken, except for the cream. Marinate the chicken pieces. Cook the potatoes for the *chaat*. Refrigerate all.

- **The Day of:**
  AM: Make the mint chutney, if using. Make the lotus root dish except for the last run under the broiler.
  PM: Chop the ingredients for the *chaat* and tightly cover the bowls with plastic wrap. Broil the chicken. Begin slowly heating the sauce for the chicken. Clean up.

- **Serving Time:** Have everyone make his or her own *chaat*. At dinnertime, make the breads. Add the cream to the sauce and then add the broiled chicken. Turn up the oven to broil, and broil the vegetables until slightly browned. Garnish the dishes and enjoy.

CRUNCHY STREET SNACK

Going for *chaat* in the bazaar in Bhatinda.

This is our daughter Raji's favorite Indian dish. In fact, all the ladies of our family love to go to Iselin, N.J., (our "Little India") for the variety of chaats we find in the shops. This version is easy to prepare at home, and your guests will love making it to their own taste. If you are short on time, buy the chutneys found in the refrigerated section of the Indian market and the ready-made masala (spice) mixtures (but they won't taste as good).

Boil the potatoes or slit and heat in the microwave until cooked but not mushy. Cool and peel. Cut into small ¼-inch dice and place in a serving bowl.

Beat the yogurt with a fork and add a little milk or water to make it very smooth. Put into a medium/large bowl.

Put the onion, chickpeas, cilantro, cayenne pepper, *chaat masala*, salt, *papardees,* and chutneys each into their own, appropriately-sized bowl. Provide a small spoon for each bowl so that your guests can choose a combination of ingredients to their own liking. *Chaat* is best assembled to the individual taste and eaten immediately so that the *papardees* stay crisp.

To assemble: Your guest takes a salad plate, puts about a ¼ cup of potatoes on it, a spoonful of chickpeas, a few fried noodles, some chopped onion and cilantro. Then she puts a sprinkle of salt, *chaat masala,* and/or cayenne pepper. Next she mixes it up slightly on the plate with some yogurt and with a chutney or two of her choice on top, like a savory sundae.

YIELD: 8 TO 10 SERVINGS

4 large Yukon Gold or 8 medium red potatoes

4 cups (32 ounces) plain yogurt

1½ cups chopped red onion

1 can (15 ounces) chickpeas, rinsed and drained

1 cup finely sliced cilantro leaves

⅛ cup cayenne pepper

¼ cup *chaat masala (page 5)*

⅛ cup salt

½ pound fried wheat wafers or fried white-flour "noodles" *(papardees*)*

Mint Chutney *(page 61),* Tamarind Chutney *(page 215),* and/or Syrupy Ginger Chutney *(page 176)*

*Note: Purchase *papardees* from an Indian market or substitute the fried, flour noodles you get with an order of Chinese food.

BUTTER CHICKEN (TIKKA MASALA)

Murgh Mukhanee   *meat*

Robin Cook, the British Foreign Secretary, said an immigrant chef invented Chicken Tikka Masala in Britain and therefore it is a "true British national dish." The authentic version is this richer dish, "butter chicken" of Punjab. This recipe is easily halved.

YIELD: 10 CUPS

For the chicken: (See Note)

3 pounds boneless, skinless chicken breasts or thighs or a combination of both

4 teaspoons salt

1 cup hung yogurt (*page 6*) or light sour cream

2 teaspoons tandoori chicken masala (*page 62*)

1-inch piece ginger, grated

2 cloves garlic, minced

For the sauce:

4 tablespoons *ghee*

½ teaspoon black cumin seeds (*shah zeera*) or regular white cumin seeds

1 teaspoon garam masala

2 medium onions, finely chopped (about 2 cups)

2 cloves garlic, minced

1½-inch piece ginger, grated

4 large tomatoes, diced or 1 (28-oz) can peeled/crushed tomatoes

2 tablespoons tomato paste

2 teaspoons dried fenugreek leaves (*kasoori methi*) (*optional*)

½ cup ground almonds

1 teaspoon salt or to taste

2 to 3 teaspoons brown sugar

½ cup cream

Garnishes: 2 tablespoons sliced cilantro leaves; sliced almonds

With kitchen scissors, clip the visible fat from the chicken. Cut into even pieces 1½ x 1½-inches. Place the chicken in a bowl of cold water mixed with 3 teaspoons salt. Refrigerate for 30 minutes. Mix the yogurt or sour cream, tandoori chicken masala, ginger, and garlic in a large bowl. Add the thoroughly rinsed and drained chicken. Marinate in the refrigerator while preparing the sauce.

Make the sauce: Heat a medium saucepan and then melt the *ghee*. Stir in the cumin seeds and heat for 5 seconds. Add the garam masala, onions, garlic, and ginger and sauté until browned. Add the tomatoes, tomato paste, fenugreek leaves, if using, almonds, salt, and brown sugar. Sauté, stirring for 10 minutes and then remove from heat. Using an immersion hand mixer purée the mixture, or purée the sauce in a blender. Return the puréed sauce to the pot and simmer over a medium flame for 6 minutes until sauce reduces.

Preheat the broiler or grill. Broil or grill chicken pieces far enough apart to brown, not stew (you will need to do this in batches). Pour off the juice from the broiler pan into the sauce part way through cooking. Return to the broiler until some brown appears and chicken is just cooked through. Repeat until all the pieces are broiled. Set the chicken aside for 5 minutes and then cut each piece in half.

Add the chicken to the reduced sauce and cook and stir for about 10 minutes or until the chicken is cooked through. Blend in the cream at the last minute, cover, and simmer until gently heated through. Taste for seasoning and garnish with cilantro and sliced almonds before serving.

Note: You can use leftover meat from the Grilled "Red" Chicken recipe (*page 62*), cut into 1½ inch cubes, and skip this part of the recipe since that chicken is already seasoned.

ROASTED LOTUS ROOTS, CARROTS, AND POTATOES

vegan   Bhey Subze

Lacy lotus root gives this mixture of vegetables an exotic flair.

The lotus is the signature flower of India and the root is a common ingredient in Chinese and Indian cooking. It is quite beautiful when sliced and is no more difficult to make than fresh carrots. You may use canned lotus root, drained and sliced, if you cannot find fresh. Try to match the diameter of the carrots, potatoes, and lotus root for a very pleasing presentation. I love these vegetables with my achar masala *pickling spice (page 24).*

Preheat the oven to 400°F. Slice the onions lengthwise into long slices ½-inch wide. Slice the lotus roots, carrots, and potatoes into ½-inch rounds. Place all the vegetables in a large glass or steel bowl. Mix the oil with the salt, mustard seeds, turmeric, masala, and cayenne pepper. Pour over the vegetables and coat them well.

Line two shallow cookie sheets with foil and spray with cooking spray. Spread the vegetables evenly on the sheets, cover with foil, and bake for 40 minutes. Uncover, turn them over, making sure they are spread evenly, and bake uncovered for another 15 minutes, turning the vegetables again halfway through. Just before serving, put each tray under the broiler for a few minutes until the vegetables are nicely browned in spots and heated through. Turn out on a heated platter, garnish with cilantro, and serve immediately.

YIELD: 10 SERVINGS

2 large onions

1½ pounds fresh lotus roots, trimmed and peeled

1½ pounds large-diameter carrots

1 pound long white potatoes

½ cup mustard-flavored oil* or canola oil

1 tablespoon kosher salt, or to taste

2 teaspoons black mustard seeds

1 teaspoon ground turmeric

2 teaspoons garam masala or 1 tablespoon *achar masala (page 24)*, or to taste

½ teaspoon cayenne pepper (*optional*)

Garnish: sliced cilantro

*Note: Do not buy mustard oil that says "for external use only."

WHOLE-WHEAT FLAT BREADS

Phulka or Chapatti   *vegan*

The staff of life, our daily bread—no salt, no fat, yet amazingly satisfying and tasty. Nothing like it when hot off the griddle! In our family, everyone sat at the table with food on the plate waiting for the freshest, puffiest phulka. *The* phulka *maker was the last to eat, but her sacrifice was appreciated.*

YIELD: 16 5½-INCH BREADS

3½ cups *chapatti* flour**

1¼ cups lukewarm water

Butter (*optional*)

In a medium bowl, mix 3 cups of the flour and ¾ cup of the water thoroughly until uniformly crumbly. Gradually add more water, sprinkling it on dough and working it in until the dough is pliable and all flour is incorporated. Remove dough from bowl and knead on a flat surface for 3 to 5 minutes. Rest dough for 30 minutes, or tightly cover and refrigerate overnight. Before making the breads, allow refrigerated dough to stand at room temperature for 20 minutes.

Heat a griddle until hot, but not smoking. Lightly flour a board and rolling pin. Turn the dough onto the board and with your hands roll it into a tube. Cut in half, then in quarters, and then in eight pieces. Roll one piece into a smooth ball; pat it flat, and with the rolling pin, roll it into a disk, turning to keep it an evenly rounded 5½-inch disk. Slap the disk between your hands to loosen the extra flour and place the bread on the griddle.

Heat until the dough starts to cook through to the other side. Flip and press edges with a folded towel (being careful to keep from flame) until bread just begins to puff with internal steam.* At this point it can be finished over a gas burner or flipped again on the griddle.

Butter the *phulka*, if you wish, by just touching with the stick of butter (wrapped in paper), taking care not to burn yourself with the hot steam. Serve immediately. Repeat with remaining dough pieces.

* If you wish to serve the breads at another time, stop the cooking at this point. Separate the partially-cooked *phulkas* so they cool, then wrap four in foil and bundle into a large freezer bag.

** *Chapatti* is the Hindi term for this bread. *Chapatti* flour is very finely ground whole-wheat flour. Substitute half whole-wheat and half all-purpose flour if you can't find *chapatti* flour.

TOASTED VERMICELLI PUDDING

A specialty of the entire Punjabi community, especially the Muslims, this dish is so comforting and delicious that it has made its way around the world. What an ambassador of sweetness! Sevian is easy to prepare, especially if you find the packaged toasted vermicelli that has already been broken into small pieces.

In a deep, heavy-bottomed pot, bring milk, cream, raisins, and cardamom to a soft boil over medium-low heat, stirring occasionally. Bring to a boil and add the vermicelli, stirring continuously until the milk boils again. Lower the heat to simmer and continue cooking and stirring until the vermicelli rises and stays at the surface. Remove the cardamom pods.

Stir in the sugar and *kewrda* and all but 1 tablespoon of the pistachios, cooking until the sugar is dissolved. (You may continue the cooking in the microwave, which prevents it from burning on the bottom as it begins to thicken.) Turn out into a serving bowl. Stir and let cool for 20 minutes.

Either cover with plastic wrap and refrigerate or serve at room temperature within an hour or so. It thickens as it cools. Check it at this point. If it is not thick enough for your taste, cook some more in the microwave. If too thick, thin with more milk or cream.

At serving time, turn pudding into a crystal bowl or tureen and touch lightly in 3 or 4 places with the silver leaf and sprinkle with the remaining pistachios.

YIELD: 10 ½-CUP SERVINGS

6 cups whole milk

½ cup cream (*optional*)

⅓ cup golden raisins

5 green cardamom pods

1 cup toasted vermicelli pieces*

1 cup sugar

¼ teaspoon kewrda** or vanilla extract (*optional*)

¼ cup unsalted pistachios, chopped

1 or 2 leaves of edible silver (*chandi verk*) (*optional*)

---

*If you can't find the packaged toasted vermicelli (*savian*) at the Indian market, lightly brown some uncooked, dry angel hair pasta in the oven and break into pieces.

**Kewrda* is the flavor of screw pine, which has a floral/pine scent. A little goes a long way. It may be found behind the counter of most Indian markets along with the *chandi verk*, edible silver foil.

CLASSIC COMBO

My courageous mother-in-law's story

I LOVED MY MOTHER-IN-LAW BEFORE I MET HER. THAT may sound strange on many levels, especially since that relationship is the comedian's most reliable workhorse. But when my future husband told me his mother's life story, I was deeply moved. I imagined her all alone in her room, praying for her only child far away and I knew her sacrifices were extraordinary.

Bebeji and my future husband on the day he left for the United States. Their emotions are clearly visible.

At the time, we were students together at the University of Michigan. While I had known from the moment I met my husband that he was the one for me, it took him a few years to reciprocate because of his concern for his mother. She was a widow at thirty-three. It is a cruel fate for most women all over the world, but especially in the hierarchical society of India. Her status in the extended family was already low, having been married to the youngest of three sons. Her chance for any happiness after the death of her husband was in the hands of a thirteen-year-old boy, an only child. When he finished his bachelor's degree in physics at the age of nineteen, instead of marrying him off to consolidate her future, she allowed him to follow his dream to go to the U.S. for a degree in engineering. That in itself was a sign of her great character. But there was so much more.

Bebeji, as I would learn to call her, suffered greatly under the thumb of her imperious father-in-law. Yet the pluck, perseverance, and generosity of her spirit grew brighter in the fire of challenge. She was an unlikely heroine, being the once pampered, some would say spoiled, only daughter among three brothers. Her father owned substantial farms in east and west Punjab. But after her son left for the U.S., her father-in-law did not allow her brothers to visit, nor did he give her money for decent clothes or personal expenses. During all of this, instead of seething with resentment, she gave service to her ailing mother-in-law, the only one of her father-in-law's five wives still alive.

Childless and stricken with metastasized breast cancer, her mother-in-law had to be fed through a tube in her throat. *Bebeji* did not hesitate. She rose during the night to change dressings, administer medications,

Bebeji's father-in-law waiting for a servant to bring him water to wash his hands.

and give tea through the tube to ease a little of the suffering. It was a true labor of love. No hot running water, no electric stove, no pre-sterilized anything. All the food had to be converted into liquid, pulverized by hand—no blenders then! She carried on this way not just for months, but for several years, with no thought of reward. To me this is the essence of virtue.

In *Bebeji*'s fantasy, her engineer son would arrive back in Punjab to marry the beautiful, only child of an industrialist, and eventually take over the factory from his father-in-law. In fact, she had already begun the preliminary arrangements for such a union. Instead, her son decided to remain in the U.S. for his master's degree.

When he finally journeyed home after seven long years, it was to ask the permission of his mother to marry an American. Can you imagine her feelings? I could. Dreams shattered, fearful, but persuaded by her brothers to agree, she finally gave in. When my future husband had asked me to live permanently in India and care for her as a condition of our marriage I said "yes" without any hesitation. I took that promise very seriously for the rest of our lives together.

Our kitchen became the playing field where we could participate in a game at which we both excelled. I cared for her, yes, but she taught me all she knew.

The "Classic Combo" Menu

The heart of this vegetarian menu is the classic combination of "washed" hulled masoor *lentils and bitter melon. Balanced in every way, it's a lot like life. The combination of flavors—sweet and sour, bitter and astringent; of textures—creamy, crunchy, and silky; the riot of colors—red, yellow, green, and white, all combine to make this meal a favorite.*

It was not easy making the transition to this country for my mother-in-law when we moved to New Jersey. She was so concerned that someone in the U.S. (me?) might give her beef disguised as chicken that she had decided to never eat meat again. I completely understood her fears and fiercely protected her from mistakenly eating any meat, although the rest of us did eat it. Anyway, I love vegetarian dishes, and we enjoyed cooking them together. Thanks, Bebeji! I could not have done it without your guidance.

Appetizer:	*MAHARANI TAMATAR* Tomatoes Stuffed with Rice, Cheese, and Marigold
Main Course:	*MASOOR DAAL* Red Lentil Curry
	KARELAY ALOO Stir-Fried Bitter Melon and Potatoes
	PHULKA/CHAPATTI Whole-Wheat Flat Breads (*see page 30*)
	PUDEENA ANAINAS RAITA Mint and Pineapple Yogurt Salad *or*
	MATEERA RAITA Watermelon or Muskmelon Yogurt Salad
Dessert:	*MASOOR PAAK* Chickpea Flour Pastry

- **One Week or More Prior:** Read completely through the recipes. Make your grocery lists and buy the bitter melons, lentils, chickpea flour, basmati rice, pistachios, *chapatti* flour, *paneer*, and spices from the Indian market.

- **Six Days or More Prior:** Make the *masoor* pastry and store it in a tin. Prepare the bitter melons and freeze the slices.

- **Two Days Prior:** Buy what you need—the yogurt, fresh fruit, mint, marigolds, cilantro, tomatoes, etc.—from the supermarket.

- **One-Day Prior:** Peel the onions, garlic, and ginger. Stuff and bake the tomatoes. Make the *phulka* dough. Refrigerate all. Make the garam masala (*page 4*).

- **The Day of:**
  AM: Boil the lentils. Make the *tardka* for the lentils and finish the bitter melon recipe.
  PM: Cut the fruit and prepare the *raita*. Refrigerate. Form the balls of dough for the *phulka*. Cover with plastic wrap. Plate the dessert.

- **About an hour before serving:** Preheat the oven to 300°F. Heat the lentils, the bitter melon, and the stuffed tomatoes. Make the *phulkas* and keep them warm in the oven. Garnish the dishes. Don't forget the *raita*!

TOMATOES STUFFED WITH RICE, CHEESE, AND MARIGOLD

Maharani Tamatar   *dairy*

Forget any preconceived notions that flowers are for gazing, not grazing. Marigolds are used as offerings to the gods and in celebrations all over India. They have a slightly spicy flavor. At the end of one summer I had lots of beautiful, ripe tomatoes and a border of marigolds, so I developed this recipe to feature their harmonious flavors.

YIELD: 8 TO 10 SERVINGS

8 to 10 medium ripe plum tomatoes

2½ teaspoons salt

¼ teaspoon pepper

¼ cup plus 1 tablespoon canola or olive oil

1 yellow onion, chopped

1 or 2 cloves garlic, chopped

1 cup basmati rice

2 teaspoons whole coriander seeds, toasted and ground

½ teaspoon ground cayenne pepper

1 cup cubed *paneer* or mozzarella cheese

¼ cup pistachios or toasted walnuts

3 tablespoons sliced mint leaves plus 8 whole leaves for garnish

2 tablespoons sliced cilantro

8 unsprayed, edible marigolds

Cut ¼ inch from the tops of the tomatoes, scoop out the seeds and pulp, and put the tomato tops, seeds, and pulp into a medium pot. Add 1 teaspoon salt, cover, and cook over low heat for about 15 minutes.

Use ½ teaspoon salt and all the pepper to sprinkle the insides of the tomatoes. Turn over to drain on paper towels.

Heat ¼ cup oil in another medium pot with a tight-fitting lid. Add the onion and garlic and sauté just until transparent.

Meanwhile, rinse the rice and drain in a sieve. Dump the rice on top of the onions in the pot. Do not stir. Cover and remove from the heat.

Mash the cooked tomato pulp with a masher or fork. The pulp should be giving up juice. If not, keep heating until it does, then pour the juice through a sieve into a 2-cup measure (if there is more than 2 cups use the rest for the lentils). Pour into the rice. Add the last teaspoon of salt, the coriander seeds, and cayenne pepper. Cover and cook over medium heat for 10 minutes. Turn the heat down to very low, give a stir, cover and cook for another 7 to 10 minutes, until all the liquid has been absorbed and the rice is done. Uncover, fluff the rice with a fork and allow to cool for a few minutes.

Preheat the oven to 400°F. In a food processor, grate the paneer and chop the pistachios. In a bowl mix together the paneer, pistachios, mint, cilantro, and the petals from 7 of the marigolds. Stir the *paneer* mixture into the cooled rice.

Spread the remaining tablespoon of oil in a 10x10-inch baking dish. Fill the tomatoes with the rice mixture mounding on top. Place them close together in the baking dish so that they remain upright, but not squeezed. You may have to put in a potato to fill in a gap in the baking dish. Bake for 30 minutes.*

Garnish each tomato with a mint leaf and a few marigold petals from the remaining marigold. The tomatoes may be eaten warm or cold.

*If making this dish one or two days ahead, bake for only 20 minutes. Then remove from oven, let sit until cool, cover with plastic wrap and refrigerate. Reheat, uncovered, in a 300°F oven for about 20 minutes.

RED LENTIL CURRY

This daal, *without its brown seed coat, cooks quite fast, so it makes a good choice for a home-cooked meal after work. All the cooked* daals *and beans freeze well, so make enough for another day. You may finely chop the tender stems of the cilantro and add them to the simmering lentils. Whey (the liquid left over from making cheese) adds even more protein.*

Pick over the lentils and rinse well. In a medium saucepan, bring the lentils, whey and/or water, turmeric, and salt to a boil; cover and simmer for 30 minutes. Stir and add more water if a thinner "soup" is desired. Keep simmering as you make the *tardka* or tempering mixture.

For the *tardka*: In a medium skillet, heat the oil and fry the onion until golden. Add the garlic and ginger and fry another minute. Add the garam masala and fry for another minute. Pour the *tardka* over the lentils. Stir in most of the cilantro, reserving a tablespoon of leaves and cook for one more minute.

Put the lentils in a serving bowl. Sprinkle with the cumin seeds, a pinch more of the garam masala, and the reserved cilantro leaves.

YIELD: 8 TO 10 SERVINGS

1 cup red lentils (hulled *masoor daal*)

5 cups (total) cold water or liquid whey or a mixture of both

1 teaspoon ground turmeric

2 teaspoons salt, or to taste

2 tablespoons canola oil or *ghee*

1 medium onion, chopped

3 cloves garlic, minced

1½-inch piece ginger, minced

1 teaspoon garam masala

¾ cup chopped cilantro leaves and tender stems

1 teaspoon toasted cumin seeds, ground

We know that this beautiful young relative of my husband was married because she has a small golden cap, an ornament called a *saghie* under her shawl, and a red *bindi* on her forehead.

STIR-FRIED BITTER MELON AND POTATOES

Karelay Aloo   *vegan*

Nubby-skinned Indian bitter melon among other vegetables.

Use either Indian (smaller, rougher, darker green) or Chinese bitter melons (smoother and light green). The juice of the bitter melon (momordica charantia) has been proven to lower blood sugar. I am one of the lucky diabetics who have been able to control the disease with diet and exercise alone. If my sugar has been somewhat high, I try to make something with bitter melon, adding some of the slices to my portion of vegetable, lentil, or meat curry. But I prepare it for myself without salt and fat. Not as tasty, but it works for me to slowly dry the slices in the oven and then freeze the surplus.

YIELD: 8 TO 10 SMALL SERVINGS

1½ pounds bitter melon (*karela*)

2 tablespoons salt

2 medium red potatoes

1 large yellow onion

⅓ cup canola oil

1 teaspoon ground turmeric

¼ teaspoon whole or ground cumin seeds

¼ teaspoon ground cayenne pepper

1 teaspoon green mango powder (*amchoor*)

1 teaspoon *chaat masala (page 5)*

1 teaspoon salt, or to taste

Black pepper to taste

The night before: Peel the melons and cut into ⅓-inch-wide rounds. (Some do not like to leave the seeds in, but I do; they add crunch.) Sprinkle with 2 tablespoons salt and toss several times.

The next day: Preheat the oven to 350°F. Oil a baking sheet. Squeeze several of the melon slices over the sink to release as much bitter juice as possible and place on the baking sheet. Repeat until you have a single layer of rounds. Spritz the slices with non-stick spray and put in the oven for 20 minutes. Turn with a spatula and continue to bake for 25 more minutes. Allow to cool. The cooled slices may be frozen to be used at another time if you aren't using them right away.

Slit the skin of the potatoes in several places and microwave them for 5 minutes. Cool. Slice the onion lengthwise into ¼-inch-thick crescents. In a wok, heat the oil and add the onions, stir-frying until golden. Peel the potatoes and cut them into wedges. Fry the potatoes with the onions for several minutes. Add the (thawed) melon slices and fry for 10 minutes. Add the spices (turmeric through *chaat masala*), salt, and pepper and fry for another minute or two, stirring constantly. Serve immediately.

MINT AND PINEAPPLE YOGURT SALAD

dairy   Pudeena Anainas Raita

This is a cooling treat that kids and grownups love. Just adjust the spices and choose the heat of the pepper to suit the taste of your guests.

Reserve a few mint leaves for garnish and finely slice the rest. Beat the yogurt with the salt, pepper, and a little water or milk. Stir in sliced mint, red onion, chile pepper, and pineapple. Put in a serving bowl and sprinkle with the cumin seeds and mint leaves to garnish.

Variation: For **Melon Yogurt Salad (Mateera Raita)**, replace the pineapple with the same amount of watermelon or muskmelon cut into ³/₄-inch cubes. Then follow the same recipe adding 3 tablespoons honey, 1 teaspoon lime zest, 2 teaspoons lime juice, and ¹/₂ teaspoon *chaat masala (page 5)* to the other ingredients. Garnish with the cumin and mint.

YIELD: 8 ¹/₂-CUP SERVINGS

¹/₂ cup packed mint leaves,

4 cups (32 ounces) plain yogurt

¹/₂ teaspoon salt, or to taste

¹/₈ teaspoon freshly ground black pepper

¹/₂ cup finely chopped red onion

1 hot or mild green chile pepper, seeded and minced

1¹/₂ cups fresh or canned pineapple, drained and chopped

¹/₄ teaspoon toasted whole cumin seeds, ground

Granddaughter Natasha Kaur practices yoga mudras.

CHICKPEA FLOUR PASTRY

Masoor Paak   *dairy or vegan*

Making this recipe is a perfect way to bond with your mother-in-law, because you will need a hand to relieve you during the stirring. My friend Baldev Dhaliwal taught me that technique is everything in this recipe. Read through it before you start! Be very careful when you add the syrup so that you do not splash yourself. It will take about 15 minutes of very fast stirring with a long-handled wooden spoon (for safety). Do not be distracted for any reason! Timesaver: Buy ready-made ghee *from the Indian store.*

YIELD: 25 PIECES

1½ pounds unsalted butter (or 2 cups of ready-made *ghee, page 7,* or vegetable shortening)

1¼ cups water

3 cups sugar

1 teaspoon ground cardamom seeds

1 cup chickpea flour *(besan)*

Make *ghee* by melting the butter in the microwave on reduced power until melted and the solids separated. Pour the *ghee* through a fine sieve once or twice into a measuring cup with a spout to catch the solids. (Discard the solids or reserve to add flavor to a vegetable dish.) Use a small amount of the *ghee* to grease a 10- to 12-inch square pan.

In a medium saucepan mix the water, sugar, and cardamom seeds and heat to the thread stage (230°F) to make a syrup. Remove from heat.

Pour 1 cup of melted *ghee* or shortening in a very large, heavy, nonstick wok. When the *ghee* is hot, add the chickpea flour and stir constantly for about 3 minutes. Very carefully pour all the syrup down the side of the wok so as not to splash yourself, stirring constantly. The mixture will bubble wildly. Do not stop stirring over high to medium-high heat, making sure nothing sticks to the bottom or sides of the pan. When you sense the mixture beginning to stick, pour in more *ghee,* about 1 tablespoon at a time, as you stir very fast. Continue stirring and adding tablespoonfuls of *ghee* as it becomes sticky until you have used about 1 more cup over 10 to 15 minutes of time. You will be stirring very fast the whole time. You may have some *ghee* left over.

At first the mixture will be very bubbly but gradually will become more sticky and taffy-like. Be alert for when it again has small bubbles. Move very quickly at this stage and carefully scrape it into the prepared pan. It is very hot! Try to distribute it evenly on the first go because it will begin to harden. Have a knife ready to immediately cut it into 2-inch pieces. Let sit in the pan until cooled completely—it will continue to cook in the pan giving the characteristic double shade of tan/brown.

BRIDE OF PUNJAB

Fabulously fun Punjabi weddings

Covered in tinsel garlands, our daughter Raji and her husband David are wished long life and happiness together.

My husband, dressed in traditional *kurta/chadra*, dances the *bhangra* to that infectious Punjabi beat.

Radiant bride Pooja dances the jaago.

An intricate henna design adorns our lovely daughter-in-law Nancy's hand.

The bride of Surinder Singh holds his ceremonial scarf, the *pullah*, to signify their union.

At a ladies' *sangeet*, Manjeet Kaur (center) leads the women in folk songs.

In Ludhiana, Punjab, the bride enters a gorgeous tent on the arm of her brother.

IS THERE ANYTHING MORE FUN THAN A PUNJABI wedding? I doubt it. And so would 99 percent of those who have attended one! If you saw the movie *Bend It Like Beckham*, you were treated to a typical one—the music and hoopla going on for days. Now double it! My husband and I were married twice, once in the U.S. and once in India. I treasure both occasions. At the first, in Hillsdale, Michigan, I wore a cream dress with a red *phulkari*, a traditional shawl that my mother-in-law had so graciously sent with my future husband when he returned to the U.S. after obtaining her permission to marry. It was a Catholic ceremony, which I had insisted on. At our second wedding, taking place in the house we rented in Bhatinda, we had a Sikh ceremony. Guests' shoes were removed and lined up outside and this time our son, who was nearly two years old by then, amused himself by playing among them. The guests found that to be most memorable!

For the second wedding, *Bebeji* chose for me a mustard-colored silk *salwar-kameez* with veil, all covered with silver embroidery. Like all brides, I looked as beautiful as I ever would. During the reception in the courtyard we didn't polka

Auntie Gobinder Kaur feeds a sweet to her son, so his words to his bride will always be sweet.

or bugaloo, but we did energetically dance and clap to the traditional *gidda* and *geets*, songs of the village women. What fun! They are usually performed before the wedding day by the bride's family at a *sangeet*.

The lyrics are rustic and usually make fun of the groom's family. Since no one from my family was present, everyone felt free to join in the laughter with the jokes on themselves.

We did not have many of the traditional ceremonies for both the groom and the bride that usually take up several days of revelry. That would come later with the next generation of our family. The ladies' *sangeet* is a special time for the bride in which she can relax a little and have some fun before her big day in the spotlight. Her hands and feet are covered with beautiful designs in henna. She can dance with abandon, and no one will mind. In the *batna* ceremony, her face is washed with yogurt and turmeric to lighten and soften the skin. Similarly, the groom's mother and aunts wash him in his village.

The men of the family usually traveled to the bride's village for the wedding. The groom would arrive on a horse, his face covered by tinsel and accompanied by the men of the family dancing and singing. The ladies of the groom's family usually stayed home, but would take turns staying up all night to watch for any intruders. The women would light the night with special brass pots fitted with candles that they carried on their heads. This is the origin of the *Jaago* ("Wake up!"), a dance performed with special lyrics that is popular at many traditional Punjabi weddings.

Nowadays in the U.S., the good-natured fun usually takes place with both families present. The men's folkdance, the famous *bhangra*, is not confined to men as it was in Punjab. Everybody is compelled to jump up and dance to the infectious, throbbing beat. Americans and Punjabis, both men and women, in clubs all over this country and in "*bhangra* blowouts" on college campuses have enjoyed this electrifying dance. In fact, at our niece Rameet's lovely wedding, we met the husband of a woman who teaches the *bhangra* on DVD (see the section "additional reading" page 227). What a great way to burn off the calories consumed in an over-the-top wedding feast!

The "Bride of Punjab" Menu

The mother in Bend It Like Beckham *exhorted her daughter, Jesminder, to "make a full Indian dinner." When you prepare this menu you would make any Punjabi mother or mother-in-law proud. It is a feast fit for a wedding!*

In the early seventies after we returned from India, we did just that. There were no Indian restaurants or caterers, and we would not have been able to afford them even if there were; so we learned from each other and "catered" our own celebrations.

Appetizer:	BHARIA BAINGAN Baby Eggplants with Potato or Tamarind Filling PAPARD Lentil Crisps (*page 16*)
Main Course:	SEEKH KEBABS Ground Lamb Kebabs AMB DA MARUBBA Mango Preserves MAHAN DEE DAAL Creamy Black Lentils with Kidney Beans NOH-RATNA PILAW Nine-Jeweled Rice Pilaf DEHIN BHALLAY Savory "Sundae" of Lentil Fritters, Yogurt and Chutney (*page 110*)
Dessert:	KHAJOOR BURFEE Date and Nut Rolls

- **One Week or More Prior:** Read the recipes from start to finish. Prepare your grocery lists. Buy the needed items from the Indian market—spices, tamarind, *papard*, lentils, green mangoes, paneer, nuts, and dates. Make the date rolls and freeze. Make the mango preserves and refrigerate.

- **Three Days Prior:** Buy the eggplants and other vegetables and the meat.

- **Two Days Prior:** Make the lentils, except for the *tardka* and refrigerate.

- **One-Day Prior:** Chop and measure the nuts for both the eggplant and kebab recipes. Make the kebabs and the stuffings for the eggplants. Refrigerate. Thaw the date rolls and slice them.

- **The Day of:**
  AM: Make the *tardka* for the lentils. Salt the eggplants, then stuff them. Begin the rice dish.
  PM: Bring the mango preserves to room temp. Finish the eggplant and rice recipes. Grill the kebabs before or after the guests arrive.

- **At Serving Time:** Warm the eggplant, lentils, and rice and heat the *papard*. Garnish the dishes.

BABY EGGPLANTS WITH POTATO OR TAMARIND FILLING

Bharia Baingan   *vegan*

Auntie Surindra makes this dish that you will find on the menu of many elegant weddings. I've developed two different fillings for you, potato and cashew or sweet and sour tamarind. They are both delicious. Choose eight 4- to 5-ounce eggplants or sixteen 2- to 3-ounce ones. But they should be uniform. Make one of the two stuffings per recipe. You will need sewing thread if you want to guarantee they stay closed. The same mixture may be used to stuff "baby" squashes or small peppers. So if you are making this recipe for a large crowd, you have six variations!

YIELD: 8 TO 16 PIECES

8 to 16 miniature eggplants

¼ cup salt

For the potato filling:

1 large potato (1 cup mashed)

3 tablespoons canola oil

1½ cups finely chopped onion

1 tablespoon grated ginger

¼ cup finely chopped cashews

½ teaspoon whole or ground cumin seeds

½ teaspoon ground or crushed coriander seeds

¼ teaspoon ground cayenne pepper

1 teaspoon garam masala

2 teaspoons salt

2 teaspoons lime juice

In a large bowl, cover the uncut eggplants with water and soak for a few minutes to release any grit. Rinse thoroughly. Fill the same bowl again with 2 quarts warm water and dissolve the salt in it. Slit the eggplants to within an inch of the calyx (green stem end) and then make another slit crosswise. Slightly separate the four sections and soak in the salted water for 30 to 60 minutes to remove bitterness.

For the potato filling: Wash and slit the potato and microwave until soft, about 4 minutes. Cool, peel, and mash. Heat the oil in a skillet and sauté the onions. Add the ginger and stir-fry until fairly brown. Add the cashews, cumin seeds, coriander seeds, and sauté for a minute. Add the cayenne pepper and garam masala and stir. Add the salt and lime juice. Mix well. Thoroughly blend into the mashed potatoes. (The mixture may be refrigerated for a day at this point.)

For the tamarind filling: Cut the onions in half and cut out the solid stem end. Cut into long slices about ¼-inch wide. Separate the slices. You should have about 3 cups. Sauté the onions in the hot oil over high heat until all the slices are transparent and beginning to brown. Add the garlic and ginger and sauté another few minutes. Turn down the heat and add the cumin seeds, garam masala, and ½ teaspoon salt and sauté until the onions are brown, being careful not to burn them. Stir in the tamarind and sugar and remove from the heat. Set aside and as it cools, push the filling to one side, leaving the oil. The filling may be refrigerated at this point. Reserve the oil.

For both recipes: Preheat the oven to 350°F. Drain and rinse the eggplants. You may wish to put on a latex glove to protect your hands from discoloration as you fill the eggplants with 1 tablespoon of filling for the small ones and 1½ tablespoons for the larger ones. Spread evenly into the four slits. Wrap each with several windings of sewing thread to keep them together. Put the filled eggplants into a glass or ceramic casserole dish. (Sixteen 2- to 3-ounce eggplants fit into a 10x10-inch one.) Brush with the reserved oil if using the tamarind filling or with canola oil if using the potato filling. Sprinkle with salt and pepper to taste. Cover and bake for about 1 hour on the bottom shelf of the oven so that the bottoms carmelize a bit.

Just before serving, place the casserole uncovered under the broiler until the top skins of the eggplants are somewhat charred, about 5 minutes. Garnish with a sprinkle of *chaat masala* and cilantro leaves.

For the tamarind filling:

2 large onions

⅓ cup canola oil

3 cloves garlic, minced

2-inch piece ginger, grated

1 teaspoon ground cumin seeds

1 teaspoon garam masala

½ teaspoon salt, plus salt and pepper to taste

1 tablespoon dark tamarind concentrate (like Tamcon®), or 2 tablespoons of the lighter

1 tablespoon sugar

A pinch of freshly grated nutmeg (*optional*)

Garnishes: *chaat masala (page 5)*; sliced cilantro leaves

Whose design do you like best? Granddaughters Sophie and Sammie at a wedding.

GROUND LAMB KEBABS

Seekh Kebabs   *meat*

*People who say they don't like lamb love these morsels. It took me
quite a while to get the recipe right. I tried to grill them on skewers,
but they are much more successful without them and broiled.*

YIELD: 24 2-INCH KEBABS

½ teaspoon saffron

½ cup chickpea flour

2 pounds ground lamb

2 teaspoons whole coriander seeds

2 teaspoons whole cumin seeds

½ cup blanched peeled almonds

3 teaspoons garam masala

2 cups finely chopped onion

2-inch piece ginger

2 cloves garlic

½ cup cilantro leaves

4 tablespoons hung yogurt (*page 6*)
    or light sour cream

¼ cup lemon juice

3 to 4 teaspoons salt

Optional garnishes: slices of tomato,
    lemon, white radish; mint
    leaves or scallions, sliced
    lengthwise in quarters,
    and soaked in ice water
    to curl them

Toast the saffron in a hot, dry pan for less than a minute.
Collect the threads on a clean piece of white paper. Pinch
between your thumb and finger until pulverized. Set aside.

Toss the chickpea flour into the same pan and heat until
light brown but not burned. In a medium bowl, mix the
saffron and the flour with the ground lamb.

Toast the coriander seeds and cumin seeds in the same pan,
tossing for 3 minutes until fragrant, being careful not to
burn. Grind in a spice grinder. Add the almonds and grind
again. Mix into the meat along with the garam masala.

Fill a cloth napkin with the chopped onion and wring it
out over a cup or small bowl. Reserve the juice. Grind
the ginger and garlic in a blender or food processor and
then add the cilantro and chop.

In a medium bowl, blend the onion and cilantro mixture
into the hung yogurt along with the lemon juice. Add 2
teaspoons salt and 1 tablespoon of the onion juice. Mix
thoroughly with the lamb mixture. Refrigerate for at
least 15 minutes. (The remainder of the onion juice may
be used in the gravy of a vegetable dish.)

Divide the lamb mixture into thin, cylindrical 2-inch-
long kebabs. Refrigerate for 15 minutes. Set the broiler
to high. Cover a broiler pan with foil and brush or spray
with oil. Place the kebabs on the pan and broil on the
first shelf below the heat for 5 minutes. Turn the kebabs
and broil for 5 more minutes until browned in spots.

Arrange some tomato and radish slices on a platter.
Sprinkle with ½ teaspoon salt or *chaat masala (page 5)*.
Arrange the kebabs on top. Sprinkle with the remaining
salt and garam masala. Top with the garnishes.

MANGO PRESERVES

vegan   Amb Da Marubba

Move over Major Grey! This is a luscious recipe by Rana K. Sidhu, which I adapted for the American kitchen. In India, Rana cooks the totally unripe mangoes until dark brown. I like to buy half-ripe mangoes and cook them just enough so they keep hints of the mango color. But the more unripe the mango, the thicker the final consistency. Like Major Grey, this is a preserve, a marubba, *not a fresh chutney.*

YIELD: 1 QUART

In a food processor, chop the almonds first, then add the dates and raisins and chop again. Set aside.

Peel the mangoes and slice the flesh off the seed. Grate the slices in the food processor leaving some small pieces. In a medium saucepan, cook the mangoes and sugar over low heat until somewhat light brown, stirring occasionally.

Grind all the spices (nutmeg through cloves) together in a spice or coffee grinder. Add them to the pot with the melon seeds, mangoes, vinegar, and salt. Stir and cook for a minute more. Remove from heat, cool, and store in a sterilized glass container. Refrigerate if not to be entirely used within a few days.

6 whole almonds

3 pitted dates, cut into pieces

2 tablespoons raisins

3 or 4 large (2½ to 3 pounds) half-ripe, green mangoes

2 cups plus 2 tablespoons sugar

1 pinch grated fresh nutmeg

Seeds from 2 black cardamom pods

½ cinnamon stick

½ teaspoon black peppercorns

3 whole cloves

1 tablespoon melon seeds (*magaz*) or pine nuts (*optional*)

2 tablespoons malt or cider vinegar

½ teaspoon salt, or to taste

1 pinch black salt (*optional*)

CREAMY BLACK LENTILS WITH KIDNEY BEANS

Mahan Dee Daal   *vegan or dairy*

Found throughout Punjab in the loftiest banquet halls swirled with cream or in a simple gurudwara langar, *these lentils are high in protein, but they also take the second longest of all the lentils to cook, making your microwave or pressure cooker a helpful friend for this recipe.*

YIELD: 7 CUPS

1 cup whole black lentils (*urad daal* or *mahan dee daal*), picked over and rinsed

½ cup dried red kidney beans or *chana daal*, picked over and rinsed

1 tablespoon salt

For the *tardka*:

1 medium onion, finely chopped

3 cloves garlic, minced

2-inch piece ginger, minced

¼ cup *ghee* or canola oil

1 long green chile pepper, seeded and thinly sliced

1 medium/large tomato, chopped

1 teaspoon garam masala (*optional*)

¼ cup plus 1 tablespoon heavy cream (*optional*)

¼ cup sliced cilantro leaves for garnish (*optional*)

Soak the lentils and beans overnight in 1 quart of water. Drain and rinse and put in a large microwavable dish with 6 cups of water and the salt. Tightly cover and heat on high for 50 to 60 minutes (or cook in a pressure cooker for the same amount of time following the manufacturer's directions carefully; or place in a large saucepan and simmer on top of the stove for about 4 hours). Stir occasionally at first and more often as they thicken. Check them and add more water if needed. Lentils will be creamy when fully cooked.

After the lentils have cooked, in a medium skillet sauté the onion, garlic, and ginger in the *ghee* or oil until lightly browned. Add the chile pepper and tomato and sauté until the tomato is cooked and the oil begins to separate. Add the garam masala and sauté a minute more. Stir in ¼ cup cream and add the mixture to the lentils. Simmer until just heated through. Place in a serving bowl, swirl with a spoon of cream on top and sprinkle with cilantro.

NINE-JEWELED RICE PILAF

vegan or dairy or egg   Noh-Ratna Pilaw

Uncle Gurcharan Singh's wedding gift to us was a beautiful jewelry set made of gold and the lucky nine gems. These jewels also symbolize the nine wise counselors or wiziers of my favorite ruler of India, the Emperor Akbar. The dish has so many additions that it is certainly fit for a king and very lucky for you and your guests! To add up to five more servings, just increase the rice to 3 cups and water to 6 cups.

Optional garnishes: 5 whole salted cashews; 5 whole pistachios; 5 whole salted almonds; 1 hard-boiled egg, sliced; slices of green chilies or scallions

YIELD: 10 SERVINGS

For the rice:
2 cups basmati rice
¼ cup *ghee* or canola oil
1 large onion, very thinly sliced
4 cloves garlic, minced
1 tablespoon minced ginger
1 long green chile pepper, seeded and chopped
2 whole black cardamom pods (*optional*)
1 cinnamon stick
¼ teaspoon ground cayenne pepper
2 teaspoons salt, or more to taste
1 teaspoon saffron, toasted slightly in a dry pan and crumbled

Optional additions:
2 tablespoons canola oil
¼ cup sliced almonds
¼ cup unsalted pistachios, chopped
¼ cup cashew pieces
1 cup frozen mixed vegetables, thawed
2 cups (¾-inch cubes) fried *paneer*, soaked in warm water
¼ teaspoon white pepper
¼ teaspoon salt
¼ teaspoon garam masala
¼ cup golden raisins, plumped in hot water
3 hard-boiled eggs, cut into eighths

Soak the rice in water to cover for 30 minutes, drain and rinse until the water runs clear. Heat the *ghee* in a large, heavy-bottomed pot and fry the onion until golden. Add the garlic, ginger, chile pepper, spices, and salt; then add the rice and fry for about 2 more minutes. Set aside.

Prepare the additions to the rice: Fry the nuts in the oil. Set aside. Cook the mixed vegetables in the microwave for three minutes on high and set aside. Drain the *paneer*. Mix the white pepper, salt, and garam masala together. Sprinkle the *paneer* with half of the spice mixture and toss. Drain the raisins. Sprinkle the cut eggs with the remaining spice mixture.

Twenty minutes before serving, bring four cups of water to a boil with the toasted saffron and add to the rice, stirring once. Bring back to a boil, and then cover tightly, lowering the heat to simmer, and cook for 20 minutes. Adjust the seasoning when the rice is cooked.

To assemble: Fold the mixed vegetables and nuts into the rice. Incorporate the *paneer* and the cut eggs into the rice. Serve immediately on a large, preferably heated, platter. Garnish with the nuts, egg, and green onions or chilies.

DATE AND NUT ROLLS

Khajoor Burfee   *dairy*

Although luddoos *(fried droplets of chickpea flour batter soaked in syrup and then molded into balls) are the very traditional Punjabi wedding sweet, my friend Baldev Dhaliwal taught me this recipe which I adapted for a garden wedding. It is not only healthful, it looks and tastes dreamy. Use any combination of nuts you enjoy. The logs may be wrapped tightly in plastic wrap, then in foil and frozen.*

YIELD: 32 PIECES

4 cups pitted dates

1 can (14 oz.) sweetened condensed milk (about 1¼ cups)

1½ cups almonds, coarsely ground

1 cup unsalted pistachios, chopped

1 cup unsalted cashews, chopped

1 cup sweetened, grated coconut (*optional*)

In the microwave, heat the dates until just soft (about 2 to 4 minutes). Then in a large, dry nonstick pan or wok over low heat, mash dates with a potato masher and add the condensed milk, stirring, until absorbed. Add the nuts and mix thoroughly. Remove from heat and allow to cool.

As soon as the date mixture cools down enough to handle, divide and roll into four equal logs less than 2-inches in diameter. Roll the logs in the coconut if you are using it. Wrap the rolls in waxed paper and store in the refrigerator overnight. Slice slightly on the diagonal with an oiled dough scraper or very heavy knife before serving.

PUNJABI SOUL FOOD

The splendid poetry of Punjab

FROM THE TIME WHEN ALEXANDER SWEPT DOWN THROUGH THE KHYBER PASS ONTO the rich plains, to the Mongols who robbed bursting granaries and looted gold from the temples, Punjab has suffered countless invasions. In fact, there is a saying about a warlord who would regularly arrive after every winter from the cold of Afghanistan: *"Khada, peeta lahe daa, Bakee Nadir Shahin daa!"* Which translates "Eat and drink whatever you can, the rest is Nadir Shah's!"

The vagaries of Mother Nature and the persecutions of the ever-changing rulers have stamped the character of the Punjabi farmer. Living in the moment as well as being resigned to one's fate are traits ingrained into daily life. Certainly the roots of that life go far back, into the Harappan civilization 5,000 years ago. Whether dancing the *bhangra*, with that infectious beat, or singing the ecstatic hymns of the *qwallee, bhajan,* or *shabad,* the Punjabi throws himself with whole heart into the task of the moment. There is passion and respect for work so intense that wherever these folks migrate or whatever profession they take up, they will be among the hardest workers and the most enterprising.

Their love of God is so strong that many rise before dawn to pray, doing *pooja, namaaz,* or *nitnem* reciting the beautiful prayers of their faith. The depth of that faith increases their appreciation of life, their joy in music and the simple pleasures of food and family that many would call "soul." That lovely word expresses patience, courage, yearning, and a little defiance thrown in for spice.

Bhulleh Shah, the great mystic poet, sums up the Punjabi philosophy: "If there is no passion in your heart, God is not pleased." Although his worldly home was in west Punjab, Bhulleh Shah belonged to the infinite. His poetry reads on many levels—the intimate lover, the social critic, a true psychologist, and the highest Sufi adept. Rarely on earth has such a soul existed, yet in his own lifetime, he and his spiritual master were shunned.

> *Mein kali te mayray mahin bee kalay.*
> I am black and my lover is black.
>
> *Ne asien kale lok sadenday.*
> People talk about us being black.
>
> *Koran majid de harf we kale*
> Yet the words of the Koran are in black [ink]
>
> *Te lok wich masit parendia*
> And people go to the mosque to read it.

Sung by Jagjit Singh Zirvi, the great interpreter of Bhulleh Shah in the *gazal*-style of music, this poem pierces my heart every time I hear it. *Qwallee* is another famous style of Sufi music employing alternating group voices, the blend of instruments, and hand clapping to build on emotion. Waves of feeling develop, transporting the audience into ecstasy. As one voice singing the poetry of a Punjabi mystic ends, another voice picks it up and sends it upward to heaven. And our souls are transported there, a place of joy, love, and light.

The "Punjabi Soul Food" Menu

This menu has many ingredients in common with the "soul food" of African-Americans of the southern U.S.—fritters, greens, cornbread, okra, and a banana dessert. Interestingly, it is also a vegan menu (if you leave off butter and ghee). For many that makes it more spiritual as well as more healthful and good for the planet.

There are more vegetarians on the Indian side of Punjab than almost anywhere else in India. Yet the great majority are not vegans because dairy plays such a big part in the diet. But the wonderful vegan recipes make the absence of meat or dairy little missed.

Traditionally, Punjabis eat stewed mixed greens served on top of a grilled cornmeal flat bread with a knob of melting butter on top. The Punjabi will break off a small piece of the bread, using it as a scoop to pick up some of the greens. The bread acts like a plate. In fact, when I first had this delicious dish in India, my husband told me the story of an Englishman who ate the greens but threw away the "plate"! That story must still be making the rounds.

Appetizer:	*SUBZE PAKORA* Chunky Vegetable Fritters
Main Course:	*SARON DA SAAG* Stewed Mixed Greens with Lentils
	MUKKEE DEE ROTEE Cornmeal Flat Breads
	ALOO BHINDEE Crispy Potatoes, Onions and Okra
	NIMBOO ACHAR Lemon Pickle
Dessert:	*KAYLA KHOPA* Baked Bananas with Coconut

- **One Month or More Prior:** Read the recipes from beginning to end and make your grocery lists. Buy the lemons, brown lentils, and greens from the market. Make the lemon pickle and cook the greens. If you double the amount of greens and freeze in batches, you save lots of time in the long run. Freeze them without adding the *tardka*, which is better added when serving.

- **One Week or More Prior:** Buy the spices, cornmeal, chickpea flour, *ghee* (if using) or coconut oil, *gurd*, and grated coconut from the Indian market. Buy a pickle or chutney if not making one.

- **Two to Three Days Prior:** Buy the vegetables, bananas, and needed staples from the supermarket. Or, if possible, combine this list with the one above, and get everything from the Indian market, saving you an extra trip.

- **One-Day Prior:** Make the baked bananas and refrigerate. Thaw the greens.

- **The Day of:**
  AM: Turn on the exhaust fan and make the *tardka* for the greens. Make the batter for the fritters. Make the dough for the *mukkee dee rotee*.
  PM: Make the *aloo bhindee*. Make the *rotees*. Cut up the vegetables for the fritters. Fry them before or after your guests arrive. Clean up.

- **Serving Time:** Warm the fritters in a 250°F oven. Serve with a chutney of your choice. Heat the greens in the microwave. Turn up the oven heat and crisp the okra and potatoes and warm the breads. Serve with the pickle. Crisp the dessert in the oven before serving.

CHUNKY VEGETABLE FRITTERS

vegan   Subze Pakora

These fritters are so good, guests of all ages will beg you to make them again and again. Everyone has a favorite vegetable among this mix, so you end up pleasing the whole crowd. Serve with a chutney of your choice, but I like Syrupy Ginger-Mango Chutney (page 176) with this menu.

Mix the chickpea flour, rice flour, baking powder, salt, cumin seeds, coriander seeds, cayenne pepper, and cold water in a large bowl. Set aside.

Trim the green end from the eggplant and slice lengthwise in half. Keeping the two halves together, cut them into 2-inch-wide slices. You will have about eight pieces. Sprinkle the cut sides with salt and let sit for 10 minutes, then drain.

Slice the potato into approximately 8 thin slices, cover and microwave on high in a little water until almost tender, about 3 minutes.

Separate the florets of the cauliflower into about 12 pieces, cover and microwave on high in a little water until almost tender, about 5 minutes. Slice the onion horizontally into 8 slices.

Cover your hand with a latex glove and slit peppers lengthwise, removing seeds and pith but leaving stems on.

In a large saucepan, add oil to a depth of at least 3 inches and preheat to 350°F. Drain the vegetables on paper towels. Drop vegetables, one type at a time into the batter. Fry one and check for salt. Fry the rest in small batches. Remove with a slotted spoon to paper towels. If there is more batter, slice another onion or potato.

These are best eaten immediately, but may be kept warm in a 200°F oven; or be refrigerated and reheated; or can be frozen in a single layer and then bagged for later use. Serve with chutney.

YIELD: 45 PIECES

2 cups chickpea flour (*besan*)

1/2 cup rice flour or use more chickpea flour

1 teaspoon baking powder

1 1/2 teaspoons salt

1 teaspoon whole or ground cumin seeds

1 teaspoon ground coriander seeds

1/2 to 1 teaspoon ground cayenne pepper

1 1/2 cups cold water

1 medium Japanese (long, thin) eggplant

1 large potato

1/2 small head cauliflower

1 large onion

5 medium long green chile peppers

Vegetable oil for frying

STEWED MIXED GREENS WITH LENTILS

Saron Da Saag   *vegan*

Healthful and satisfying, stewed mixed greens with lentils and corn flatbread.

Mustard greens are the star in this Punjabi recipe that is famous throughout India. My mother-in-law would sit on a wood and rope peedee *or low stool with piles of fresh mustard next to her and cut it, not with a knife, but with a* daatt, *a curved sharp blade with a wooden base that she would hold between her feet. That way she could use both hands to hold the mustard. Her extra pair of hands we all wish we had sometimes were her feet!*

YIELD: 8 CUPS

2 bunches mustard greens or kale, about 1 pound each, or 2 (16-ounce) packages frozen mustard greens, thawed

1 bunch broccoli rabe, about 1 pound, or 1 (20-ounce) package frozen chopped broccoli, thawed

3 bags fresh spinach (about 12 ounces each) or 2 (20-ounce) packages frozen spinach, thawed

1 large onion, sliced

4 cloves garlic, sliced

½ to 1 teaspoon dried red pepper flakes, according to taste

2 teaspoons dried fenugreek leaves (*optional*)

½ to 1 cup brown flat lentils (*sabat masoor*), picked over and rinsed

2 teaspoons salt, or to taste

¼ to ½ cup coarse cornmeal

For *tardka* (for 4 cups of *saag*):

¼ cup vegetable oil

1 medium onion, chopped

2 cloves garlic, minced

1-inch piece ginger, minced

6-inch mild or hot green chile pepper, seeded and chopped

Garnish: ¼ teaspoon *ghee* per person (*optional*)

Wash fresh greens thoroughly by soaking in a pan or sink of cold water. Rinse, drain, and coarsely chop. Put the fresh or thawed greens in a pot with 4 cups fresh water, and the onion, garlic, red pepper, fenugreek leaves, lentils, and salt. Bring to a boil, reduce heat and cook this mixture on medium/low heat for 1 hour. Reduce heat to low and continue to cook for 4 hours, stirring occasionally. (Or you may then transfer to a crock-pot and continue cooking slowly.) Allow to cool enough to safely handle, about 20 minutes (mixture will be watery). Purée in a processor or in batches in a blender. Return the pureéd greens mixture to medium heat, add ¼ cup of cornmeal, and cook stirring for 10 more minutes until somewhat thick. Add more cornmeal if still watery. Take out as much *saag* as you are going to use and freeze the rest in your choice of containers.

Each time you are ready to serve the *saag*, make the *tardka* by frying the onion, garlic, ginger, and chile pepper in the hot oil and then pouring it over the *saag* in the serving bowl and lightly stirring it in. You may give each person a little melted *ghee* on her portion, which is very Punjabi, but that is not the vegan thing to do.

CORNMEAL FLAT BREADS

vegan   Mukkee Dee Rotee

This bread is unusual because the dough is partially cooked by boiling water—just enough to hold the dough together. The best corn breads are made by our dear Auntie Sanghera, best friend of my mother-in-law during the last fifteen years of her life. Watching Auntie work is like watching a master artist, hypnotic. We have all learned more than bread-making from her example. Her patience, humility, and faith have matched her artistry in the kitchen.

Auntie Sanghera makes the best corn breads.

In a large bowl, mix the cornmeal and salt very thoroughly. Add half the boiling water and stir with a long wooden spoon that does not conduct the heat. Keep stirring until the mixture is uniformly crumbly. Gradually add more water and continue stirring until the dough holds together. (Or you can use the dough arm of a mixer.) Allow the dough to rest for 30 minutes or more, covered, and then knead thoroughly in the bowl with oiled hands.

Heat a griddle on high until very hot. With oiled hands divide the dough into 16 pieces and roll each piece into a ball and cover them with a damp towel. Flatten a ball in your oiled hand and then roll with a rolling pin or pat with your hands between sheets of clear wrap into a 5-inch disk. Remove one side of the wrap and flip the *rotee* onto the griddle. Try to keep the edges from crumbling. Heat until you can see that it is almost cooked through on one side and then flip it. It should be a little brown in spots. Wrap in a towel or serve immediately. Or cool and wrap tightly before freezing. Continue until all the dough balls are cooked.

YIELD: 16 5-INCH BREADS

4 cups fine to medium-course cornmeal*

1 scant tablespoon salt

4 cups boiling water, or less

Vegetable oil for greasing hands

*Do **not** use very finely ground corn as in cornflour or the *masa harina* used in tamales and tortillas.

CRISPY POTATOES, ONIONS AND OKRA

Aloo Bhindee   *vegan*

Crispy Okra and Potatoes, a dish that would be at home in Punjab or Louisiana.

Can you fall in love with a vegetable? After you taste this sophisticated dish you will agree with me that the answer is yes. Yes!! Fresh okra and other "exotic" vegetables were not available where I grew up in Detroit. But my mother would take me downtown to a cafeteria that had all kinds of vegetable dishes and I astonished the servers by piling my tray with every single one. This greedy little kid took no desserts, just fried eggplant and okra, cauliflower au gratin, stuffed peppers, and stewed tomatoes! Yum!!

YIELD: 8 ½-CUP SERVINGS

1 pound fresh okra

2 large Yukon Gold potatoes, peeled

2 cups vegetable oil for frying

1½ large onions, thinly sliced

2 teaspoons ground turmeric

1 teaspoon ground cumin seeds

2 teaspoons salt, or more to taste

½ teaspoon freshly ground black pepper

¼ teaspoon dried red pepper flakes, or to taste

½ teaspoon black salt (*optional*)

1 tablespoon dried green mango powder (*amchoor*) or juice of ½ lemon

Garnish: 1 small tomato, sliced into wedges

Cut off the "caps" of the okra and slice lengthwise into four sections. Cut the potatoes into sticks 2 to 3 inches in length and ½-inch wide. In a large pan or wok, heat the vegetable oil over high heat. Begin stir-frying the okra in batches, turning infrequently until they begin to brown slightly in places. Remove from the oil with a slotted spoon and lightly spread across a slotted broiler pan.

Fry the potatoes in batches until brown, being careful not to break them. Remove with a slotted spoon to the broiler pan. Add the onions to the hot oil in batches and fry until brown. Remove with a slotted spoon and lightly spread across the broiler pan.

Before serving, preheat the oven to 250°F. Mix together the turmeric, cumin, salt, black pepper, red pepper, black salt, and green mango powder (if using lemon juice do not add at this point). Sprinkle over the vegetables. Place in the oven for 15 minutes. The excess oil will drip into the tray and the heat will crisp the vegetables. Toss lightly in a serving bowl to evenly distribute the spices. If using lemon juice instead of the *amchoor*, sprinkle it on now, give another toss, and serve immediately. Garnish with tomato wedges.

Note: You may substitute 1½ tablespoons *chaat masala (page 5)* for the ingredients listed after cumin seeds.

LEMON PICKLE

I love all kinds of Punjabi pickles and chutneys, but my husband is faithful to this very plain one—especially with saag and mukee di rotee or aloo paurantha. I always have to make sure to start a batch curing when we are running low because he will not touch a commercial product. Use a jar with a plastic lid if possible, so that the salt and acid in the pickle will not corrode the lid.

Soak the whole lemons in light soapy water or veggie wash to remove the wax. Rinse and dry with a clean cloth. Trim stem end. Cut 5 of the lemons into quarters. Put the quarters in a sterile glass quart jar (like a mayo jar). As you put the quarters in, pour some salt around each layer. The lemons should fit snugly in the jar. Cut up and add another lemon if there is not a snug fit. Squeeze the juice from the last ½ lemon over the top of the lemons or use a full lemon if the others are not very juicy. Finish with salt. If using a metal cap, cover the opening with a piece of plastic wrap so that the metal will never touch the contents even if turned upside down.

Set out on a sunny shelf if possible for several weeks to months, turning the jar often. If mold is detected, remove that section and add a little vinegar to the lemons. Every couple of weeks, shake the jar and turn it upside down for a few hours to redistribute the juice.

YIELD: DEPENDS ON THE AGE OF THE PICKLE*

6 or 7 lemons

1 cup kosher salt (approximate)

*The lemons shrink and "melt" as they get older and browner. Preserved lemons are used in Moroccan, Greek, and Italian cuisine as well as Punjabi. The Mediterranean countries tend to use the lemons sooner (within a few weeks of preserving), cutting slivers into pasta and meat dishes, while Indians prefer their pickle "well done."

BAKED BANANAS WITH COCONUT

Kayla Khopa

vegan or dairy

I wanted a vegan recipe for this menu and made several traditional fried chickpea flour confections that just seemed too heavy. This recipe is one I adapted from an historic cookbook of the British Raj that attributed it to the state of Punjab. It seems quite the British fusion dish to me, but hey, it's delish!

YIELD: 12 SERVINGS

¼ teaspoon saffron (*optional*)

4 tablespoons coconut oil or *ghee*

1½ cups grated coconut (fresh; frozen and thawed; or unsweetened dried)

½ cup all-purpose flour

1 cup crumbled *gurd* or light brown sugar

Juice of 1½ lemons (¼ cup)

6 bananas or very ripe (black) plantains

Preheat the oven to 350°F. Heat the saffron in a small dry pan over high heat for a few seconds until fragrant. Crush the saffron and dissolve it in 2 tablespoons boiling water.

Spread 2 tablespoons of coconut oil or melted *ghee* in a 10x10-inch, preferably glass, baking pan. Sprinkle with the coconut and toast the coconut for about 8 minutes until very lightly brown in spots.* Stir in 2 more tablespoons of oil or *ghee*, the saffron, flour, and sugar. Mix well.

Put the lemon juice into a bowl. Cut the bananas in half lengthwise and then into 2-inch lengths and put into the bowl. Toss the pieces in the lemon juice. Top the coconut with the bananas. Turn with a spatula so that most of the coconut mixture is on top. Bake for 20 minutes or until bubbly.

*Thawed coconut needs more time to brown in the oven and may need to be stirred halfway through cooking.

MOST POPULAR

A story about the downside of celebrity

I GOT MY FIRST TASTE OF CELEBRITY IN BHATINDA. THE COAL-DRIVEN TRAIN CARRYING us and hundreds of others had just screeched to a grinding halt at 4 AM, the great engine still steaming and sputtering in the night. Donkeys were braying and roosters crowing. Men were jostling each other, vying for the chance to carry our bags. The bell tones of hawkers cried out, "*Chai garam! Chai garam!*" Delicious smells of spiced tea and fried noodles competed with the stench of animals and humans. This was Bhatinda, the great rail junction town in south Punjab, our new home.

The air was cool, but my mother-in-law and I were warm in our new Chanel-style rabbit fur and wool sweaters that I had splurged on for us back in the U.S. She in light blue, me in pale yellow, we perched in the peddie-cab, my two-year-old in my lap, the preposterously thin legs of the driver, standing straight with the strain, pumping up and down, luggage piled behind us.

As we arrived on Birla Mill Road, the whistle of the departing train seemed to have announced our presence because somehow the word was out. "*Ma'am ahgee! Ma'am ahgee!*" ("Madam has come!") echoed in the narrow, grimy street from a horde of children. Somehow I got into the house, but found we were not alone. Through the bars of the windows and the wooden shutters (there was no glass), I could see eyes follow me as the children raised the slats with little sticks. Sparrows flew around the room while I washed my dust-streaked face in a basin. And then I performed a ritual I would practice every morning and evening. I threw a white sheet over my head, and under it I changed my clothes.

Whenever I left the house, even if I were in the open courtyard, the excited chant would begin, and people would appear from nowhere to crowd on the rooftops or the street, their necks straining to get a glimpse of a rarely seen American woman. Boys would take turns standing on shoulders to try to peek over the wall. I found that the "*gusselkhana,*" a stark room with bolted door, very high concrete walls, and no windows, was my only refuge from prying eyes for months. It was the place where I would place a bucket of cold water on the concrete floor, stand and bathe, one steel cup poured over me at a time, the soapy water running to the open drains along the perimeter.

Recent research has shown that a chimpanzee will do just about anything to look at a photo of the leader of the troop. Since our genes are 98.77 percent the same as the chimps, it may explain our human interest in celebrities. But sorry, the "Most Popular" title, even with all of its glamorous connotations, will, for me, be forever suspect.

Spinning in the street for Bhatinda's kids.

The "Most Popular" Menu

A large tandoor, a cylindrical oven made of clay bricks covered by a thick slurry of clay, stood waist high, not far from the entrance to our village compound. The owners would start the fire with dried dung cakes at the bottom and cotton sticks piled on top of that. As the ashes fell, the rotees were slapped directly onto the walls that remained at temperatures approaching 700°F for several hours. Only breads were baked in that oven, so it did not have the usual vertical spits used to grill meats.

This menu and its recipes were developed for the first cooking class I ever taught. It became the favorite for beginners because it has five well-known and wonderful dishes. The zucchini, although not found on restaurant menus, is very popular in our extended family.

Whether preparing this menu to raise money for a playground, or for scholarships, as I do now, or for the first of your many Indian Gourmet Club dinners, you will soon discover why these dishes are so popular.

Appetizer:	SAMOSA Small Vegetable and/or Meat Turnovers PUDEENA CHUTNEY Mint Chutney
Main Course:	TANDOORI MURGA Grilled "Red" Chicken TANDOORI ROTEE Broiled Whole-Wheat Yeast Flat Breads TORIAN NAL BUDDIAN Home-style Zucchini
Dessert:	KHEER Rice Pudding or AMB KHEER Mango Rice Pudding

- **One Week or More Prior:** Read the recipes from beginning to end and make your grocery lists. Buy the spices, basmati rice, and *buddian* from the Indian market. Make the garam masala (*page 4*) and the tandoori chicken masala (spice mixture for Grilled "Red" Chicken, *page 62*). Mix the salt and spices for the vegetable *samosa* (except for the mustard seed).

- **Two to Three Days Prior:** Buy the meat, vegetables, and staples from the supermarket. Skin the chicken when you get home and rinse in salt water, then marinate it in the salt and lemon juice for half an hour before rinsing again and storing in a plastic bag in the refrigerator. Make the meat filling for the meat *samosa*, if chosen. Make the rice pudding. Refrigerate everything.

- **One Day Prior:** Make the vegetable filling for the *samosa*, if chosen. Make the rest of the marinade for the chicken. Rinse the chicken and dry on paper towels and then place it in the marinade. Make the mint chutney. Peel and cut up the zucchini. Refrigerate all.

- **The Day of:**
  AM: Make the dough for the *tandoori rotee*. Make the zucchini. Make the garnish for the chicken. Refrigerate.
  PM: Get the gang together! Turn on the exhaust fan and finish making the *samosas*. Don't forget the chutney. Grill the chicken.

- **Serving Time:** Make the *rotees*, warm the zucchini and the chicken if needed, and garnish. Garnish the rice pudding.

vegan or meat   Samosa

Irresistable samosas just out of the fryer.

Everybody loves samosas! This is probably the snack that converts people to Indian food. My recipes for the fillings are really outstanding; guaranteed to be the best you've ever tasted. My friend Daljeet Sandhu taught me to take the shortcut using tortillas for the pastry. You'll be surprised by how well they turn out.

I like the meat filling made with lamb, but any ground meat would be delicious. I usually buy a leg of lamb on sale and ask the butcher to halve it. Some butchers will grind half the meat from the shank (long bone end) if you ask. If not, I grind it myself. The other half I freeze for raan *(page 70) or cut into pieces for roghan josh (page 166).*

For vegetable filling: Slit the skin of the potatoes and microwave on high for 6 minutes or until barely tender. Cool and peel. Cut into ¹/₂-inch cubes. You should have about 3¹/₂ cups of cubes. Microwave the peas on high for a minute or two. Set both aside.

Heat the oil in a wok and add the mustard seeds, if using. Fry until they pop, and then add the onion. Stir-fry until soft and brown, and then add the ginger. Stir in the coriander seeds, turmeric, cumin seeds, and fennel seeds. Fry for a minute, and then add the cayenne pepper, pomegranate seeds, potatoes, peas, salt, and water. Reduce heat, cover and simmer for 5 minutes. Stir in cilantro and cook 5 more minutes. Add the garam masala. Mix and cool before making the *samosas*. Taste and adjust the salt and cayenne pepper.

For meat filling: Toast the saffron for a few seconds in a hot, dry pan just until fragrant. Turn out onto a clean sheet of paper and pulverize between your thumb and finger. In a small *cowlee* or ramekin, stir the saffron into the boiling water to dissolve.

YIELD: 20 TURNOVERS

1 package (10-count) 8-inch flour tortillas (or 2 packages if making both fillings)

Canola oil for frying

Flour and water for paste

Vegetable Filling:

4 medium to large red potatoes

³/₄ cup frozen green peas, thawed

3 tablespoons canola oil

¹/₂ teaspoon mustard seeds (*optional*)

1 medium onion, finely chopped (³/₄ cup)

2 teaspoons grated ginger

¹/₄ teaspoon crushed or ground coriander seeds

(continued on next page)

SMALL VEGETABLE AND/OR MEAT TURNOVERS *(continued)*

½ teaspoon ground turmeric

½ teaspoon whole or ground cumin seeds

¼ teaspoon whole or ground fennel seeds *(optional)*

⅛ to ¼ teaspoon ground cayenne pepper, to taste

2 teaspoons dried ground pomegranate seeds *(optional)*

1½ teaspoons salt, or to taste

1½ tablespoons warm water

1½ tablespoons sliced cilantro leaves

½ teaspoon garam masala

Meat Filling:

½ teaspoon saffron, loosely packed

1 tablespoon boiling water

3 tablespoons vegetable oil

½ cup minced onion

2 cloves garlic, minced

1 scant tablespoon grated ginger

1 pound lean ground lamb or other ground meat

½ teaspoon ground cayenne pepper

1 scant teaspoon salt, or to taste

Juice of ½ a lime

1½ teaspoons garam masala

⅓ cup dried cranberries or currants, coarsely chopped *(optional)*

⅓ cup pistachios, melon seeds *(magaz)*, or pine nuts, coarsely chopped

Heat the 3 tablespoons oil in a wok. Fry the onion, garlic, and ginger until golden brown. Add the meat and break up in the wok as you stir-fry for 10 minutes. Drain off most, but not all, of the fat. Add the cayenne pepper, salt, lime juice, garam masala, dissolved saffron, dried cranberries, and pistachios. Fry for 5 more minutes. Cool or refrigerate if not assembling the *samosas* within 15 minutes.

To assemble *samosas*:

Heat 3 inches of oil to 350°F in a deep wok. In a small bowl or *cowlee*, mix a few tablespoons of flour and water into a paste. Heat 4 of the tortillas at a time in folded paper towels in the microwave on high for about 10 seconds, until they are just warm and pliable (**very important**). Place on a cutting board and cut the stack in half with a sharp, heavy knife. Cover with a clean kitchen towel.

Take half a tortilla and make a cone in your left hand by overlapping the straight edges. Glue with a little of the flour paste. Fill it with a rounded spoonful of vegetable or meat filling. Make sure that the bottom of the cone is pinched tightly. Close the top of the cone by smoothing a little paste between the two top edges and pressing firmly—even folding the edge slightly. You have made a triangular pillow. Continue to make four more, pinching them closed again before setting carefully in the hot oil.

Fry the *samosas* until light brown. Drain on paper towels. Repeat process with remaining ingredients. *Samosas* are best eaten immediately but can be kept warm in a 200°F oven. Or refrigerate for a day and re-warm in the regular (not microwave) oven.

MINT CHUTNEY

Purely and simply this is Bebeji's recipe. It is so refreshingly delicious; you will make it whenever you can to serve with everything—it is great on toasted cheese sandwiches. The onion must be mild, please!

A snake charmer entertains us as we look on from next door.

Wash the mint leaves thoroughly in cold water. In a food processor, grind the onion with 2 tablespoons of the lemon juice and gradually add the washed mint leaves, grinding after each addition. Add the rest of the ingredients and grind to combine. Taste, and then add more sugar or lemon juice if needed. Best eaten immediately, but keep refrigerated until ready to use (within 5 days).

YIELD: 2 CUPS

2 cups packed mint leaves

1 large mild Vidalia onion

2 to 3 tablespoons lemon juice

6-inch long mild or hot chile pepper, seeded and white membrane removed

2 teaspoons green mango powder (*amchoor*) (*optional*)

1 teaspoon ground dried pomegranate seeds (*optional*)

1 teaspoon salt, or more to taste

3 to 5 teaspoons sugar, or to taste

GRILLED "RED" CHICKEN

Tandoori Murga   *meat/dairy*

The kids' (of all ages) favorite food! This recipe should really be called "Clay-Oven Chicken" which is what the tandoor is. But our nephew, Alex, always asked for "red" chicken when he came to visit. He loved it so much and I thought it was charming to call it for the coloring we use. In a pinch you can substitute a commercial tandoori paste or a dry tandoori mixture for the spice mixture here.

YIELD: 16 PIECES OF CHICKEN

4 to 5 pounds chicken pieces (4 roaster legs, 4 roaster thighs, 8 chicken breast halves, or 16 pieces of one kind), skinned and trimmed of fat

3 tablespoons salt, preferably kosher

4 tablespoons lemon juice

For the spice mixture (Tandoori Chicken Masala):

2 teaspoons whole cumin seeds

1 scant teaspoon whole cloves

2 teaspoons black peppercorns

1½ teaspoons green cardamom seeds

Seeds from 3 black cardamom pods

For the marinade:

3 cloves garlic, sliced

2-inch piece ginger, sliced

4-inch green chile pepper, seeded and coarsely chopped

½ teaspoon salt,

1 tablespoon paprika

1 cup hung yogurt (page 6) or light sour cream

4 to 6 drops red food color (*optional*)

The day before serving:

Cover the chicken with cold water and 2 tablespoons salt and soak for 10 minutes. Rinse thoroughly and drain. Make diagonal cuts on the larger pieces and place in a non-reactive bowl. Sprinkle with the remaining 1 tablespoon salt and the lemon juice and refrigerate while making the spice mixture and marinade.

For spice mixture: Heat the spices in a dry pan for 3 minutes until fragrant, then remove from heat and grind in a spice or clean coffee grinder.

For marinade: Grind the garlic, ginger, and chile pepper in a food processor. Then combine the spice mixture (tandoori chicken masala) with all the ingredients for the marinade, mixing them thoroughly.

Drain the meat again. Roll the chicken pieces in the marinade until all are coated. Cover and refrigerate overnight.

The day of serving:

The cooking times will vary depending on the size of the chicken pieces and the heat of the oven or grill.

Grilling: Preheat the grill and spray with cooking spray. Spray the chicken pieces lightly with cooking spray. Grill on indirect heat for 30 minutes for large dark meat pieces, 15 minutes for white. Finish over direct flame. Poke with a fork to see if juices run clear.

Roasting: Preheat the oven for 30 minutes to 450°F. On a cookie sheet covered with oiled foil, place the chicken pieces from the same part of the chicken. Do not crowd them. Brush or spray lightly with oil. Roast for 15 minutes. Turn once and bake for 5 more minutes. Remove the breast pieces first if the juice runs clear when pricked with a fork or the temperature reaches 175°F on a meat thermometer. The legs and thighs may need an additional 10 minutes. You may wish to run the chicken under the broiler or put it on the grill for a few minutes just to get a few charred spots to mimic a *tandoor* oven.

Mix the garnishes with a little of the *chaat masala* and arrange around the edges of a large platter. Sprinkle the chicken with more *chaat masala* and pile in the center of the platter. Top with some of the cilantro and lemon slices.

Optional garnishes: Grilled onion slices; cucumber slices; cilantro; lemon wedges; chilies, seeded and slivered; daikon slices; *chaat masala (page 5)*

Note: Leftover tandoori chicken may be removed from the bone, and used for Butter Chicken (*see page 18*).

BROILED WHOLE-WHEAT YEAST FLAT BREADS

Tandoori Rotee   *vegan*

This recipe came from California via my husband's cousin and her husband, Raj and Sat Dewan. Satjee is a nutritionist who worked for NASA in the early days of the space program. He and his wife are known for making the freshest food on this planet! Use the kitchen table to roll out the breads if you are short on counter space.

YIELD: 8 7-INCH BREADS OR 10 5-INCH BREADS

1 package active dry yeast

1 teaspoon sugar

2 cups whole-wheat flour (not *chapatti* flour), plus some for dusting

2 cups all-purpose flour

1 teaspoon salt

Oil for your hand and ball of dough

Ghee, butter, or oil (*optional*)

Dissolve the yeast and sugar in two tablespoons warm water. Set aside until foamy. Mix the flours and salt in a large bowl. Add the yeast mixture and 1 cup warm water all at once. Mix with an oiled hand until thoroughly crumbly. Gradually add more warm water to the flour, mixing constantly, until you have a fairly stiff dough. Knead the dough until elastic, 6 or 7 minutes.

Spread a thin layer of oil on the entire ball of dough. Cover it with a damp cloth, and leave in a warm place for 2 hours or until nearly doubled.

Divide the dough into 8 or 10 balls. Cover them with a damp towel and allow them to rest for 5 minutes. Dust your work surface with whole-wheat flour and flatten each ball into the loose whole-wheat flour and roll into disks approximately 5 or 7 inches in diameter with a lightly floured rolling pin. Cover the breads with a clean tea towel. Allow the breads to rest again for 5 minutes.

Broiler method: Preheat the oven to broil if you are going to serve the breads immediately upon finishing them. Heat a griddle over medium heat. Slap a *rotee* on the hot griddle for a minute to halfway cook it. Turn over with a spatula and repeat. (At this point, you may cool the *rotees*, put waxed paper between them, and wrap the breads in foil to finish the next day.)

When ready to eat, apply a layer of water to the bread with your palm. Then broil on the second rack of the broiler, turning once. Brush with *ghee* or butter before serving.

Grill method: Preheat the grill to 400°F. Prick the rested breads with a fork and then apply a layer of water to the bread with your palm. Put them on the grill over indirect heat for a few minutes. Cover the grill for a minute and then turn them. Put over direct heat to finish. Brush with *ghee* or butter before serving.

HOME-STYLE ZUCCHINI

vegan   Torian Nal Buddian

This is another of Bebeji's great recipes. She and I loved buddian *(dried, spiced lentil balls) so we outnumbered my husband who does not. Try using them in this recipe to see with whom you agree. (Bet it's me and Bebeji!)*

Heat a large nonstick skillet and add the oil. Sauté the onion until transparent. Add the garlic and ginger and brown lightly. Add the spices (turmeric through cinnamon) and salt, stirring constantly. Add the chopped tomato and chile pepper and stir for a minute. Add the zucchini and stir for 2 minutes on high heat. Cover, lower heat, and simmer for 25 minutes. Stir in the cooked *buddian* and garam masala and sprinkle with cilantro.

YIELD: 8 SERVINGS

3 tablespoons vegetable oil

1 large onion, finely chopped

3 cloves garlic, minced

2-inch piece ginger, minced

1½ teaspoons ground turmeric

1 teaspoon whole or ground cumin seeds

½ teaspoon crushed or ground coriander seeds

Pinch ground cinnamon

2 teaspoons salt, or to taste

1 large tomato, chopped

1 green chile pepper, seeded and minced

6 medium zucchini (about 3 pounds), peeled and cut into 1-inch cubes

2 to 4 crushed Punjabi *buddian** (*optional*)

½ teaspoon garam masala

¼ cup chopped cilantro (*optional*)

*Buddian (photo on page 2) are rarely, if ever, made at home except in the villages since they need to be dried outdoors in strong, bright sunlight, usually spread out on *dhurrie*-covered cots. Make sure you buy the "Punjabi-style" dried lentil balls which come in cellophane packets. If using the *buddian,* wrap them in a clean towel and break them up a little by striking them with a rolling pin. Lightly fry them in a tablespoon of oil in a separate small pot with lid. Add one cup of water, cover and cook over low heat until soft, about 20 minutes, then add to the zucchini.

RICE PUDDING

Kheer   *dairy*

This is the most popular Punjabi dessert. Please taste it to ensure that it is sweet enough for you and your family. If not, add more sugar. Use rose flavor or extract, usually found behind the cashier in the Indian grocery store. Don't substitute rose water.

YIELD: 10 ½-CUP SERVINGS

¾ cup basmati rice

⅓ cup golden raisins

½ teaspoon ground cardamom seeds or 10 whole pods

½ gallon whole milk, or more to taste

¼ cup slivered, blanched almonds (toast a few and reserve for garnish)

½ cup heavy cream or non-fat half and half

½ cup sugar, or more to taste

1 teaspoon rose flavor (*optional*)

Soak rice in tap water for 5 minutes and rinse until water runs clear. Drain. In a deep, heavy pot put the rice, raisins, cardamom, and milk and bring to a boil over medium heat, stirring occasionally. Lower heat and simmer, stirring often, until the milk is reduced by a third (about 40 minutes).

Add the almonds, heavy cream, and sugar and cook and stir over low heat for 10 more minutes. Remove from heat and stir in rose flavor, if using. Mixture will be slightly runny but will thicken as it cools. If it is not thick enough to your liking, you can always transfer it to a glass bowl and heat it in the microwave for several more minutes. Garnish with reserved nuts.

Variation: To make **Mango Rice Pudding** (*Amb Kheer*) stir in 1 cup canned mango purée to the pudding after removing from the heat. Do not use rose flavor.

PRINCELY FEAST

The fabulous Maharaja of Patiala, a distant relative

THERE WERE FEW MORE FABULOUS RULERS THAN the late Maharaja of Patiala, Bhupinder Singh. We were staying in our favorite hotel in the world, the Imperial in New Delhi, where the regal halls are filled with etchings and paintings of old Delhi and its denizens. In its charming mahogany pub, the Patiala Peg, we were surrounded by pictures of the Maharaja playing cricket during the heyday of the British Raj. It was there that my husband casually related to me that he was directly, but distantly, related to His Highness. Their common ancestor, Phul, lived in the eighteenth century, twelve generations ago. And his ancestor was Sidh, a descendant of the Rajput king of Jaisalmer. Of course I was intrigued, knowing only that His Highness was one of the most extravagant men to have lived on earth in the last century.

His Highness, Bhupinder Singh, wearing the fabulous diamond necklace by Cartier.

My husband and I were dazzled by his jewels as were the thousands who also attended the Cartier exhibit at the Museum of Natural History in Chicago in 1999. According to Cartier's president Stanislas de Quercize, one necklace was the largest ever produced on earth, and the first to be made in a platinum setting. It contained 2,930 diamonds, the centerpiece of which was a golf-ball-sized pale yellow diamond of 234 carats. Alain Boucheron's family also crafted many jewels for the maharaja.

He wrote in the book, *The Master Jewelers (on page 89)* of the dramatic scene of 1927 when the Maharaja of Patiala arrived in Paris "accompanied by a retinue of forty servants all wearing pink turbans, his twenty favourite dancing girls and, most important of all, six caskets filled with diamonds, pearls, emeralds, sapphires, and rubies, all of incomparable beauty ... then valued at about 1800 million francs." "(That is not a misprint! What would they be worth today?)

A master of the grand gesture, he traveled in a motorcade of twenty Rolls Royces. He sat on silk-cushioned furniture made of pure crystal. In order to spite a clerk who snubbed him, he bought an entire store's stock of chandeliers in one go. Yet Bhupinder Singh was a world-class cricketer and his leadership skills were as evident as his athletic prowess. Of the six hundred maharajas alive during his heyday, he was chosen to lead their consortium. The magnificent buildings and schools of Patiala remain as proof of his family's largesse.

In the Motibagh Palace in Patiala, behind the eleven acres of beautiful pink sandstone walls and in the magnificent gardens and outbuildings, lived at least four thousand souls dependant on him. His dining was no less magnificent. On one of our trips we had the pleasure of meeting His Highness' aide de camp, Mehar Singh Kalouria, the father of our dear friend Jasbir Singh. Mehar Singh had also been in charge of the palace kitchen, the *lussee khana*. You can imagine! It was like being in charge of the meals for an

An outdoor kitchen at the Motibagh Palace.

entire city every day, day after day. Kings and queens dined at his table, including Britain's Edward, the Duke of Windsor.

What stories the guests have told, passed down to us eager listeners! The dishes prepared in the courts of the day were covered in edible gold and silver leaf. It was common for certain cooks to specialize in only one dish, the secret recipe passed down from their fathers. The famous "turducken" of Louisiana has nothing on the type of dishes served in the courts of the maharajas—dishes such as a whole goat stuffed with boned birds, largest to smallest, then stuffed with eggs and rice. Colonel Mit Singh, Auntie Surindera's father, was a guest of the Maharaja of Patiala when bread, fried with a live bird inside, was cut at the table to allow the bird to fly free. Live entertainment at the Patiala palace!

The "Princely Feast" Menu

Wow your guests with food that is extraordinary in flavor and appearance. Is it rich? You bet! But it is also beautiful, and the richness is balanced with the sweet/sour of fruit and the fragrance of screw pine (kewrda) and roses. This meal is surprisingly easy to prepare if you spread the tasks throughout the week.

Appetizer:	*KALAYJEE KEBAB* Chicken Liver Kebabs with Pineapple
Main Course:	*TANDOORI RAAN* Moghul-style Leg of Lamb
	PEELEE DAAL TE BANGAN Yellow Mung Lentils with Eggplant
	CHAIL NAAN Grilled White Flat Breads with Almonds and Raisins
	RAJA RAITA Saffron Yogurt with Peaches and Pistachios
	MITHA CHAVAL Sweet Rice Pilaf
Dessert:	*GULAAB TE LAAL* Roses and "Rubies" Mousse

- **One Week or More Prior:** Read the recipes from beginning to end. Make the grocery list for the Indian market and the supermarket. If you wish to have a formal dinner, make the breads and freeze them.
- **Three to Four Days Prior:** Buy the food from the supermarket and Indian market. Remove the tough fell (the skin-like covering) from the lamb if the butcher has not done so.
- **Two Days Prior:** Prepare the marinade for the lamb. Refrigerate. Prepare the marinade for the chicken livers; prepare the chicken livers and put them into the marinade. Refrigerate.
- **One Day Prior:** Make the mousse and the *raita*. Refrigerate. Add the lamb to the marinade and refrigerate.
- **The Day of:**
  AM: Make the lentil dish. Measure the dry ingredients for the breads if you have not made them. Make the rice pilaf. Drain the pineapple and add it to the chicken livers and refrigerate.
  PM: Make the dough for the bread and let it rest (or thaw the breads you have already made). Three and a half hours before serving time, remove the lamb from the refrigerator, preheat the oven, and begin roasting the lamb.
- **About an hour before serving:** Broil the chicken livers and pineapple. Heat the lentils in the oven. While the lamb is resting, make the breads.

CHICKEN LIVER KEBABS WITH PINEAPPLE

meat   Kalayjee Kebab

The liver is considered by many cultures to be the "prize" of the meal. This was so in the villages of Punjab as well as at the palace in Patiala. My husband remembers that while he was a college student, he and his friends would eagerly visit the second floor of the Lahorian Da Hotel in Ludiana to be served drinks with their chicken-liver kebabs.

Rinse the chicken livers and soak in salted water for 10 minutes. Rinse again and drain in a colander. Turn out onto several thicknesses of paper towel, cut away any obvious fat or thick membrane, and pat dry.

Mix the oil, honey, spices (paprika through black pepper), and salt in a small bowl.

Preheat the toaster oven or regular oven to maximum broil. Combine the livers with the spice mixture. Brush or spray a slotted broiler pan with oil and space the livers across the pan. Broil them a few inches from the heat for 5 minutes. Turn the livers and broil until just firm. Set aside.

Wipe the broiler pan with a damp paper towel and then brush or spray with oil. Add the pineapple to the remaining spice mixture in the bowl and toss to coat. Place the pineapple chunks on the broiler pan, spacing them, and broil until slightly charred. If not serving immediately, refrigerate the livers and the pineapple at this point on paper towels and covered with plastic wrap. Then before serving, uncover and return to the broiler for 3 to 5 minutes until the pieces have developed some crunchy edges.

To serve, place one liver and one pineapple chunk on pretty toothpicks and arrange on a platter. Serve immediately on a plate with some chutney in a small bowl at the center.

Variation: Place the livers in a food processor with a few drops of the accumulated juice. Grind and spoon the mixture onto 16 buttery crackers like the *Matthian* on page 196. Crown each with a broiled pineapple chunk.

YIELD: 16 SMALL APPETIZERS

20 ounces chicken livers

3 tablespoons *ghee* or canola oil

1 tablespoon honey

1 tablespoon paprika

1½ teaspoons ground cumin seeds

¼ teaspoon ground cayenne pepper

¼ teaspoon whole or ground fennel seeds

¼ teaspoon freshly ground black pepper

1 teaspoon salt

1 (15-ounce) can pineapple chunks, drained

MOGHUL-STYLE LEG OF LAMB

Tandoori Raan   *meat/dairy*

A grand, impressive dish inspired by Mrs. Balbir Singh's recipe. Lamb is so tender now, it does not need to be over-cooked, as it had to be in her day. This dish tastes best cooked medium, but if you like medium-well, leave it in the oven in 10-minute increments. Allow it to rest before carving. You may also completely debone two smaller legs, butterfly, marinate and then grill them over medium-high, direct heat, about 20 minutes per side.

Equipment to have on hand: *a roasting pan, a rack that fits inside the roasting pan, a clean plastic kitchen garbage bag, a meat thermometer, and cotton butcher's twine.*

YIELD: 8 TO 10 SERVINGS

1 tablespoon whole coriander seeds

1 teaspoon whole black peppercorns

6 whole cloves

1½ teaspoons whole black or white cumin seeds

4 or 5 dried fruits of *kachri** (*optional*)

1½ teaspoons ground turmeric

1 teaspoon garam masala

1-inch piece ginger

6 cloves garlic

1 tablespoon lemon juice

2 tablespoons canola oil

1 tablespoon kosher salt

¾ cup hung yogurt (*page 6*) or Greek yogurt

6 to 7-pound semi-boneless leg of lamb

Garnishes: whole chives with flowers; green garlic; or sprigs of cilantro

Toast and toss the coriander seeds, peppercorns, and cloves in a hot, dry skillet until just fragrant. Add the cumin seeds and toast for another 20 seconds. In a spice grinder, grind them along with the *kachri*. In a small bowl, mix the spice mixture with the turmeric and garam masala and set aside.

In a food processor, grind the ginger and garlic cloves with the lemon juice to a paste, and then add the spice mixture, oil, and salt. Remove from the food processor and mix thoroughly with the yogurt.

Remove the thick papery skin (the fell) which may still be covering the leg, and any excess fat, or ask a butcher to do it. If the butcher has not already done so, cut the leg of lamb to the bone across the inside portion, open the leg and check for a lymph node—a flat nodule usually covered with fat that has a bitter flavor; remove it whole and discard. Rinse the leg and pat dry with paper towels inside and out.

Put the roast inside a large, clean plastic kitchen garbage bag with the sides rolled down, or in a large non-reactive stainless or glass container. You may wish to put on disposable gloves for the next step. With a spatula, smear the spice paste over the inside of the lamb. Turn the lamb over, rolling it somewhat back into shape and tie with the twine in at least three places to hold it together during cooking. Smear the surface with the paste. Allow the roast to marinate for 1 hour on the counter or overnight in the refrigerator.

About 30 minutes before roasting, remove from the refrigerator and place the lamb with the fat side up on a rack in the roasting pan so that it can come to room temperature.

Preheat the oven to 400°F for 20 minutes to make sure the heat is evenly distributed in the oven. Roast the lamb, uncovered, for about 2 hours and 20 minutes for medium (some parts will be medium-rare). The internal temperature should be 135°F, tested in several places; if not, continue to roast until it reaches that temperature. Remove roast from the oven and allow to rest for 15 minutes, covered loosely with foil. The lamb will cook more as it sits. When done to medium, the internal temperature will rise to 140°F.

To serve, place the whole roast on a platter, sprinkle with cilantro leaves for garnish and present to your guests before slicing. Then carve ¼-inch-thick slices and fan artistically on a heated platter and garnish with whole chives, green garlic, or sprigs of cilantro.

* Some substitutes for the *kachri* might be 1 tablespoon of green mango powder *(amchoor)* or 1 tablespoon of mango chutney ground with some garlic.

YELLOW MUNG LENTILS WITH EGGPLANT

Peelee Daal Te Bangan   *vegan*

Our favorite Indian restaurant in Mountainside, New Jersey, is Raagini. The chef, Sat Nam Singh, served this dish and I promptly went home and tried to copy it. It is so easy and fast that I'm sure it will become one of your favorites also.

YIELD: 8 ½-CUP SERVINGS

For the lentils:

2 cups yellow (split) mung lentils (hulled *moongee* are best but *masoor daal* [red lentils] would do)

6 cups cold water

2 teaspoons salt, or to taste

2 teaspoons ground turmeric

For the eggplant:

2 (long) Chinese eggplants, stem ends removed

¾ cup canola oil for frying

½ teaspoon ground toasted cumin seeds

½ teaspoon garam masala

½ teaspoon green mango powder or ½ teaspoon *chaat masala* (page 5)

½ teaspoon salt

For the tempering or tardka:

¼ cup canola oil (leftover from frying the eggplant)

1 large onion, chopped

3 cloves garlic, minced

2-inch piece ginger, grated

1 tablespoon sliced cilantro leaves

For the lentils: Check the lentils for any debris or stones and rinse thoroughly. In a large pot, bring all the lentil ingredients to a boil and immediately reduce the heat to simmer. Cover and continue cooking until the lentils are creamy, about 30 minutes, stirring occasionally.

For the eggplants: Cut the eggplants in half lengthwise and then diagonally into 2-inch chunks. Heat the oil in a wok until nearly smoking. Add half the chunks and sauté until brown. Drain on paper towels. Repeat with the remaining eggplant. Mix the cumin, garam masala, mango powder, and salt together and sprinkle on the eggplant slices. Just before serving, stir them into the hot lentils.

For the *tardka*: In a medium skillet, heat the oil leftover from frying the eggplant, add the onion, garlic, and ginger and sauté until golden brown. Stir into the lentil mixture just before serving. Garnish with cilantro.

Variation: To make **Yellow Mung Lentils with Spinach (Peelee Daal Te Paalak)**, instead of the eggplant mixture add 7 ounces of baby spinach and the *tardka* to the creamy, cooked lentils.

GRILLED WHITE FLAT BREADS WITH ALMONDS AND RAISINS

dairy   Chail Naan

Bebeji and I relaxing in the foothills of the Himalayas.

The Maharaja of Patiala was quite an athlete. The hill station he developed in Chail after he lost Simla has the highest cricket ground in the world. In this Shangri-La, dried fruit and nuts are ambrosia. You may wish to top your breads with silver leaf after they are finished to give them a royal touch. These are best made on the barbecue grill.

In a small bowl, stir the yeast and sugar into ½ cup of warm water until dissolved. Set aside until foamy, about 5 to 10 minutes depending on room temperature.

In a large bowl, fluff the 4 cups of flour, salt, and baking powder with a fork. Then with a wooden spoon, make a well in the flour. Pour the yeast mixture and yogurt into the center all at once, and begin stirring in one direction from the center out, trying to incorporate all the flour. You may have to give up the spoon and use your hand since the batter will be sticky.

Sprinkle the dough with some flour. Oil your hand and begin kneading the dough until elastic—about 5 minutes. The motion is to scrape the dough from the bottom and sides of the bowl and fold it as you turn the bowl in one direction with your other hand. When you are finished, the dough should be in a smooth ball and leave your hand and bowl. Don't over knead. Wash and dry the bowl and replace the ball of dough. Brush dough with some oil or *ghee* and cover with a cloth. Leave in a warm place for 1½ to 3 hours (depending on room temperature), until the dough is light.

Mix the almonds, raisins, 1 teaspoon flour, and sea salt in a mini-processor and grind, then set aside.

YIELD: 8 BREADS

1 teaspoon active dry yeast

2 teaspoons sugar

½ cup warm water

4 cups all-purpose flour, plus 1 teaspoon and more for dusting

1½ teaspoons salt

½ teaspoon baking powder

⅔ cup hung or Greek yogurt (*page 6*)

Oil for greasing dough and your hands

2 tablespoons melted *ghee* or butter

⅓ cup ground almonds

⅓ cup golden raisins

¼ teaspoon sea salt (*optional*)

Coarse cornmeal (only if using the oven method)

(continued on next page)

GRILLED WHITE FLAT BREADS
WITH ALMONDS AND RAISINS *(continued)*

With a dough scraper (if you have it), divide the dough in half; divide each half into four equal sections (you will have eight balls of dough). Oil your hands and roll each ball between your palms until smooth. Flatten the balls in some loose flour and lightly dust a flat surface. With a rolling pin, roll out the balls of dough into circles as flat as possible. As they are rolled, put them on a cookie sheet sprayed with oil or on the clean counter or table. Cover with clean, slightly damp towel(s) and let rest for 5 minutes as you roll out a few more. Use a rolling pin or with your thumbs and the heels of your palms, rapidly move the rested dough in a circle to stretch it. Using gravity and your hands, keep stretching as you go until the circles are about 7 inches round. Put them on cookie sheets sprayed with oil or on the clean counter or table. Cover with clean, slightly damp towel(s) and let rest for 10 minutes. Then stretch the *naan* into a teardrop shape about 9 inches at the top. (Don't worry if not even. The center should be thinner than the edges. When baked, some parts will get crispy, others chewy.)

Brush each circle with melted *ghee* or butter. Sprinkle a spoonful of the raisin/nut mixture evenly on each circle and then lightly press in.

On the grill: Preheat grill to 450°F. Put the stretched breads on indirect heat and close the lid for a minute. Open the lid and move to direct heat until that side is brown, the center cooked through, and the top bubbly. Repeat with the other side. Eat immediately (best) or wrap in a clean tea-towel.

On the griddle: Preheat the griddle on medium-high. Place a prepared dough circle on the griddle. When bubbles form on the top, turn it over. Keep turning until the bread is cooked through and browned in spots. Remove from the griddle with tongs and wrap in a clean towel. Repeat with the other *naans*.

In the oven: Remove racks from oven and put a baking stone or tile on the bottom of the oven. Preheat the oven to 500°F. Sprinkle the stone with coarse cornmeal. Place one or two *naan* on the stone. (You may have room to bake only two at a time.) Bake until bottom is cooked, about 2 to 3 minutes. Turn over and repeat. Repeat with the other *naans*. If the *naans* have not browned, replace the top rack of the oven. Turn on the broiler. Turn the *naans* over and broil on the top shelf for less than a minute to ensure they are browned. Remove from the oven with tongs and wrap in a clean towel. Serve immediately.

Note: The dough may be wrapped in plastic and refrigerated for a day or two. But then it will take longer to warm to room temperature and to rise.

SAFFRON YOGURT
WITH PEACHES AND PISTACHIOS

dairy Raja Raita

This is a beautiful recipe inspired by Julie Sahni. She uses mango and ground crystallized ginger in a raita. I like using peaches, since I am more likely to find them in my local market. Use only the ripest fresh fruit or use canned, available any time of year.

In a serving bowl beat the yogurt with a whisk until smooth.

Toast the saffron in a dry, hot pan and then soak in the hot water.

Stir the cardamom, ginger, and salt into the yogurt.

Drain the peaches (if using canned) and reserve ¼ cup of the syrup. Cut the peach slices so that they are at least halved. Beat the saffron into the yogurt and then mix in the peach syrup and/or sugar. Stir in the peach slices and cover and refrigerate for 2 hours or overnight.

Just before serving, stir in the pistachios and *kewrda* flavor. Garnish with the silver or some more ground pistachios.

YIELD: 10 ½-CUP SERVINGS

4 cups (32 ounces) plain yogurt

¼ teaspoon saffron threads

1 tablespoon hot water

2 pinches ground cardamom seeds

2 pinches ground ginger

½ teaspoon salt

3 peaches, blanched, peeled, and sliced, or 2 cups (24-ounce can) sliced peaches, drained

2 tablespoons sugar or ¼ cup light syrup from canned peaches plus 1 tablespoon sugar

¼ cup unsalted pistachios, chopped

⅛ teaspoon *kewrda* flavor (*optional*)

2 sheets silver leaf (*chandi werk*) (*optional*)

This inlaid table might grace the palace of a prince.

SWEET RICE PILAF

Mitha Chaval · *vegan or dairy*

This elegant dish that Bebeji often made for our community meal in the gurudwara *can be part of the main meal or a dessert, just vary the amount of sugar. The orange zest adds a Persian touch, which is probably the origin of the dish.*

YIELD: 8 OR 9 ½-CUP SERVINGS

1 rounded cup basmati rice

⅓ cup golden raisins

Pinch of salt

½ teaspoon saffron or 5 drops yellow food color

2 teaspoons orange zest (*optional*)

3 tablespoons coconut oil or *ghee*

⅓ to 1 cup sugar

4 cloves

1 cinnamon stick

¼ teaspoon cardamom seeds

½ cup dried thin slices of coconut, broken into pieces (*optional*)

½ cup slivered and lightly toasted almonds

Rinse the rice under cold water until water runs clear. In a large saucepan, bring 6 cups water to a rolling boil. Add the rice, raisins, and salt and boil for exactly 5 minutes. Drain thoroughly.

If using the saffron, pulverize in a mortar. Add the saffron or food coloring and orange zest to the rice.

Over low heat, warm the coconut oil or *ghee* in a nonstick pan or pot with a tight-fitting cover. Add the sugar, cloves, cinnamon stick, and cardamom seeds, stir for only a few seconds and then stir in the rice mixture. Add ¼ cup water and coconut slices. Cover tightly and cook over very low heat until all water is absorbed and rice is cooked, about 20 minutes. If the rice is undercooked, sprinkle a teaspoon of water into it and check after 5 minutes. Rice grains should be separate. Serve warm with the almonds sprinkled on top.

Two great cooks—Bebeji's nieces Hardarshen Kaur and Birinder Kaur.

ROSES AND "RUBIES" MOUSSE

dairy/egg   Gulaab Te Laal

Add elegance to your meal with a lovely Roses and Rubies Mousse.

You will love this light and different dessert that is "fit for a prince charming." I developed it as a make-ahead but spectacular finish to an extraordinary meal. It is not too sweet. If you like very sweet things, add more sugar—up to two more tablespoons. If using the rose flavor rather than the rose petal spread, add 4 to 6 more tablespoons sugar.

In a small pan, sprinkle the gelatin into the water, thoroughly wetting it. Let it sit for 1 minute to soften. Warm it over a very low flame, stirring until the gelatin is completely dissolved. Add the rose spread, sugar, and food coloring and continue to stir until the spread has dissolved. Cool.

Beat the egg whites until soft peaks form. Gently fold in the gelatin mixture.

Remove the cream from the refrigerator. In a separate, larger bowl, beat the cream until stiff peaks form. Gently fold into the egg-gelatin mixture. Put in the freezer for 5 to 10 minutes so that the gelatin begins to set.

Put a few raspberries into the bottom of a glass bowl or into individual parfait glasses. Reserve some raspberries for the garnish and fold the rest into the mousse. Spoon the mousse into the bowl or glasses. Garnish with the reserved raspberries and rose petals. Cover and refrigerate until serving time.

YIELD: 8 ¾-CUP SERVINGS

2 envelopes unflavored gelatin

⅔ cup cold water

4 tablespoons rose petal spread, or
    1½ teaspoons rose flavor

2 tablespoons sugar

8 drops red food color (*optional*)

4 egg whites, at room temperature

2 cups heavy cream (very cold)

1 pint (12 ounces) raspberries

THE HEART OF PUNJAB

A vignette about two historic Sikh temples

The Har Mandir Sahib or Golden Temple is truly an example of "interfaith" cooperation, and may be unique in the whole world. Part of the land was donated by the Emperor Akbar and the foundation stone laid by a Muslim Sufi saint, Mian Mir. Its four doors welcome all from each direction. Meals served from the free kitchen and recitation from the Sikh scriptures never cease here. Reminiscent of some of the psalms of David, the scriptures contain the divine message received by Sikh gurus (teachers), *bhagats* (Hindu saints) and *pirs* (Muslim saints)—representatives of all the major faiths of the day and several castes.

MANY WOULD CONSIDER THE strikingly beautiful Golden Temple of Amritsar to be the heart of Punjab. The name of the city means "tank of nectar" or another name for God's grace. Certainly it was God's grace for my husband and I to make our way across the wide swathe of marble that led to the temple. It was still dark, well before 4 A.M., *amritvela,* the time of nectar, when the procession bearing the holy book, the *Guru Granth Sahib* wound its way into the hall. After making our obeisance to the holy book, we found a small spot on the floor to sit amid the crush of the crowd. Everyone present must have felt the magical energy of the moment when the music began. There was a collective surge, the anticipation of renewal that transforms the heart and the soul—the music, the *shabad* energy that seemed to swell from the very heart of the universe.

Entirely covered in gold leaf, the temple sits serenely in the center of a huge pool of water. Outside, devotees were taking a dip as the rays of the sun glinted off the gold reflecting the shining image. The Golden Temple, *Har Mandir Sahib*, like most Sikh temples or *gurudwaras,* is built to have four doors open to each direction and to every soul—no matter what race or religion. In fact, the word *gurudwara* means God's door.

My favorite *gurudwara*, however, is in Old Delhi in Chandni Chownk, the center of the most chaotic, most bustling place I have ever been. Yet, when we first entered the temple forty years ago, I was surprised to feel a great peace surround me. It was, and is, a very special place.

In the eighteenth century, the Hindu Kashmiri Brahmins were being persecuted by the Emperor Aurengzeb and they suggested that he would stop if a prominent person would offer his head as a sacrifice to end their sufferings. Guru Tegh Bahadur answered the call. His body was callously left in the streets. At great peril, under cover of night, his head was collected by a brave Sikh who cremated it by burning down his own house. The

The bustling intersection of Chandni Chownk in Old Delhi.

martyrdom occurred where *Sis Ganj Gurudwara* stands in Chandni Chownk. The resonance of these unselfish acts lives as a palpable and uplifting presence. The doors there truly seem more open to the eternal truths that are beyond place, culture, or systems of belief.

A few years ago I learned more of why I resonated with that center of peace. We knew that our son-in-law, Jonathan, had visited India while he was still in the Peace Corps before he met our daughter, Sheila. But what we didn't know until recently was that he had written an article called "The Sikh" about his serendipitous visit to find the peace of the *Sis Ganj Gurudwara* in the center of the chaos of Old Delhi.

A large Sikh man with a carefully braided beard and a mustache tucked into his immaculate purple turban came to us and welcomed us to the temple and gently asked us if we would like a tour ... We climbed to the second floor and saw Sikh boys continuously reading their holy book. They don't stop, we were told. It is so that Sikhs can count on someone, somewhere in the world always reading the book.

As I am writing this, my husband is reading from that same holy book in the room we reserve for prayer in the center of our house. Guru Nanak taught us that by singing hymns together the whole being is lifted and

A mother's prayer answered. Jonathan and Sheila make a handsome couple on their wedding day.

transformed—the scars of many lifetimes are erased. "Lift up your hearts!"—this exhortation from the Catholic and Episcopal mass has its equivalent in *"Chardi kalaa!"* from the *Ardaas* or prayer of the Sikhs. We **can** expand into the peace of our universal nature. This is one message of *Sis Ganj* and of the *Guru Granth Sahib*.

The "Heart of Punjab" Menu

Some tastes, like some places, will forever be etched in my memory. I tasted kadee for the first time at a roadside open-air "restaurant," a dhaba, in the Hisar district that was then part of Punjab. It was served with tandoori rotee and was a revelation! What was essentially a vegetarian gravy became a savory ambrosia! When I returned to the states, my mother-in-law taught me the basics of the dish. She put the besan into the liquid and began stirring slowly for hours. Then, when the gravy was sufficiently thickened, she added the tardka and the pakoras.

I became impatient with that method and borrowed the French technique of making a roux for gravy—sautéing the besan in the tardka before adding the liquid. The result was richer tasting and cut the cooking time in half. Everyone loved it when I would make it at the gurudwara, the Sikh temple, for the free community meal, the langar. No one could guess why it tasted so good. It became our signature langar meal.

Appetizer:	*PEESIA SUBZE PAKORA* Chopped Vegetable Fritters *DHANIA NIMBOO CHUTNEY* Cilantro Lime Chutney
Main Course:	*RAAJMA* Red Kidney Beans in Gravy *KADEE* Buttermilk Stew *TANDOORI ROTEE* Broiled Whole-Wheat Yeast Flat Breads (page 64) *SAADA PILAW* Simple Rice Pilaf
Dessert:	*SOUKHA RAS MALAI* Easy Ricotta Squares in Creamy Syrup

- **One Week or More Prior:** Read each recipe from beginning to end and make a shopping list. Buy the ingredients for the *pakoras* and staples like chickpea flour and *kewrda* from the Indian market. Make the *pakoras* and freeze them.

- **One to Three Days Prior:** Do your grocery shopping. Make the beans, the *kadee,* and the *ras malai,* if you have room in your refrigerator to store them. If not, save the *ras malai* to be made the morning of the party.

- **The Day of:**
  AM: Make the chutney. Turn on the exhaust fan and sauté the onions, spices, and rice for the *pilaw.* Make the *ras malai* and refrigerate. Defrost the *pakoras.* Separate the number you will need for the *kadee* dumplings, if using.
  PM: Remove the *kadee* and the beans from the refrigerator. Chop the cilantro for the garnishes. Clean up.

- **About an hour before serving:** Boil the water and add it to the rice. Plate the cold dessert, and either bring to room temperature or re-refrigerate. Preheat the oven to 200°F and warm the *pakoras.* Heat the other dishes and garnish them.

CHOPPED VEGETABLE FRITTERS

vegan   Peesia Subze Pakora

These delicious fritters are on "double duty." If serving as an appetizer, the batter can rest in the refrigerator separate from the chopped vegetables which should then be added just before frying, since they are best eaten immediately with chutney. If made as dumplings for the kadee *(page 84), they can be prepared ahead and frozen, since their quality is not compromised when eaten this way. Just make them smaller.*

Combine the chickpea flour, rice flour, baking powder, salt, cumin seeds, coriander seeds, and cayenne pepper with the water to make a batter. Set aside.

Sprinkle the potatoes or zucchini with a little salt. Place the potatoes or zucchini in a glass bowl, cover with water and heat in the microwave on high for 4 minutes. Drain.

Heat 3 inches of oil to 350°F in a deep wok.

Mix the potato or zucchini, spinach, ginger, onion, and chile pepper into the batter. Drop a spoonful of batter (for the appetizer, use a rounded tablespoonful; for the dumplings, use half of that) into the hot oil and fry until crispy. Remove with slotted spoon and drain on paper towels. Taste and check for salt before making the rest. If needed, add more salt to the batter. Fry in small batches, maintaining the oil temperature so that the *pakoras* are crispy. Remove with a slotted spoon to paper towels.

These are best eaten immediately, but may be kept warm in a 200°F oven, reheated, or frozen. Freeze in a single layer on a cookie sheet and then place in a plastic bag. Serve with tamarind or cilantro lime chutney *(page 82)*. Or use as dumplings in the *kadee* recipe on page 84.

YIELD: 45 PIECES

For the batter:

2 cups chickpea flour (*besan*)

1/2 cup rice flour (or use more chick-pea flour)

1/2 teaspoon baking powder

1 1/2 teaspoons salt

1 teaspoon whole or ground cumin seeds

1 teaspoon crushed coriander seeds

1/2 to 1 teaspoon ground cayenne pepper

1 1/2 cups cold water

Vegetables:

2 large potatoes or 2 large zucchini, peeled and cut into tiny cubes (about 2 cups)

3 cups fresh baby spinach (6 ounces), chopped; or 1/2 cup frozen chopped spinach, thawed and drained

2 tablespoons grated ginger

1 large onion, finely chopped

3 tablespoons minced green chile pepper

Canola oil for frying

CILANTRO LIME CHUTNEY

Dhania Nimboo Chutney   *vegan*

When my students taste this chutney, they want to eat it right out of the bowl! It is the most "delicate" of all the chutney recipes in this book because of the tenderness of cilantro leaves and stems. Be sure to use a Vidalia or other sweet onion. It makes a world of difference.

YIELD: 2 CUPS

½ cup grated unsweetened or sweetened coconut (fresh, frozen, or dried)

2 cups cilantro leaves and tender stems, packed

1 teaspoon finely grated lime zest

2 medium sweet onions, sliced

¼ cup lime juice

2-inch piece ginger, sliced

5-inch green chile pepper, seeded and sliced

1½ to 2 teaspoons sugar

1 teaspoon salt, or more to taste

⅛ teaspoon freshly ground black pepper

If using dry unsweetened coconut, soak it in some boiling water. If using dry sweetened, you do not have to soak it, and you can omit the sugar.

Soak the cilantro in a bowl of cold water to allow any sand to sink to the bottom. Swish and rinse.

Combine lime zest, onions, and lime juice in a food processor and grind. Add the ginger, chile pepper, and cilantro, grinding after each addition. You may need to add a very small amount of water to facilitate the grinding.

Drain the coconut, if soaked, and add to the processor with the sugar, salt and black pepper. Grind again. Refrigerate.

RED KIDNEY BEANS IN GRAVY

vegan   Raajma

Red beans are a favorite in both northwestern India and the southwestern United States. This is a flavorful, hearty dish wherever you enjoy it. It also freezes well; just leave out the cilantro until ready to reheat.

Pick over the beans and rinse; drain and rinse again. Add dried beans to a pot* with 3 quarts fresh water. Add the turmeric, pepper flakes, and salt and bring to a boil. Reduce heat, cover, and simmer for 2 to 3 hours. Beans should be tender but not mushy. (If using canned beans, place them in a large saucepan, add ¹/₂ cup water, turmeric, and pepper flakes [no salt] and bring to a simmer before proceeding.)

In another pan, heat the oil and fry the onion, garlic, and ginger until brown. Add the spices (cumin seeds through garam masala) and fry for 1 minute. Add the chopped chile pepper and tomatoes and sauté for 5 minutes.

Add the tomato mixture to the beans and simmer, covered, for 10 minutes. Stir in the ground cilantro leaves. Taste and adjust seasoning. Continue to simmer, covered, for 10 more minutes.

Turn out into a serving dish. Sprinkle with more garam masala and the tablespoon of cilantro leaves.

YIELD: 12 ¹/₂-CUP SERVINGS

1 pound (2¹/₂ cups) dried kidney beans, presoaked, or use 4 (15-ounce) cans cooked kidney beans, rinsed and drained

1 tablespoon ground turmeric

¹/₂ teaspoon dried red pepper flakes

1 tablespoon salt

¹/₄ cup canola oil

1 large onion, chopped

3 cloves garlic, minced

2-inch piece ginger, minced

1 teaspoon whole or ground cumin seeds

5 teaspoons ground coriander seeds

¹/₂ teaspoon dried fenugreek leaves (*kasoori methi*) (*optional*)

1 teaspoon garam masala

1 or 2 green chile peppers, chopped

1 (15-ounce) can diced tomatoes with juice

¹/₂ cup cilantro leaves and stems, ground plus 1 tablespoon cilantro leaves for garnish

* If using a slow cooker or pressure cooker, the time will vary. Presoak the beans in any case.

BUTTERMILK STEW

Kadee   *dairy*

This is the amazing dish I mentioned at the start of this chapter that has me salivating just thinking about it. I use the French technique of making a roux to speed the cooking. Kadee *tastes even better if refrigerated and served the next day, which makes it a great dish to serve to guests when you don't have time to be in the kitchen the day they arrive. Just leave out the additional ingredients until you have reheated it and restored it to the consistency you like.*

YIELD: 12 ½-CUP SERVINGS

2 medium onions, finely chopped

½ cup canola oil

2 or 3 large cloves garlic, minced

2-inch piece ginger, minced

2 teaspoons ground turmeric

1 teaspoon whole or ground cumin seeds

2 teaspoons ground coriander seeds

2 whole black cardamom pods (*optional*)

2 whole bay leaves

2 teaspoons dried green mango powder (*amchoor*)

¼ teaspoon dried, crushed fenugreek leaves (*kasoori methi*) (*optional*)

½ teaspoon cayenne pepper, or to taste

1 green chile pepper, seeded and chopped

1 cup chickpea flour (*besan*)

5 or 6 cups lukewarm water

3 cups buttermilk or 2 cups plain yogurt

2 teaspoons salt, or to taste

½ cup chopped cilantro leaves

1 teaspoon garam masala

Additional ingredients:

12 small *pakoras** and 1 cup diced red bell pepper (cooked on high in the microwave for 2 minutes)

or 1 (1 lb.) package thawed pearl onions and peas (cooked on high in the microwave for 2 minutes)

or 2 cups fresh spinach, packed, and ½ pint grape tomatoes

In a large saucepan, sauté the onions in the oil until transparent. Add the garlic and ginger and sauté until lightly brown. Add the spices (turmeric through cayenne pepper) and sauté for 1 minute, and then add the green chile. Add the chickpea flour and sauté over low heat for 2 minutes, stirring constantly until the flour is very lightly browned.

(Note: If using buttermilk, use 5 cups of water; if using yogurt, use 6 cups of water.) Slowly add the water a little at a time to the flour mixture, whisking constantly to keep from lumping. Bring the mixture to a boil, stirring constantly. Whisk in the buttermilk or yogurt and salt. Lower the heat and continue to simmer for 30 minutes to blend the flavors, stirring often so it doesn't stick or burn. (At this point it will be fairly thick and will thicken more as it cooks. If you are going to freeze it, do so at this point after cooling).

After 30 minutes, taste and check for salt. If you are going to add *pakoras*, stir in an additional cup of water. Then you may fold in any additional ingredients but do not stir vigorously after that. Continue to heat over very low heat for another 10 minutes. Check the consistency and cook a little longer or add a little more water. Some people like it thin, like cream soup; others like it thicker. Garnish with the cilantro and garam masala before serving.

*If using frozen *pakoras*, rinse, defrost, then soak for 30 seconds in warm water and carefully squeeze dry before adding to the stew. You may do this to the fresh ones as well to make them softer, but don't burn your hands with fritters hot out of the oil.

SIMPLE RICE PILAF

vegan   Saada Pilaw

There are so many complicated rice dishes in India, but this is one you can make quickly after work. In our home we always made it for guests. It has lots of flavor even without the optional ingredients, but becomes almost a meal with them.

Rinse the rice thoroughly until the water runs clear. Drain. Cover the rice with clean water and soak for 20 minutes.

If using onion, in a medium saucepan begin frying the onion in hot oil or *ghee* over medium heat until golden. Add the cinnamon stick, cardamom and/or cumin, cloves, bay leaf, and salt. Continue to fry until the onions are fairly brown.

Drain the rice thoroughly in a sieve. Add rice to pot with the spices and stir-fry, gingerly tossing it with a spatula until it is just uniformly opaque. Try not to break the grains of rice. (You can make the rice ahead to this point and then cover and set the pot of rice aside until about a half hour before serving.)

Thirty-five minutes before serving, add the boiling water to the rice mixture. Bring to a rolling boil over high heat. Stir well, and then cover tightly, reducing the heat to very low and cook for 25 minutes. Meanwhile heat the peas in the microwave for several minutes until barely cooked, about a minute. Stir the peas gently into the rice. Remove from heat and cover the pot with a cotton tea towel and then the lid and allow to steam for 10 minutes. Fluff with a fork and turn out onto a heated platter. Garnish, as you like.

YIELD: 10 SERVINGS

2½ cups basmati rice

1 medium onion, sliced (*optional*)

¼ cup canola oil or *ghee*

1 cinnamon stick

4 black cardamom pods and/or 1 teaspoon whole cumin seeds

4 whole cloves

1 bay leaf

2½ teaspoons salt, or to taste

5 cups boiling water

1 cup frozen green peas (*optional*)

Optional garnishes: cilantro; toasted salted almonds or cashews; fried onions

EASY RICOTTA SQUARES IN CREAMY SYRUP

Soukha Ras Malai   *dairy*

Everyone is wild about this recipe that "Ooma" taught me because it is so yummy and yet so easy to prepare. It will become a standard "company" dish in your repertoire. Do not substitute rose water for the rose flavor or extract. The rose flavor is usually found behind the cashier at the Indian market.

YIELD: 25 1½ X 1½-INCH PIECES

4 cups (32 ounces) ricotta cheese

¼ cup farina

1 cup cold water

1½ cups sugar, divided

10 green cardamom pods

2 cups (1 pint) heavy or light cream

½ teaspoon rose flavor or extract

2 tablespoons unsalted pistachios, chopped

Preheat the oven to 350°F. Mix the ricotta with the farina and ½ cup sugar and spread evenly in a buttered or sprayed glass 10-inch or 12-inch square baking dish. Bake the ricotta for 1 hour. Turn off the oven and allow to rest in the oven for 15 more minutes.

Meanwhile make a simple syrup by combining the water, remaining sugar, and cardamom pods in a medium saucepan and heating until boiling. Continue to boil until it reaches 230°F, the syrup stage. Cool for 10 minutes. Remove the cardamom pods from the syrup.

Remove the cheese from the oven. Cut into 25 pieces in the pan. Mix the syrup with the cream and rose flavor. Pour half of the syrup over the cheese squares and cool the rest. Cool the cheese squares in the refrigerator for 1 hour or more until completely chilled and until all the syrup is absorbed. Pour the reserved cream-syrup over the squares just before serving and sprinkle with pistachios.

Darling Meghan and Madie have stayed close to their grandmother Surindera whom they call "Ooma."

BUFFALO DREAMS

The prominence of dairy in Punjab

WHEN I WAS GROWING UP, SUNDAY AFTERNOON DINNER WAS THE BIGGEST PRODUCTION of the week—and therefore, to me, the most satisfying. And yet my husband said that of all the meals he had as a child, he loved a plain glass of milk best. I had a difficult time processing that the most-simple meal could be the most satisfying. In fact, during his school days, the only thing he had for breakfast was a glass of plain milk. But what milk! Thick and rich, it was more like a milkshake and would fill him until lunchtime when he returned from Khalsa School to eat his *subze, rotee,* and *dehin.*

Punjab is the land of bread and dairy. Not the dairy produced from the cow, which most people would assume, but from the water buffalo. Instead of the 4 percent butterfat in the milk of most dairy cows, buffalo milk contains much more, sometimes double! No wonder the yogurt and *paneer,* let alone a plain glass of milk, cannot be duplicated with cow's milk, and only weakly imitated with the addition of cream.

My husband's family kept twelve brown and black buffalo. The brown were thought to produce more butterfat in their milk. In addition, the family had about seven cows, and two to three horses and camels. The stalls and mangers for the animals were in their large home/compound, called the *heveli.* A servant couple cared for the cattle, taking them by turns to one of the very large ponds on either end of the village. *Babaji*, my husband's grandfather, made sure that the cattle were well fed. Cottonseed, grams (chickpeas), and wheat chaff made their milk unusually rich—even for Punjab!

The whirring sound of the butter churn was the first thing my husband heard in the morning, every morning, even before the roosters began crowing. The man doing the milking and churning was hired by *Babaji* after losing his property due to mental illness and drink. The trust was not misplaced. This unforgettable character churned out the treasures of the farm—fresh butter, cream, and buttermilk.The most precious of all, *ghee*, was carried by my husband and his cousins to college in padlocked tins to be doled out by their servant a spoon at a time.

The useful buffalo could pull a plow, or be hitched to a water wheel at the well. When we would drive into a village, we could tell how wealthy it was by the number and height of the pyramids or hillocks of buffalo dung cakes drying in the sun. That is because buffalo also manufacture an important source of fuel. Punjab is generally dry except for the monsoon months, so trees are not abundant and kindling wood is scarce. People rely on very fast-burning cotton sticks or slower-burning buffalo dung cakes for

Our son, Herpaul Singh, is dwarfed by a water buffalo and a huge pile of cotton sticks used to fuel cooking stoves.

cooking. There would be no slow-cooked curries without this fuel. In the self-sustaining villages of India, nothing is wasted.

One very hot Sunday afternoon, we learned that the versatile buffalo could also double as the siren, Lorelei. Our two-year-old son, our precious, went missing in Bhatinda. He was supposed to be taking a nap in the bedroom. We made a frantic search throughout the house and courtyard. Nearly hysterical, I was ready to do anything to find him. My husband seemed calmer. He reassured me while methodically organizing a search party to look throughout the neighborhood. Actually, his fear was that our son had been kidnapped.

After the longest hour of my life, one of the servants found our son next door, sitting peacefully, fascinated by a mother buffalo and her newborn calf. That time of terror and wild grief would be repeated much later in our lives in another generation as it had been in the village of my husband when he was a child. But on that day, in Bhatinda, we had a happy ending.

The "Buffalo Dreams" Menu

I tasted khoa paneer *for the first time in Rohtuk, a city that was then part of Punjab, now in the state of Haryana. My husband's cousin, Mithi, was in medical school there and she took us to a restaurant that specialized in this wonderful dish. Rich buffalo cheese squares in creamy, tomato-kissed gravy, eaten with fresh, fluffy* kulchas—*could it get any better? Yes! Add the delicious accompaniments and you have a meal fit for your most discerning guests!*

Appetizer:	SUBZE TIKEE Vegetable Cutlets
	KAJOO KHOPA CHUTNEY Cashew Coconut Chutney
Main Course:	KHOA PANEER Cheese Squares in Creamy Gravy
	PAPEETA SALADE Papaya Salad
	GUNDAYWALA KULCHA Grilled White Breads with Onion
Dessert:	PISTA BADAAM FEARNEE Pistachio-Almond Milk Pudding

- **One Week or More Prior:** Read the recipes from beginning to end and make your grocery lists. Buy the *paneer*, the spices, butter, and nuts at the Indian market or make your own paneer *(page 216)*.

- **Three to Four Days Prior:** Make the *ghee* for both the bread and cheese recipes and fry the *paneer*.

- **Two Days Prior:** Buy the vegetables and fruit. Make the nut pudding. Cover tightly and refrigerate.

- **One Day Prior:** Make and refrigerate the gravy for the *khoa paneer*. Prepare the vegetable mixture for the cutlets. Make the coconut chutney except for the finishing *tardka*.

- **The Day of:**
  AM: Defrost the *paneer*, if frozen, and soak it. Chop and cut the fruit and the vegetables for the salad. Fry the onions for the *kulchas*.
  PM: Make the dough for the *kulchas*. Measure the ingredients for the "sauce" for the chutney. Bread the cutlets. Finish the *paneer* dish.

- **Within the hour before serving time:** Fry the cutlets. Make the *tardka* for the chutney. Reheat the *paneer* dish in the microwave. Make the *kulchas*. Add the cilantro to the salad and the *khoa paneer*.

VEGETABLE CUTLETS

vegan   Subze Tikee

In India, breaded leftovers made into patties are a staple of high tea, a remnant of the colonial era. Some dishes, and even the names of dishes became melded, neither Indian nor British. This recipe is one. They are called "cutlets" or "cutlass" in many parts of India, but in my husband's family they were called "small pieces"—tikee.

Slit the potatoes slightly and heat in the microwave on high for 6 minutes or until just cooked. Cool. Peel the potatoes and mash in a large bowl.

Microwave the thawed vegetables or your own mixture a few minutes until cooked but not mushy. In a food processor, coarsely chop the vegetables into very small pieces (do this using PULSE to be sure they do not get puréed). Add to the potatoes.

Trim and then finely slice the white part of the green onions and up to 1 inch of dark green. Grind the green onions, ginger, and chile pepper in a food processor. Add to the potatoes along with all the remaining ingredients except the breadcrumbs and oil. Mix well. Taste for salt.

Spread the breadcrumbs or *panko* on a plate. Pack an oiled measuring cup (⅓ cup) with some of the vegetable mixture and tap out onto the crumbs. Lightly press into a patty; turn and repeat, coating with crumbs. Repeat with remaining mixture. Place the cutlets on a cookie sheet and refrigerate for at least 1 hour.

Brush or spray a heated griddle with oil and fry the cutlets until brown on one side; turn carefully and brown on the other side. Serve hot or warm with Cashew Coconut Chutney *(page 90)* or Tamarind Date Chutney *(page 215)*.

YIELD: 15 CUTLETS

3 medium red potatoes

20-ounce package frozen Italian medley (cauliflower, carrots, Italian green beans), thawed

3 green onions

1-inch piece ginger

2-inch piece green chile pepper, seeded

½ cup dried, unsweetened grated coconut

½ teaspoon garam masala *(optional)*

½ teaspoon ground toasted cumin seeds

½ teaspoon ground coriander seeds

¼ teaspoon dried red pepper flakes *(optional)*

¼ cup cilantro *(optional)*

2 teaspoons salt, or to taste

Black pepper to taste

Panko (Japanese breadcrumbs) or dry breadcrumbs

Canola oil for frying or non-stick spray

CASHEW COCONUT CHUTNEY

Kajoo Khopa Chutney   *vegan*

*Adapted from a recipe by Devika Teja, this chutney has a typical
south Indian topping, another version of* tardka *that can be just as
delicious as the north Indian tempering mixture of onions, garlic,
and ginger. Also try this topping over boiled lentils or rice.*

YIELD: 2 CUPS

For the chutney:

2 cups grated fresh* or frozen
    coconut

2-inch piece ginger

2 cloves garlic

1 mild or hot long green chile
    pepper, seeded

1 tablespoon lemon juice or more
    to taste

¼ cup cilantro leaves

1 teaspoon salt, or more to taste

For the tardka:

2 tablespoons canola oil or *ghee*

2 teaspoons mustard seeds

6 curry leaves

2 tablespoons coarsely ground
    cashews

Pinch of salt

Place grated coconut in a serving bowl. Grind the rest of
the chutney ingredients in a food processor and mix into
the coconut. Taste for seasoning.

Just before serving, in a small pan, heat the oil. Fry the
mustard seeds for a minute until they "pop." Add the curry
leaves, cashews, and salt and then fry for 1 more minute.
Pour over the coconut chutney. Refrigerate leftovers.

*If using fresh, the brown peel should be scraped off the coconut
before chopping coarsely. You may have to add a small amount of
water in order to grate the coconut in a food processor. Grate in
two batches.

90

CHEESE SQUARES IN CREAMY GRAVY

This 100 percent Punjabi dish is a paean to milk—comfort food par excellence! Khoa is whole milk that has been slowly concentrated into a solid, an important way to preserve it when there was no refrigeration in the village. Paneer, or fresh pressed cheese, was used less in the village, but more in the city. Both may be found in the dairy case of Indian supermarkets. Or make your own cheese from the recipe on page 216. I like the contrasting texture of the fried cheese, and the cubes won't crumble in the sauce.

Garnishes: 2 tablespoons cilantro leaves, finely sliced, and/or 1 tablespoon small red or sliced green chilies; chopped cashews or sliced almonds

YIELD: 8 ³/₄-CUP SERVINGS

4 large, ripe tomatoes or 1 (28-ounce) can diced tomatoes

3 tablespoons *ghee*

2 tablespoons canola oil

1 teaspoon whole cumin seeds

1 medium onion, chopped

3 cloves garlic, minced

1¹/₂-inch piece ginger, grated

1 green chile pepper, seeded and chopped

2 teaspoons ground coriander seeds

¹/₂ teaspoon ground cayenne pepper (*optional*)

1 teaspoon dried fenugreek leaves (*kasoori methi*)

1 (14-ounce) package *paneer*, cut into 1-inch cubes and fried (4 cups cubes)

1¹/₂ cups milk

1 tablespoon tomato paste

1 teaspoon brown sugar

1 teaspoon garam masala

4 ounces *khoa*, finely grated, or ¹/₂ cup *mava* (powdered whole milk) plus ¹/₄ cup cream*

1 to 2 teaspoons salt, or to taste

Blanch the fresh tomatoes in boiling water until the skin cracks—a minute or two. Cool, peel, and chop. Set aside.

In a large wok, heat the *ghee* and oil and sauté the cumin seeds for several seconds. Add the onion, garlic, ginger, and chile pepper and sauté until golden brown, stirring often. Add the coriander seeds and cayenne and sauté for a few more minutes. Add the tomatoes, the fenugreek leaves, and ¹/₂ cup water. Simmer over very low heat, stirring often, for about 25 minutes or until the tomatoes are "saucy" and cooked.

Soak the fried *paneer* cubes in very warm water.

In a blender, purée the tomato sauce, milk, tomato paste, brown sugar, garam masala, and *khoa* or *mava*/cream until smooth. Pour into a microwavable serving dish. Taste for seasoning and add salt as needed. Microwave on half power for five minutes. Drain the *paneer* cubes and add to the tomato mixture. Heat at half power until warmed through. Add water in small increments if you like a thinner gravy. Stir in 1 tablespoon cilantro and then top with another tablespoon cilantro and the other garnishes.

*If neither *khoa* nor *mava* can be found, substitute ¹/₂ cup of powdered skim milk mixed with ¹/₂ cup heavy cream.

PAPAYA SALAD

Papeeta Salade   *vegan*

Nature's mouthwatering digestif—and work of art—the papaya.

In Punjab, papaya is usually eaten for breakfast with only a splash of lime. But I thought a salad would be a great addition to this meal. This one is not only beautiful but the enzymes in the papaya are a great digestif. This salad is best prepared an hour or less before serving.

YIELD: 8 1-CUP SERVINGS

3 tablespoons lime or lemon juice

1 clove garlic, minced

1 tablespoon crumbled gurd or brown sugar

2 teaspoons *chaat masala* (page 5)

½ teaspoon salt

¼ teaspoon black pepper

5 cups peeled and cubed (1-inch) ripe papaya

1 cup halved red or green grapes

3 cups ½-inch cubes green or red apple

1 small to medium red onion, finely chopped (*optional*)

½ cup sliced cilantro leaves

Mix the lime or lemon juice, garlic, brown sugar, *chaat masala*, salt, and pepper together until smooth.

Combine the fruits and the onion in a large salad bowl. Pour the dressing over the salad and toss carefully. Refrigerate until serving time and add the cilantro just before serving.

GRILLED WHITE BREADS WITH ONION

dairy   Gundaywala Kulcha

These breads are a real treat, especially fine with the khoa paneer *(page 91). Each time the dough rests you will be able to roll it out a little further. For best results, make on a very hot (above 450°F) grill.*

In a small bowl, dissolve the yeast and sugar in the warm water. Set aside until foamy. In a small pan, sauté the onions in the *ghee* until brown. Add a ¼ teaspoon salt and the black pepper. Set aside.

In a medium bowl, whisk the yeast mixture, warm milk, yogurt, remaining salt, and one tablespoon of the *ghee* in which you cooked the onions.

In a large bowl, whisk together the flour and baking powder. Make a well in the center of the flour and pour in the milk mixture. Stir with a wooden spoon or dough hook until thoroughly mixed. If the dough is too stiff, add a few spoonfuls of water at a time until the dough is workable.

Grease your hands and begin to knead the dough until it is elastic and does not stick to your hands and the bowl. Then knead in earnest for at least 6 more minutes. Oil the ball of dough and cover the bowl with a tea towel. Leave it in a warm place for 2 hours or until the dough has doubled in size—the time will depend on the warmth of the room.

Divide the dough into eight equal, smooth balls. Let the dough rest while you begin heating one or more iron griddles, the charcoal or gas grill, or a skillet on high heat for five minutes. Roll out the balls to 4 inches in diameter. Cover with moist tea towels and let rest for a few minutes. Roll out again to 7 inches. Take a spoonful of onions and slather on only half of each circle of dough. Fold in half and roll out again, crimping the edges. Let rest for another 5 minutes and then roll some more, until they have reached 7 inches again. Slap one or two onto the griddle, grill, or skillet, keeping the other dough circles covered with a towel. Cover and cook one side for about 1 minute or until little "hills" begin to form on the uncooked side. Flip and cook the other side for 2 minutes. Flip again and cook for 2 more minutes. Repeat if the bread is not quite done or if you like it more brown. Place the cooked bread on a rack and brush with the melted *ghee*.

Repeat the process until all are grilled. They are best served immediately or kept warm wrapped in a tea towel.

YIELD: 8 7-INCH BREADS

2 teaspoons active dry yeast

1 tablespoon sugar

2 tablespoons warm water

1½ cups very thinly sliced onion (about 1 medium)

3 tablespoons *ghee*

2¼ teaspoons salt

¼ teaspoon freshly ground black pepper

1¾ cups warm milk

2 tablespoons plain yogurt

4½ cups all-purpose flour

2 teaspoons baking powder

Oil for hand and bowl

PISTACHIO-ALMOND MILK PUDDING

Pista Badaam Fearnee   *dairy*

When I first went to Punjab, my mother-in-law was proud to use custard powder, one of the very few commercial foods available then. This pudding is the "old-fashioned" kind—all "from scratch" ingredients, an Indian-style blancmange *(white pudding).*

YIELD: 12 ½-CUP SERVINGS

¾ cup whole milk powder (*mava*) or non-fat dry milk

¼ cup heavy cream

6 cups whole milk

⅔ to ¾ cup rice flour (depending on how thick you like your pudding)

1 cup sugar

1 teaspoon rose, almond, or *kewrda* flavor

1 tablespoon *ghee*

¼ cup sliced or slivered almonds

¼ cup ground pistachios (*optional*)

In a heavy wok, whisk the dry milk and cream into 1 cup of the milk until it is dissolved, and then whisk in the rice flour and another 1 cup of milk. When smooth, add the remaining 4 cups of milk to the wok. Over medium heat, whisk until boiling. Turn down the heat and cook, stirring for a few minutes. Add the sugar and cook, stirring, over medium-low heat until the pudding is thick. Stir in the desired flavoring. Pour into a serving bowl and refrigerate until thoroughly chilled, about 4 hours (putting it in the freezer for 20 minutes may speed up cooling).

Heat the *ghee* in a small frying pan and toast the nuts until lightly browned. Drain on paper towels before sprinkling on the firm pudding. You may leave the nuts on the surface or gently fold them in with a rubber spatula.

Pista Badaam Fearnee with crunchy almond topping.

AT THE DHABA

The outdoor restaurants of Punjab

WHEN MY HUSBAND AND I ARRIVED IN INDIA in 1966, there were very few restaurants, but every town had at least one or two *dhabas,* "permanent" outdoor stalls, little more than tarp-covered outdoor campfires with rope cots strewn about for seating. Wonderful aromas tempted us as we watched the cook stirring a big pot of fragrant chickpeas or stir-frying colorful vegetables in a giant *kardhai* or wok over an open fire. We could order anything the cook made—sometimes grilled meat or lentils, or perhaps only the fabulous bread fried or grilled right before our eyes. Unlike at an indoor restaurant, there were no menus at the *dhaba,* each *dhabawalla* specialized in a few dishes made extremely well. So whatever we ordered, we knew it would be absolutely delicious!

Sometimes we wandered through the streets of the crowded city center. There we found smaller stalls, with vendors who called to invite you to try their wares—special snacks such as the myriad *chaats. Chaats* are close to what westerners think of as a salad, and they are always spicy and refreshing, with cooked legumes or fruit, yogurt, and chutney featured in some way. Crispy or crunchy bits of lentil or wheat flour wafers or noodles give the *chaats* an interesting texture.

Even in Chandigarh, designed by Le Courbousier to be the modern capital of Punjab, there were no grocery stores, and certainly no supermarkets. One might find a narrow stall with prepackaged items like matches, a few

A street vendor hawking fruit outside Uncle's house in Chandigarh.

canned goods, and biscuits (cookies). Even in the residential area where we were guests of Uncle Gurcharan Singh and his family, the air was filled with the musical cries of the vendors—vegetable hawkers, milk hawkers, and spice vendors. Tailors, shawl merchants, gardeners, house cleaners, cooks, and washer folk, who pressed clothes in front of the house with irons filled with live coals—all could be hired from your doorstep. I was amazed at how specialized the vendors and *dhabawallahs* were. A cook was the owner of a recipe that may have been passed down through the family for generations. The cook could be a Brahmin, but if he were, he could not eat the food prepared by a lower caste person. The laundress would not sweep the floor, and the tailor would not launder the clothes. No one considered living any other way.

Émigrés of my husband's generation and background were usually of the college-educated upper-middle classes. These men had never made a sandwich for themselves, let alone mowed a lawn, painted a room, or changed a tire. Their marriages were arranged for them, and their wives went off to a strange country with husbands they hardly knew. Back home the women had clothes sewn especially for them, and most had never so much as chopped a vegetable. But now in the "land paved with gold" everyone was required to wear ten "hats"—including the one worn by the untouchable who cleaned the bathroom. It was a shock for both the men and the women to discover how much they had to do with their own hands. But basically, their nature was enterprising, and they had respect for all types of work due to an important example in their Sikh faith: Guru Nanak, who, despite his travels from Punjab to Medina and to Sri Lanka and his status as a great teacher, would come home to personally farm his land.

On the way to the dhaba. Parmpal gives cousin Sati a ride on a motorcycle.

Waves of immigrants to the U.S., through hard work and sacrifice, have turned into prosperous Americans. Many South Asians also had to give up their status to enjoy the freedom of being "equal." They, like so many before them, have made a comfortable home here, but sometimes still dream of that special *chaat* at the *dhaba* in the town of their birth.

The "At the Dhaba" Menu

Luckily, most of the ingredients for this typical menu should be found in a grocery store not too far away. Whether you are second generation Punjabi or fourth generation Irish, I hope you will enjoy preparing this dhaba-style menu yourself with and for friends and family. The main course, especially the bhatura *and* chunnay *can be served on paper plates in an informal setting. Yet the fruit salad and the halva are fancy enough for china. Use the bread Punjabi-style—tear off a piece to scoop up a small amount of the delicious vegetable and gravy—no need for forks or knives.*

Appetizer:	*SEKUNJBEE* Lemonade Punjabi-Style *PHUL CHAAT* Spicy Fruit Salad
Main Course:	*KAABLEE CHUNNAY* Sweet and Sour Chickpeas *BHATURA* Puffy Fried Leavened Breads *ALOO MIRCH DUDHWALI* Potatoes and Peppers in Milk Curry
Dessert:	*GAJJERELLA* Carrot Almond Halva
Next-Day Lunch:	*TASTY TOAST* Vegetable Panini

- **Three to Four Days Prior:** Read the menu and recipes all the way through and make your grocery lists. From the Indian market buy the lemons, mint, cilantro, carrots, ginger, yogurt, plus the groceries such as the spices, nuts and chickpeas that are much cheaper there. A fresh guava and *gurd* might only be found in the Indian market. Buy the remaining vegetables and fruit.

- **Two to Three Days Prior:** Make the *chaat masala* (page 5). Make the carrot halva; refrigerate. Soak the dried chickpeas.

- **One-Day Prior:** Make the chickpeas and refrigerate. Prepare the dough for the *bhatura*. Refrigerate, oiled and covered with plastic wrap. Make the syrup for the lemonade.

- **The Day of:**
  AM: Make the potatoes and peppers.
  PM: Make the fruit salad and the lemonade. Refrigerate. Remove the bread dough and the halva from the refrigerator to allow to come to room temperature. Clean up.

- **At Serving Time:** Pour the drinks and serve the *chaat*. Turn on the fan. Reheat the chickpeas and the peppers. Enlist help in making the breads. Watch in awe as the breads balloon when you fry them. Garnish the vegetables. Serve and enjoy!

LEMONADE PUNJABI-STYLE

vegan   Sekunjbee

On a hot day, there is nothing more refreshing than lemonade. I've incorporated lemon zest—a western touch—with the traditional Punjabi salt and pepper. This drink tastes lots better than a sports drink, and yet is restorative. I bring the pre-made concentrate along on our RV trips because it takes up very little space in the refrigerator.

In a medium pan, boil the sugar, water, lemon zest, and peppercorns for 10 minutes over low heat, stirring occasionally. Strain and set aside to cool. Add the lemon juice and refrigerate this concentrate if you are not using immediately.

To serve, fill 10 tall glasses with ice. Stir the salt and pepper into the concentrate. Pour ⅓ cup of concentrate over each glass of ice and then fill the glass with cold water. Finish with a slice of lemon and a sprig of mint.

YIELD: 10 TALL GLASSES

2 cups sugar

1 cup water

3 teaspoons grated lemon zest (yellow part only)

1 teaspoon whole black peppercorns

1 cup fresh lemon juice (from 4 to 6 lemons)*

1 tablespoon salt

Freshly ground black pepper, to taste

Garnishes: Lemon slices; mint sprigs; pinch of toasted, ground cumin

*8 to 10 limes may be used instead for delicious limeade.

SPICY FRUIT SALAD

Phul Chaat *vegan*

Although my Dad always put salt on his watermelon, it was surprising to taste salt and spices on fruit salad when we arrived in New Delhi at Auntie Avtar's home. I have loved phul chaat *ever since. I really like this particular mixture of fruit, but you can dream up your own signature combo.*

YIELD: 5 CUPS

3 sweet, unpeeled apples

2 tablespoons lemon juice, divided

3 pears, peeled, or 1 large, ripe guava, peeled*

3 large bananas

1 can (14 ounce) lychees, drained (*optional*)

2 teaspoons *chaat masala*, divided (*page 5*)

1 tablespoon sugar (*optional*)

Garnish: 1 tablespoon fresh mint leaves, finely sliced (*optional*)

Cut the apples into 1½-inch chunks and toss in a serving bowl with 1 tablespoon of the lemon juice. Cut the pears or guava into 1½-inch chunks and add them to the bowl of apples.

Cut the bananas in half lengthwise, then crosswise into 1-inch chunks and put into a smaller bowl. Sprinkle immediately with 1 tablespoon lemon juice and toss lightly. Combine with the other fruit. Add the lychees, if using.

Sprinkle all the fruit with 1½ teaspoons *chaat masala*. Toss lightly but thoroughly. Check the taste and then add sugar and/or ½ teaspoon more *chaat masala*, depending on whether you prefer it sweet or spicy. Refrigerate up to 2 hours or serve immediately. Garnish with mint, if desired.

*To choose a ripe guava, sniff it as you would a melon. They are quite fragrant when ripe.

SWEET AND SOUR CHICKPEAS

vegan   Kaablee Chunnay

This dish is a standout and could make you the most popular guy in town. Try to use dry chickpeas, but in a pinch, substitute 4 (15-ounce) cans, rinsed and drained. Tastes even better reheated and it freezes well.

Soak the chickpeas overnight, changing the water at least once. Drain and rinse. In a pressure cooker or large, heavy pot with a tight lid, cover the chickpeas with fresh water plus 2 inches. Make a strong cup of tea with the two bags. Add the tea, tamarind, and salt to the chickpeas and bring to a boil over high heat. When the steam starts (in the pressure cooker) or the water boils (in the pot), turn down the heat to medium and cook for 40 minutes under pressure or 2 hours without pressure (adding water, if needed). Let the chickpeas cool in the pot for 15 minutes. They should be fully cooked.

Heat the oil in a large, heavy pot. Fry the onions until transparent and then add the ginger and garlic. When they begin to brown, add the turmeric, cumin seeds, black cardamom, and coriander seeds. Continue to stir-fry for a minute, and then add the tomatoes, brown sugar, garam masala, salt, and cayenne, if using. Simmer for 10 minutes, stirring occasionally.

Check to see how much water is left with the chickpeas. If little or none, add 1½ cups water to the onion mixture and then add the chickpeas. Simmer, covered, for 20 minutes. Turn into a serving bowl and garnish as desired.

YIELD: 12 SERVINGS (6 CUPS)

1 pound (3 scant cups) dried chickpeas

2 teabags

¼ cup dark (Tamcon®) tamarind concentrate or ½ cup light (like Lakshmi®)*

3 teaspoons salt, or to taste

⅓ cup canola oil

3 medium onions, chopped

2-inch piece ginger, minced

2 cloves garlic, minced

2 teaspoons ground turmeric

1 tablespoon ground cumin seeds

2 black cardamom pods, crushed (*optional*)

1½ tablespoons crushed or ground coriander seeds

2 tomatoes, chopped, or 1 small (8-ounce) can tomato sauce

3 tablespoons *gurd* or brown sugar*

2 teaspoons garam masala

1 to 2 teaspoons ground cayenne pepper (*optional*)

Garnishes: Seeded and slivered green chilies; 1 small red onion sliced into rings; a small tomato sliced into wedges

*You can substitute ⅓ cup tamarind chutney for the tamarind concentrate and the brown sugar, but add it at the end.

PUFFY FRIED LEAVENED BREADS

Bhatura *dairy/egg*

Our nephew Andy's favorite meal in the world is chunnay *with* bhatura *and* sont *chutney (see pages 99 and 176). Everyone loves this bread; so make sure you have made enough (2 to 3 per person)!*

YIELD: 6 TO 8 BREADS
Very large breads are the professional norm, but the size of your breads will be determined by the size of your wok.

4 cups all-purpose flour

1 teaspoon salt

1 teaspoon baking powder

1 large egg

½ cup plain yogurt

²/₃ cup warm water

Canola oil for frying, and for greasing the bowl and hands

Whisk the flour, salt and baking powder in a large bowl. In a small bowl, beat the egg, yogurt, and water with a fork.

Grease your hands with some of the oil. Make a well in the flour and slowly pour in the yogurt mixture, stirring one way from the center outward, combining the flour and yogurt mixture. Knead the dough until it no longer sticks to your hands and then for 2 more minutes. Lightly grease the bowl and ball of dough and cover with plastic wrap or a wet cloth and set in a warm place for 1 hour.

Pour the oil in a large wok to a depth of at least 3 inches. Have a large, slotted spoon ready. Cover a cookie sheet or large tray with paper towels.

Oil your hands and the rolling pin. Divide the dough into 6 to 8 balls. Flatten one ball at a time in a little oil and roll into a disk of about 4 inches. Cover the disks with a slightly damp towel and let rest for 10 minutes. Heat the oil to 375°F.

Roll one disk at a time to a diameter of 5 to 7 inches. Carefully slide the *bhatura* into the hot oil. Immediately press down once to cover the top in hot oil. It will begin to puff. Turn it over, it should be lightly brown. Remove to the paper towels when the underside is also lightly brown. This takes less than a minute. Then roll out the next bread and fry.

Do **not** stack these breads on top of one another as they will become soggy (unless you put several paper towels between them). Serve immediately. Or, if carefully stacked sideways, they may be reheated a few hours later in a pre-warmed 200°F oven. Do not leave them in the oven past the time they are just warmed, they will quickly dry out.

Who could resist Puffy Bhatura with Chunnay?

POTATOES AND PEPPERS IN MILK CURRY

dairy

Aloo Mirch Dudhwali

My mother-in-law would make this subze when we were out of other fresh vegetables on Friday. It's great to make when you need to add another dish for unexpected guests because it's fast and the ingredients are readily available. Use ⅓ cup grated khoa plus 10 ounces water in place of evaporated milk; and red potatoes—if you have them."

Wash and peel the potatoes, cut in half lengthwise and heat in the microwave on high until just cooked, about 7 to 10 minutes. Cut into 1¼-inch dice. Set aside.

Cut the peppers into 1¼-inch squares, place in a bowl, cover and microwave on high until just tender, about 7 minutes. Set aside.

Heat the oil and sauté the onions until transparent. Add the garlic and ginger and sauté until golden brown. Add the turmeric, cumin seeds, fenugreek seeds, cayenne pepper, and chile pepper; sauté for 1 minute. Add the garam masala and salt. Stir in the milk and cook on medium heat for 3 minutes. Add the potatoes and peppers (with their juices).

Turn into a serving dish and garnish with cilantro. If needed, re-warm in the microwave until just hot so as not to curdle the milk.

YIELD: 8 ½-CUP SERVINGS

- 3 large or 4 medium potatoes
- 3 medium green bell peppers
- 1 red bell pepper (*optional*)
- ¼ cup canola oil
- 2 medium onions, finely chopped
- 3 cloves garlic, minced
- 1½-inch piece ginger, grated
- 1 teaspoon ground turmeric
- 1 teaspoon whole or ground cumin seeds
- 1 teaspoon ground fenugreek seeds (*methi*) (*optional*)
- ¼ to ¾ teaspoon ground cayenne pepper
- 4-inch green chile pepper, seeded and chopped
- 1 rounded teaspoon garam masala
- 1½ to 2 teaspoons salt, or to taste
- 1 (12-ounce) can evaporated milk
- ¼ cup sliced cilantro

Bebeji's Friday night special, Aloo Mirch Dudhwali.

CARROT ALMOND HALVA

Gajjerella *dairy*

Although this dessert can be made over an open fire, it is sumptuous enough for a banquet, especially if piled high on a platter and garnished with edible silver. Both yummy and healthful, it is a dessert popular throughout India and Pakistan. Maybe I'm prejudiced, but I love my mother-in-law's version which I have streamlined to prevent burning on the stovetop.

YIELD: 8 ⅓-CUP SERVINGS

5 (about 1 pound) medium carrots, trimmed, peeled, and grated

1 cup whole milk

½ cup heavy or light cream

½ teaspoon ground cardamom

½ cup chopped golden raisins

½ cup ground almonds

¼ cup white sugar

½ cup crumbled *gurd* or dark brown sugar

3 tablespoons *ghee*

1 cup whole-milk powder (*mava*)*

Garnishes: Silver leaf (*chandi verk*) and/or a spoon of slivered or sliced almonds

Put all the ingredients (except the *mava* and garnishes) into a glass container with lid. Cover and heat in a microwave oven on high for 6 minutes. Uncover, scrape the bottom of the vessel, and stir. Cook uncovered on medium (50 power) for increments of 5 minutes for a total of 20 minutes, stirring after each 5 minute period. When ready the mixture should be somewhat thick so that a wooden spatula or spoon clears a path in it as it is scraped. If not, keep cooking it. Once done, stir in the milk powder and heat in the microwave oven for another 5 minutes on medium (50 power).

Spread the halva on a platter, mounding in center and decorate with the silver leaf and slivered almonds. Serve warm or at room temperature. Leftovers keep well if covered tightly with plastic wrap and refrigerated.

*If whole milk powder (I use Deep™ brand) is unavailable, use 1 cup skim milk powder and the heavy cream (not light).

NEXT-DAY LUNCH

Lives very well-lived. His Honor, Gurcharan Singh Dhaliwal
with his loving wife Rasham Kaur ever by his side.

VEGETABLE PANINI

Tasty Toast   *dairy or vegan*

Traditionally these Anglo-Indian sandwiches are made in an iron press with a long handle and held over an open fire—that's how Auntie Surindra makes them. You may use a panini maker or George Foreman-type grill or the oven method.

YIELD: 8 SANDWICHES

3 cups leftover *aloo gobee* (page 108) or *kaablee chunnay* (page 99)

½ cup *ghee*, melted butter, or canola oil

16 slices substantial sandwich bread

1 cup grated cheddar or asiago cheese (*optional*)

Put the vegetables on several layers of paper towel to remove any excess water or oil. Chop finely. Butter or oil only one side of the bread slices.

Griddle method: Put ⅓ cup of the drained vegetables on the unbuttered side of half of the bread slices. Sprinkle with some cheese, if using. Top with another bread slice, buttered side up. Preheat a panini maker or George Foreman-type grill. Press a sandwich in the hot griddle until browned on both sides. Cut in half and trim the crusts if you like. Keep warm in a 200-degree oven until all are cooked. Serve immediately with or without chutney.

Oven method: Preheat the oven to 475°F. Place the brushed slices of bread, buttered side down, on 2 cookie sheets. Toast the slices for 10 to 15 minutes, rotating the baking sheets once. Meanwhile, heat the vegetables in the microwave for 2 minutes. Drain on paper towels. Put ⅓ cup of the drained vegetables on the unbuttered side of half of the bread slices. Sprinkle with some cheese, if using. Top with another bread slice, buttered side up. Cover the sandwiches on the baking sheet tightly with foil. Heat in oven for 5 minutes. Cut in half and trim crusts if you like. Serve immediately with or without chutney.

KID'S CHOICE

Memories of our grandson

IN PUNJAB, CHILDREN USUALLY DO not have the opportunity to cook. The open fires in the *chula* are hot and dangerous, and in the cities, most middle-class families have a cook. It is different in the U.S. We have so many wonderful memories centered on food and cooking with our grandchildren—the most poignant with our grandson, Bennett. A fresh mango shake is the last thing I made with him. Although he was not quite five when he was admitted to the hospital with a fever that wouldn't relent, he was showered with love every day of his short life.

Lined up for lunch. Parmpal (left) and his cousin-brothers, Gurpal, Surinder, Charnpal, and Avtar Singh.

His temperament was apparent from the start—basically shy, but fiercely protective of his sisters. Benny was very serious when it came to something he perceived was his "job," something that he needed to master. He put a great effort into learning and was so proud he had memorized the credo for his karate class. This extended to his "work" as a rescue hero, which even at two and three years of age, he was convinced that he was. When I came over to the house, Ben would have me lie down on the floor. Because he was so small, it was impossible to move me onto his pretend stretcher or pretend ambulance, so he would "rescue" my feet. Grabbing them, he would lift and very carefully place them in some position of which only he knew the meaning. I was not allowed to move until he was satisfied that I was sufficiently "rescued." I would thank him for rescuing my feet. He was pleased and solemnly acknowledged my thanks.

Benny was enjoying his world as he developed mastery over his emotions. On the last outing Grandpa and I had with Ben, we went to McDonald's. He used to pronounce it "McDowell's" when he was younger. As always, he was very well behaved there. He told Grandpa what meal he wanted (almost always nuggets and fries); this time with an orange soda. Grandpa got him a Sprite. Ben was upset, but we explained that Grandpa would get him what he wanted. So Grandpa went back and this time brought him an orange juice. With brow furrowed and lips in a pout, at that point he was ready to blow. I said to him that Grandpa meant well and that when we are upset or angry, it's a good time to practice patience—"Taking a deep breath is very helpful." Ben's desire for mastery kicked in, and sure enough, he listened carefully. He sucked in the air like a vacuum and expelled it in a deep, long sigh. He quietly drank the juice and ate his nuggets. As we were leaving, we passed a young woman in the next booth. She had overheard the entire conversation and stopped us to compliment Ben on his patience. We were so very proud of him.

Through the heartache we focus on the joy he brought us. And the joy we are so lucky to experience today. Benny's lively sisters, Sophia and Samantha, who are twins, help keep our spirits high. Our daughter, Raji, was a very quiet child like Benny, but her daughters have a chatter going at all times. I'm sure my mother-in-law would have called them *chirdian*—little sparrows. Their noisy laughter keeps us in the present. What a blessing!

The girls have never forgotten Benny. Although they were only three when he passed, they keep his memory alive by talking about him and taking delight in his photographs. Raji and David chronicle their children's lives so well. It is a blessing of God's grace that gives them the determination to be strong for their girls. It is their strength that keeps us alive.

The "Kid's Choice" Menu

We all love surprises that taste good; yet introducing new foods and new flavors to kids may take some time. The recipes in this menu are kid-friendly because they take something a child may already be familiar with—fried chicken, potatoes, plain yogurt, custard— and add another element. To the chicken and potatoes, the recipes add some mild spicing; to the yogurt, we add chutney; and to the custard, mango.

Chickpeas with fried breads, as well as mild cauliflower and potatoes, have always been the staple food of children in Punjab. I've found that most kids in the U.S. enjoy them as well. In fact, these dishes are always a big hit when I demonstrate Indian food to entire classrooms! Another fun aspect of this menu is the contrasting textures and pleasing forms these recipes take—the decorative foil at the end of the chicken pieces; the surprise of the yogurt dish that looks like a chocolate sundae; and of course, the entertainment of the breads that rise up as they are made. Fun in taste, form, and texture!

Appetizer: *MURGA PAKORA* Chicken "Lollipops"

Main Course: *MUTTER YA ALOO GOBEE BHOOJIA* Stir-Fried Cauliflower with Peas or Potatoes
KABLEE CHUNNAY Sweet and Sour Chickpeas *(page 99)*
POOREE Puffed Whole-Wheat Breads
DEHIN BHALLAY Savory "Sundae" of Lentil Fritters, Yogurt, and Chutney

Dessert: *AMB FEARNEE* Mango Custard

- **One Week or More Prior**: Read the recipes from start to finish. Prepare your grocery lists. Buy the spices, tamarind, *gurd*, ginger, garlic, chickpea flour, *chapatti* flour, rice, lentils, chickpeas, dates, mango purée, mangoes, and other staples from the Indian market. Make the *imlee* chutney. Make the lentil balls and freeze them.

- **Three Days Prior**: Buy the chicken, cilantro, onions, yogurt, cauliflower, potatoes or peas, and other vegetables. Make the chickpeas. Refrigerate.

- **Two Days Prior**: Measure the dry ingredients and mix with the spices for the chicken. Make the custard; cover and refrigerate.

- **One-Day Prior**: Prepare the chicken and marinate it in the refrigerator.

- **The Day of:**
AM: Make the potatoes or peas and cauliflower. Prepare the vegetable garnishes. Defrost the lentil fritters.
PM: Soak and squeeze the fritters. Assemble the *dehin bhalay*. Slice the mangoes if serving with the custard. Bake the chicken and keep warm in the oven.

- **At Serving Time**: Warm the chickpeas and cauliflower. Fry the breads (but if there are vegetarians among your guests, do not fry in the same oil as the chicken). Garnish the dishes.

CHICKEN "LOLLIPOPS"

meat/dairy   Murga Pakora

Chicken "lollipops" with foil booties to protect little fingers.

I first saw a chicken lollipop in Little India in New Jersey—perfect for a kid's menu. Serve my version to children with ketchup or tamarind chutney on the side. Adults may also like chili-garlic sauce for dipping. You may either bake or deep-fry the winglets.

Although they are simple to cook, there is some prep work on the chicken, so enlist help if you need it. You will need a small, very sharp, pointed knife, sharp kitchen scissors, paper towels and a large cookie sheet with a rim to ensure browning of the chicken.

Prepare the winglets: Take the bone of the winglet in one hand. Push the blade of a paring knife against the bone, about 1 to 1½ inches above the end of the bone, below the thickest tendon. Scrape up the bone (away from you) and around, releasing the tendon. Repeat around the bone until all of the tendons are scraped from the bone. Finish cutting and scraping all the winglets. With sharp kitchen scissors, cut away the inch or so of tendon hanging from the meat and discard. (Your goal is to have about 2 inches of bare bone below the meat.)

Stir the garlic, ginger, lemon juice, sour cream, spices, and salt in a large bowl. In a large plastic bag toss the prepared winglets in the marinade until they are thoroughly coated. Refrigerate for 2 hours or overnight.

Heat the oven to 450°F. Mix the cornstarch and rice flour in a plastic bag or large bowl. Shake the winglets in it until coated. Pour the *ghee* smoothly over a cookie sheet with a rim. Scrape the meat down on each winglet. Cover the bone ends with aluminum foil to make them easy to hold and place as far apart as possible on the baking sheet. Turn on the fan! Bake the drumettes, turning once, until crispy and brown, about 20 minutes. Serve immediately, sprinkled with *chaat masala* if desired.

*Removing skin is optional. If using unskinned winglets, do not use *ghee* on the cookie sheet because the skin releases fat, but do brush or spray the pan and wings with oil and bake for an additional 10 minutes.

YIELD: 16 WINGLETS

2½ pounds chicken "drumettes" (the section of the wing with only one bone is best), skin removed*

3 cloves garlic, finely minced or ½ teaspoon garlic powder

1 teaspoon grated ginger or ½ teaspoon ground ginger

Juice of 1 lemon (about 2½ tablespoons)

2 tablespoons sour cream or plain hung yogurt (page 6)

2½ teaspoons paprika

1 teaspoon *tandoori chicken masala (page 62)* or *chaat masala (page 5)*

1 teaspoon garam masala or seasoned salt

1 teaspoon salt

1 cup cornstarch

¼ cup rice flour

3 tablespoons melted *ghee* or oil

Garnish: *chaat masala (optional)*

STIR-FRIED CAULIFLOWER WITH PEAS OR POTATOES

Mutter Ya Aloo Gobee Bhoojia   *vegan*

This dish is a favorite of Indian kids. You may make it milder by leaving out the mustard seed, garam masala, and/or cumin. Like it hot? Add chile peppers or cayenne. If you like the cauliflower somewhat browned in spots, just add a little more oil to fry it and don't use the microwave or a nonstick wok.

YIELD: 8 SERVINGS

1 medium/large head of cauliflower, washed and trimmed of gray or brown spots

1½ teaspoons salt, or more to taste

⅓ cup canola oil

1 teaspoon black mustard seeds (*optional*)

1 medium onion, thinly sliced (*optional*)

1 teaspoon ground or whole cumin seeds (*optional*)

2 teaspoons ground turmeric

1 teaspoon crushed coriander seeds

1 teaspoon garam masala, divided (*optional*)

2 cloves garlic, minced

2-inch piece ginger, grated

3 large red potatoes, peeled and cubed into 1-inch pieces, *or* 2½ cups frozen green peas, thawed

¼ cup sliced fresh cilantro leaves

Break the cauliflower into florets and cut the stem into small pieces. Slice the nicer green leaves. Pour ¼ cup water into a microwavable dish or bowl and dissolve ½ teaspoon of salt in it. Add the cauliflower leaves, stems, and florets. Cover and microwave for 5 to 6 minutes on high.

In a large wok, heat the oil over medium heat. Add the mustard seeds first and stir-fry for 30 seconds. Add the onions, if using, and stir-fry until golden brown. Add the cumin, turmeric, coriander seeds, ½ teaspoon garam masala, garlic, and ginger. Fry for another 1 to 2 minutes. Add the potatoes now, if using, and stir-fry until they are evenly coated with spices. Cover and cook over low heat for 5 minutes, stirring once. Add the drained cauliflower and the peas, if using. Sprinkle with the remaining salt. Mix thoroughly, stir-frying vigorously over high heat for at least 5 minutes, adding more oil if necessary, until all the spices are evenly distributed and the cauliflower is browned, if desired.

Turn down the heat and finish cooking until tender, 10-15 minutes, stir-frying uncovered (if you like your vegetables dry) or covering (if you like them wetter). Sprinkle with the remaining ½ teaspoon of garam masala and garnish with cilantro before serving.

PUFFED WHOLE-WHEAT BREADS

vegan

Pooree

Rolling dough for poorees, Sher Singh and his grandmother work together.

When my kids were small, I used to take a hot plate, a pot of chickpeas, a wok, oil, and dough to their classroom to demonstrate making poorees. The kids loved to watch the breads puff up. Even the fussy kids ate them if I left out the carom seed that tastes like caraway and aids digestion.

In a deep bowl combine the flour, farina, salt, carom seeds, and half of the water. Mix until crumbly. Slowly add the remaining water until all the loose flour is incorporated and makes a loose ball. If more water is needed, just sprinkle on a few drops at a time and knead. Remove the dough from the bowl, and knead on a flat surface for approximately 6 minutes or until dough is elastic. Coat the ball all over with a tablespoon of oil. Let the dough rest in a covered bowl for at least 30 minutes or up to 2 hours. You may refrigerate the dough overnight, but allow it to reach room temperature (30 minutes) before continuing.

Divide the dough into 3 parts. Roll each part into a cylinder. Cut or pinch each cylinder into eight pieces. Roll into smooth, even balls between the palms of your hands. Cover the balls with a damp towel.

Oil the rolling pin and either oil the workspace or use a little loose flour. Taking one ball at a time, flatten the ball in your oiled hand or in the flour and roll out into a disk. Turn the disk several times to make thin, even circles about 5 inches in diameter.

Heat at least 2 inches of the oil in a deep wok to 350°F. Carefully slide one *pooree* at a time into the hot oil. Press it down as it rises and as it begins to puff, turn it over until it is evenly golden.

Remove to a paper towel-lined tray and continue frying until all the *poorees* are cooked. Do not stack them. Serve immediately; or these breads may be kept warm for a few minutes in a 200°F oven if stood on their sides without crushing them.

YIELD: 24 BREADS (SERVES 8)

3 cups *chapatti* flour, or 1½ cups whole-wheat flour plus 1½ cups all-purpose flour

¼ cup farina (regular Cream of Wheat® is fine)

¼ teaspoon salt

½ teaspoon carom seeds (*ajwain*), (*optional*)

1½ cups warm water

3 cups vegetable oil for frying

SAVORY "SUNDAE" OF LENTIL FRITTERS, YOGURT, AND CHUTNEY

Dehin Bhallay   *dairy*

A savory "sundae" makes any meal a party.

These fritters, called vade *in Hindi, are very versatile—two recipes in one. They may be eaten immediately with chutney as a snack; or be made days ahead and then frozen for the "sundae." To save time, buy the commercially prepared fritters frozen in the shape of a ball or small donut. Soak them in warm water for a minute before using. They taste fine in the yogurt. But, if eating them as a snack, the homemade ones taste much better.*

YIELD: 10 TO 12 SERVINGS

For the fritters:

¾ cup white lentils, (washed or split *urad daal* or *mahan di daal*)

½ cup basmati rice

¼ cup farina (regular Cream of Wheat® is fine)

1¼ teaspoons salt

1½ teaspoons baking powder

1 teaspoon toasted cumin seeds

Canola oil for frying

For the yogurt sauce:

4 cups (32 ounces) plain yogurt

1 teaspoon salt

1 teaspoon toasted cumin seeds

¼ teaspoon ground cayenne pepper

½ cup sliced fresh cilantro

½ teaspoon *chaat masala (page 5)*

½ cup tamarind *imlee* chutney *(page 215)*, thinned with water if very thick

Make the fritters: Pick over and rinse the lentils. Place in a large bowl. Rinse the rice until water runs clear and add to the lentils. Add plenty of water so that they will be completely covered even after soaking. Soak for 4 hours or overnight. Drain in a colander and rinse again. Grind in a food processor, thinning with a little water if necessary. In a large bowl, mix the lentil mixture thoroughly with the farina, salt, baking powder, and cumin seeds to form a batter. Heat 2 to 3 inches of the oil to 350°F in a wok. Drop the batter in by tablespoons, a few at a time, and cook until brown, turning once. Drain on paper towels.

Make the yogurt sauce: Beat the yogurt with the salt, cumin seeds, cayenne pepper, and half of the cilantro. You may add a little milk or water if it is too thick.

Dip the fritters in lukewarm water and squeeze gently. Place balls in a large shallow bowl or dish and cover with the yogurt sauce. Sprinkle with *chaat masala* and drizzle some chutney over the surface like a sundae. Sprinkle with remaining cilantro and serve within 30 minutes.

MANGO CUSTARD

dairy/egg
Amb Fearnee

Our grandson Benny loved his ripe mangoes! This recipe is very nutritious. It encompasses all the food groups, so is a little meal in itself. I usually use Ratna brand canned purée, but you may use fresh, ripe mangoes you purée yourself. Just add a quarter cup more sugar.

In a heavy-bottomed medium/small pan or double boiler, mix the eggs with the sugar. Gradually add the milk, whisking constantly over medium heat until thickened.

In a separate small bowl, soften the gelatin in the water. Stir some of the hot milk mixture into it to dissolve the gelatin and then add to the milk mixture. Whisk briskly for 2 more minutes.

Add the cream and ¾ cup of mango purée, lemon juice, and salt and whisk until blended. Reserve a few mango pieces and then mix in the rest. Cool in the refrigerator in an attractive glass bowl. When almost solid, swirl the tablespoon of purée into a design on the surface of the custard and/or decorate it with the reserved mango pieces.

YIELD: 8 ½-CUP SERVINGS

2 extra-large eggs or 3 medium eggs

1 cup powdered sugar

1¼ cups whole milk

1 envelope (1 tablespoon) unflavored gelatin plus ¼ cup water

1⅓ cups light cream or non-fat half and half

¾ cup plus 1 tablespoon mango purée

2 teaspoons lemon juice (*optional*)

1 pinch salt (*optional*)

1 ripe mango, diced *or* 1 cup canned mango slices (*optional*)

A moment of hilarity—Benny and his sisters

COLORFUL!

My first shopping adventure in India

THE BEGINNINGS OF THINGS ARE IMPORTANT. I HAVE NEVER FORGOTTEN THE generosity and thoughtfulness of my mother-in-law who, before I had even met her, sent her own jewelry and a colorfully embroidered chiffon stole, a *phulkari*, for our wedding in the U.S. Red is the color of life and is traditional for the bride in India. The stole trimmed with gold looked unusual but lovely with my traditional, ivory-colored lace gown and veil. The combination of red, orange, and gold in my bouquet of Tropicana roses was an exotic echo of the colors in the stole. I loved it, but there was so much more to come.

Colorful glass bangles wrapped in cellophane.

The colors, the riot of colors! It was India and it was nearly overwhelming. My mother-in-law and I sat in the Sari Palace of Bhatinda on low wicker stools. In front of us white sheets were spread on the floors and row upon row of carefully folded colorful fabrics marched up and down and across the walls. The owner of the store sat cross-legged on the sheets. He offered us tea or a Limca soda. At his side was a young boy who rose, hefted a bolt of magenta silk from a row and shook it out, unfurling the shimmering fabric high in the air. He dropped that bolt, and as it crumpled to the floor, in rapid succession came sapphire, teal, deep purple, hot pink. There were glints of silver, of extravagant embroidery in maroon and gold and peach. I was breathless!

The owner was confident, expecting a bonanza. But there I was, only six years removed from the convent. "Who was going to have to roll up all that silk?" I thought, feeling guilty. I looked over at my mother-in-law wearing a faded gray cotton *salwar-kameez*. How could I buy silk?

What I did not know then, and what she was trying to explain to me in Punjabi, was that brides wore bright colors. Even after the wedding they were expected to dress up like dolls in their finery for days, weeks, or even months (depending on their status) until the "honeymoon" with their husband's family wore off.

I chose a cotton print, a pale gray and pink Pennsylvania Dutch design I was surprised to see there. I had no idea that widows must wear white or gray or risk the censure of the community. As a bride, it was bad luck for me to wear white or gray! But there I sat, thinking it unseemly for me to dress more richly than my mother-in-law.

The owner was in shock. There was going to be no bonanza for him that day.

But there were definitely other days. India is a shopper's paradise. The clothes, the jewels, the paintings, and the carpets, the trays of sweets, even the lentils—what an array of wonderful color and design! I certainly learned to enjoy it. And still enjoy the experience today when we shop or window shop in "Little India"—the neighborhood of Indian stores and restaurants near our present home in New Jersey.

Circa 1966, the bazaar in Bhatinda on the way from the cloth merchant.

To think that in the early sixties, when we were just married, one could not find a cumin seed or a knob of fresh ginger, or even a cup of yogurt outside of an ethnic enclave in a very large city. Amazing, really, how far we have all come!

The "Colorful" Menu

This menu luxuriates in color! Dress up humble dumplings in pink froufrou. Forget any preconceived notions that turnips aren't tasty. And just because shrimp are not native to Punjab doesn't mean they can't appear on the menu. Your guests will be delighted with these delectable and healthful offerings.

Appetizer:	*JINGHA SALADE* Shrimp Salad Rolls *SOWA ACHAR CHUTNEY* Dilly Pickle Chutney *TEJ NIMBOO ACHAR* Hot Ginger and Lime Pickle in Oil
Main Course:	*HARIALA MURGA* Chicken in Green Sauce *SHALGAM GAJJER MUTTER* Turnips with Carrots and Peas *PUDEENA KULCHA* Grilled White Breads with Mint
Dessert:	*CHUM CHUM* Sweet Cheese Dumplings Dressed in Pink

- **Five Weeks Prior:** Read through the recipes from beginning to end. Make grocery lists. Salt the limes for the pickle if you are making your own.

- **Three Weeks Prior:** Buy the ginger, mustard oil, and spices from the Indian market. Add the ginger and spices to the pickle.

- **Three Days Prior:** From the Indian market buy the *kewrda* flavor and coconut as well as the vegetables, mint, dill, and cilantro. Buy the lime-ginger pickle if you haven't made your own. Wash and wrap the greens in paper towels and then place in plastic zip bags and refrigerate.

- **Two to Three Days Prior:** Make the *chum chum*, refrigerate. Buy the chicken and shrimp, and remaining ingredients from the supermarket. Skin the chicken and soak in salted water in the fridge.

- **One-Day Prior:** Make the dough for the *kulchas*. Cover with plastic wrap. Peel and dice the turnips. Make the Dilly Pickle Chutney. Refrigerate all.

- **The Day of:**
  AM: Slice the mint, dill, and cilantro for the bread and chicken. Chop the onions, garlic, and ginger for the turnips and chicken. Begin frying them with the spices. Thaw the peas and carrots.
  PM: Finish cooking the turnips, peas and carrots, and the chicken. Prepare the shrimp salad. Clean up.

- **At Serving Time:** Make the shrimp rolls and serve with a beverage of choice. Get everyone to pitch in—making the *kulchas*, setting the table, and reheating the dishes.

SHRIMP SALAD ROLLS

Jhinga Salade   *shellfish*

Since there are no oceans on the Punjabi border and therefore no shrimp used in traditional Punjabi cuisine, I borrowed from the Vietnamese for this recipe. I like to alternate chickpeas with beans or peas as another source of texture and nutrition in this salad, and you could substitute tuna or salmon for the shrimp.

YIELD: 12 APPETIZER SERVINGS

¼ cup light sour cream or good mayonnaise

½ cup Dilly Pickle Chutney, or more to taste *(page 115)*

1 (15-ounce) can chickpeas

2 pounds precooked and peeled shrimp, thawed and coarsely chopped

1 small red bell pepper, seeded and finely chopped

¼ teaspoon salt, or to taste

12 large, soft lettuce leaves like butter, Boston, or leaf, stiff ribs removed

Garnishes: Red bell pepper slices; red onion rings; fresh dill

Mix the light sour cream or mayo with the chutney to make a dressing. Drain the chickpeas, rinse and lightly mash. Mix with the dressing. Toss in the shrimp and the chopped bell pepper. Add salt, taste and, if you like, add more chutney. You may refrigerate the salad at this point.

Just before serving, wash the lettuce, drain, and wipe dry with paper towels. Divide the shrimp salad between the twelve leaves. Fold the sides of the leaves over the salad and roll up like a spring roll. Refrigerate until serving time. To serve, place the shrimp salad rolls on a platter and garnish as desired.

Variation: Instead of in lettuce rolls, serve the salad on top of the lettuce leaves.

DILLY PICKLE CHUTNEY

vegan   Sowa Achar Chutney

Its name is a verbal pun, of course, but the fun is in tasting its bright flavors. I developed this recipe as an accompaniment for assertively flavored fish like smoked whitefish or grilled sardines. Use a sweet onion if you want to tame its strong flavors. Mix with mayonnaise as a dressing for shrimp or smoked salmon.

Wash the dill and remove the tough stems before measuring. Put it in the food processor with the pickle, lime juice, oil, and honey. Grind coarsely. Mix in the onion.

YIELD: 1½ CUPS

1 cup fresh dill, packed

¼ cup Hot Ginger and Lime Pickle in Oil* *(page 116)*

Juice of ½ lime

2 tablespoons oil from Hot Ginger and Lime Pickle in Oil

4 tablespoons honey or corn syrup (for vegans)

1 cup finely chopped red or Vidalia onion

This chutney is an important flavor component of the spectacular Shrimp Salad on page 114.

*You can use the recipe given here or a commercial product. I've seen one made by Priya®. If the store does not have ginger and lime pickle in oil, they definitely will have either lime or lemon pickle in oil. If so, then stir-fry 1½ cups of matchstick slices of ginger in mustard oil and stir into the jar of lime or lemon pickle in oil.

HOT GINGER AND LIME PICKLE IN OIL

Tej Nimboo Achar   *vegan*

I like the combo of lime and ginger and made this pickle at home for ourselves. I was pleasantly surprised when I saw a similar one a few years later in the Indian store. "Great minds…!" Use a very clean and dry glass quart jar with a plastic, rather than metal, lid to prevent corrosion from the salt and the acid in the limes. Remember to start this recipe well ahead of time because the pickle takes several weeks to ferment before it is ready to eat.

YIELD: 3 CUPS

6 limes

⅔ cup kosher salt

1 cup edible mustard oil

2 teaspoons mustard seeds

2 teaspoons fenugreek seeds (*methi*), toasted and ground

½ teaspoon asafoetida (*hing*)

1 (mild) to 4 (very hot!) teaspoons ground cayenne pepper

1 cup slivered ginger

¼ cup slivered green chilies

10 dried small red chilies

At least five weeks ahead: Soak the limes in sudsy, hot water. Scrub with a brush to remove wax. Rinse and dry with a clean cloth. Wash your hands thoroughly and use a very clean knife and cutting board. Cut the ends off the limes and quarter them, removing the visible seeds. Scatter some salt on the bottom of a jar. Add a layer of limes and some more salt. Repeat, pressing slightly to get as many limes into the jar as possible and then close the jar. Shake the jar every few days. The limes will shrink as they ripen.

After two to three weeks: Heat the mustard oil while measuring out the rest of the ingredients. Add the mustard seeds to the oil first. When the seeds "pop," add the other spices, then the ginger and both chilies. Stir-fry for 5 minutes. Remove the limes (without their juice) from the jar and add them to the spice mixture. Cover and cook for five more minutes. Add the lime juice and stir. Allow the mixture to cool and then put into a crock with a cover or into very clean jar(s). Fill to the very top if possible. Put a double layer of paper towel over the jar and fasten with a rubber band. Leave for a day, so all the moisture is absorbed by the paper towel. Remove the paper towel and cover the crock or jars. The pickle will be ready to eat in another few weeks.

CHICKEN IN GREEN SAUCE

meat   Hariala Murga

I first had this dish at a banquet hall. They used chicken pieces with the bones and you can too, but I have used just the breast here since it can then be made very quickly and is so healthful for all the family. Add chile peppers or cayenne if you like it hot.

Cut each chicken breast into 2-inch pieces.* Set aside. In a food processor, chop the onion, garlic, and ginger and then sauté in the hot oil until golden. Add the cumin seeds, coriander seeds, turmeric, and cinnamon stick and sauté for 1 more minute. Add the chicken and salt and stir-fry for 5 minutes on high heat.

Thoroughly wash the cilantro, dill, and mint. Finely chop or grind the cilantro stems and half of the leaves. Add to the chicken, stirring for a few minutes on medium heat. Cover, lower the heat and simmer for 10 minutes. Coarsely chop the dill and mint. Add them to the chicken and simmer, covered, another 10 to 15 minutes, until the chicken is cooked.

Slice the remaining cilantro leaves. Turn up the heat, add them to the chicken, and stir-fry for a minute. Sprinkle with the garam masala and serve.

YIELD: 8 SERVINGS

2½ to 3 pounds skinless, boneless chicken breasts

1 large yellow onion

4 cloves garlic

2-inch piece ginger

3 tablespoons canola oil

2 teaspoons whole or ground cumin seeds

3 teaspoons ground coriander seeds

2 teaspoons ground turmeric

1 cinnamon stick

2 teaspoons salt, or more to taste

1 large bunch (2 to 3 cups leaves and small stems) cilantro

1 cup fresh dill (*optional*)

1 large bunch (2 cups) mint leaves

1 teaspoon garam masala

*If substituting any other cut or type of meat, cut into 1½-inch cubes.

TURNIPS WITH CARROTS AND PEAS

Shalgam Gajjer Mutter   *vegan*

My mother-in-law got our kids to eat their vegetables with this one. It's amazing how delicious turnips can be, especially fresh from the farmer's market or garden. If you like, you may increase the sugar to 1 tablespoon.

YIELD: 6 CUPS

2 medium yellow onions, chopped

3 tablespoons canola oil

3 cloves garlic, grated

1½-inch piece ginger, grated

1 teaspoon ground turmeric

1 teaspoon whole or ground cumin seeds

1½ teaspoons ground coriander seeds

2 tomatoes, chopped

3 (about 1½ pounds) white turnips, peeled and cut into 1-inch pieces

1 teaspoon salt

2 cups frozen peas and diced carrots, thawed (or fresh equivalent)

2 teaspoons gurd or dark brown sugar

¼ cup chopped cilantro (*optional*)

In a large skillet, sauté the onions in the heated oil until golden. Add the garlic and ginger and sauté for 1 minute; then add the turmeric, cumin seeds, and coriander seeds. Sauté for another minute. Add the tomatoes and sauté for 2 minutes; then add the cubed turnips and salt. Sauté for 1 minute, cover, and cook over low heat for 30 minutes.

Add the peas and carrots. Dissolve the sugar in a little warm water. Add to the vegetables, cover, and cook for 15 more minutes over the lowest heat or until the carrots are tender. Serve with the chopped cilantro as a garnish.

GRILLED WHITE BREADS WITH MINT

It's fun to experiment with a variety of breads. This one is beautiful and delicious. You may add finely chopped scallions (green onions) to the dough or top with sesame or poppy seeds. These are best made on the barbecue grill.

In a large bowl whisk the flour, salt, baking powder, baking soda, and sugar with a fork or whisk. Combine the milk, buttermilk, and water. Then with a wooden spoon, make a well in the flour. Pour the milk mixture in the center all at once, stirring in one direction from the center out, trying to incorporate all the flour. Mix in the mint and the onion seeds. The batter will be sticky.

Sprinkle the dough with some flour, oil your hands and begin kneading the dough until elastic, from 6 to 10 minutes, adding more flour as you go. You may use over a ¼ cup more flour, depending on the moisture in the flour and the humidity. The motion is to scrape the dough and fold it as you turn the bowl with your other hand. When you are finished, the dough should pull away from your hand and the bowl and be in a very smooth ball. Wash and dry the bowl and put the ball of dough back in. Coat the dough with some oil and cover with a cloth. Leave in a warm place until light, up to 3 hours depending on room temperature.

With a dough scraper (if you have it), divide the dough in half. Divide each of those halves into four equal balls. (You will have eight balls.) Oil your hands with a little oil and roll each ball between your palms until smooth. Flatten the balls and then turn them sideways. With your thumbs and the heels of your palms, rapidly move the dough in a circle to stretch it. Using gravity and your hands, keep stretching as you go until they are about 5 inches round. Put them on cookie sheets sprayed with oil or on the clean counter or table. Cover with clean, slightly damp towel(s) and let rest for 10 minutes. Then stretch the dough circles again until 7-inches wide and thicker around the edges. (When cooked, parts will get crispy, others chewy.)

YIELD: 8 BREADS

4 cups all-purpose flour, plus more for dusting

2½ teaspoons salt

1½ teaspoons baking powder

½ teaspoon baking soda

1 tablespoon sugar

¾ cup whole milk

¼ cup buttermilk

¾ cup warm water

1 cup mint leaves, washed, finely sliced, and packed tightly

2 teaspoons onion seeds (*kolonji*), toasted in a dry pan for 1 minute (*optional*)

Oil for greasing dough and your hands

Coarse cornmeal (if using the oven)

2 tablespoons melted *ghee* or butter (*optional*)

(continued on next page)

Three ways to grill the breads:

On the barbecue grill: Preheat to 450°F. Put the stretched breads on indirect heat and close the lid for 1 minute. Open the lid and move them to direct heat until one side is brown and the top bubbly. Turn over and cook the other side. Brush with *ghee* or butter. Eat immediately (best) or wrap in a clean tea towel.

On the griddle: Place a *kulcha* that you have stretched onto a medium/hot (350°F) griddle. When bubbles form on the top, turn it over. Keep turning until the bread is cooked through and browned in spots. Repeat with the other *kulchas*.

In the oven: Remove the racks and place a baking stone or tiles on the bottom. Preheat the oven to 450°F for at least 30 minutes. Sprinkle baking stone with coarse cornmeal. Place two *kulchas* on the stone (you may have room to cook only two at a time). Bake the *kulchas* for about 2 to 3 minutes. Turn over and cook on the other side. Remove from the oven with tongs and wrap in a clean towel. Repeat with the other *kulchas*. If the *kulchas* have not browned, re-place the top rack of the oven. Turn on the broiler. Turn the bread over and broil each on the top shelf for a minute to ensure they are browned. Keep warm in a clean towel until all are done. Brush with *ghee*. Serve immediately.

SWEET CHEESE DUMPLINGS DRESSED IN PINK

dairy   Chum Chum

I love going to "Little India" (the Indian neighborhood of shops and restaurants in Edison, NJ) to look at the beautiful silk clothes and gorgeous jewels. But just as attractive are the colorful sweets. There are so many varieties. This is one you can learn to make easily at home. You will be proud of the results.

In a large saucepan, bring the milk just to a boil. Add the lemon juice and stir until the curds separate from the whey. Allow to cool. Line a colander with a cheesecloth or very clean cloth napkin and pour the curds and whey into the colander. (You may do this over another bowl to catch the whey that is high in protein and can be used as the liquid in making lentils or in soup.) Drain for 10 minutes. Squeeze the curds fairly dry. Knead in the farina thoroughly by hand or in a food processor. Wrap tightly in plastic wrap and refrigerate for a few hours or up to a few days.

Make a syrup by boiling 2 cups water with the sugar and cardamom pods in a wide vessel with lid. Add the *kewrda* flavor, if using.

Divide the cheese into 4 even sections. Make 8 balls from each section, kneading them between your palms to smooth them out. Roll the balls between your palms into a cylindrical shape. When all are formed, carefully place them in the syrup. All the dumplings should fit in one layer and be covered with syrup. If not, add a little water. Gently bring the syrup up to a soft boil. Turn down the heat to the lowest point and cover the pot. Simmer the dumplings for 20 minutes. They should puff up slightly. At this point the dumplings can be cooled or frozen in their syrup.

At serving time, drain the thin syrup from the dumplings into a small pot and boil until thick like corn syrup. Cool until just warm to the touch. In a zip-top plastic bag, mix the food color thoroughly with the coconut by rubbing the coconut through the closed bag. Roll the dumplings one by one in the warm syrup first and then in the coconut. Place on a serving plate. (Alternately, you may roll the dumpling in jimmies or colored sugar.)

YIELD: 32 PIECES

1 gallon whole milk

½ cup lemon juice

1 tablespoon farina (regular Cream of Wheat®)

3 cups white sugar

4 green cardamom pods

1 teaspoon *kewrda* flavor (*optional*)

1½ cups sweetened grated coconut, (*optional*) or colored sugar or jimmies

Few drops red food color (*optional*)

ON THE FARM

The story of my husband's village

IT WAS WITH GREAT ANTICIPATION THAT I CLIMBED INTO THE JEEP THAT WOULD TAKE us to my husband's village for the first time. I hung on for dear life as we bumped along, raising clouds of dust behind us. There was no road—we traveled along the canal built in the late fifties that brought the wealth of water from the Bhakra Dam. Yet it was so much easier than prior times when my husband rode bareback on a horse or saddled a camel. Water was still so precious, that as we drove along the banks of the canal I was startled to see the menacing figure of a man with rounds of ammunition across his chest, ready to shoot anyone diverting more than his share. The crops—cotton, wheat, and mustard—rotated throughout the year, needed that water. The lives of the villagers depended on it.

The sky was an intense, cloudless blue. The flat, endless fields were bright green and yellow with mustard flowers. I noticed that the canal was almost dry and wondered aloud why the villagers didn't cooperate to line the bed with bricks and cover it to avoid loss of water as it traveled from the river. "You are so naïve! Survival is seen in a different way here," my husband smugly chuckled and then told me some stories about his village.

Over 100 years ago, his great-great-grandfather, Chard Singh, was bold enough to leave his original village of Juindan and persuade his distant kinsman, the Maharaja of Patiala, to sell him 2,400 acres of miserably dry land for 100 rupees. He made a down payment of 60 rupees. But it rained only every five or seven years, so after 10 years, Chard Singh returned to beg him to take back the land, since he was unable to raise the remaining 40 rupees. The maharaja forgave him the debt.

My husband as a toddler, a rifle always close by.

Chard Singh went back to the village and eventually had three sons, among whom he divided the land. It was a hardscrabble life. Each son had children. Fateh Singh, his middle son, died young, leaving a widow with two children, a teenager and a toddler, Bhag Singh. Bhag Singh's rivals saw an opportunity to increase their share of the land and it is said that they poisoned his unsuspecting teenage brother. His mother ran off with her surviving child to her own village where her brothers could protect them.

Bhag Singh, my husband's grandfather, became a student of survival. Schooled by his maternal uncles, he made alliances with young toughs from surrounding villages who became his bodyguards. Fifteen years after his brother's death, he successfully returned to claim his land. But the terrible price was vigilance and ruthlessness. Almost to the end of his life, he kept a gun near, even when bathing or sleeping.

Vying for his affections became a game among his maternal uncles. When one uncle arranged a marriage for him, the other uncle did so as well. On his own, he arranged a third. And when one of the wives died, he married a fourth, a sister from the same family. When another died, he married a fifth. Sadly, none of his wives and none of his five children survived him.

Strong of mind even in her nineties, Sheikpura Masijee told us her life story the last time we met.

An ancient Indian text lists 12 survival tricks for men and 440 tricks for women. When we visited the sister of my husband's grandmother, Sheikpura Masijee, she told us that Bhag Singh wanted her to be his wife, but she had refused. And unheard of in those days, prevailed! Eventually, she married another. But in order to protect the gold she received with her dowry, she buried it in the yard. When she needed some of it, she would tell her servant to dig in a certain place but not why and then would cry, "Snake!" when the servant got too close to the gold. Late, on a moonless night, she would finish the digging—tricks of survival.

Today, the brick-lined canal provides water to lush vineyards and orchards. Could it be that cooperation is not so naïve? Could it be a basic principle of survival?

The "On the Farm" Menu

Eating a meal in our village was very different from in the city where the customs of the English have spread into everyday life. Instead of the family sitting all together at a table with plates, knife, fork, and spoon, only two people at time were fed so that the bread would be hot and fresh from the tawa *or griddle. Either the children or the eldest men or guests were fed first. In our village, Grandfather sat on the* munja, *an unadorned rope bed that doubled as a settee. He sat sideways facing a small stool that doubled as a table. When it was their turn, the others sat cross-legged, facing each other, two to a bed, a large* thali, *or metal tray between them. Each person had individual small bowls that held their own portions of lentils, vegetables, and yogurt—but everything was served at once. Sliced onions and sometimes lemon pickle were on the tray as the hot-off-the-tawa breads were brought, topped with a lump of melting butter. There was little or no conversation. As in most of Asia, people paid attention to eating their food.*

This menu is one you would find served at the main (noon-time) meal. Everyone who could would then retire for a little nap. At the evening meal in my husband's village, only bread and green lentils were served, every day, seven days a week.

Main Course:	*LOBIA DAAL* Black-eyed Peas
	ALOO PAALAK Spinach and Potatoes
	DEHIN Homemade Plain Yogurt
	SHALGAM GAJJER MUTTER Raita for Vegans
	MISSEE ROTEE Chickpea and Onion Flat Breads

Dessert:	*CHOOREE* Whole-Wheat Crumble
	MASALA CHA Hot Spiced Tea
For the Evening Meal:	*MOONGEE DEE DAAL* Green Mung Lentil Curry
	[*PHULKA/CHAPATTI* Whole Wheat Flat Breads *(page 30)*]

- **Three to Five Days Prior:** Prepare your grocery lists. Buy the spices, *chapatti* flour, chickpea flour, black-eyed peas, fenugreek, spinach, mint, and cilantro from the Indian market. Make the *phulkas* for the dessert and freeze.
- **Two Days Prior:** Make the black-eyed peas. Refrigerate.
- **One-Day Prior:** Make the dough for the breads and the yogurt or *raita*. Refrigerate.
- **The Day of:**
  AM: Make the spinach. Thaw the breads to be used for the dessert.
  PM: Make the *missee rotee*. Make the dessert. Clean up.
- **At Serving Time:** Warm the black-eyed peas, the spinach, and the breads. Garnish the peas and the *raita*. Warm the dessert before serving.

The canal, now brick-lined, holds precious water.

BLACK-EYED PEAS

vegan   Lobia Daal

This is a dish served in rural areas, whether in India or down South in the U.S., just tweaked a little more in India. Beans are nutritious, cheap, and filling. But you do not need to be down on your luck to enjoy them. In fact, in the southern U.S. black-eyed peas are considered good luck and eaten on New Year's Day. If not adding potatoes, use 3 packages frozen black-eyed peas or 2 cups dried.

In a large saucepan, heat the oil and sauté the onions until golden. Add the garlic and ginger and lightly brown. Add the spices (turmeric through garam masala), reserving ½ teaspoon garam masala for garnish.

Add the potatoes to the onions and stir-fry for 3 minutes over high heat. Add the tomato and chile pepper, and stir again for a few minutes. Stir in the tomato paste until blended. Add the black-eyed peas, 2 cups water, and salt. Bring to a boil, then cover and simmer for about 1 hour, stirring occasionally. Garnish with the cilantro and remaining garam masala.

YIELD: 8 SERVINGS

¼ cup canola oil

2 medium onions, chopped

3 cloves garlic, minced

2-inch piece ginger, minced

1½ teaspoons ground turmeric

1 teaspoon whole or ground cumin seeds

1½ teaspoons ground coriander seeds

2 teaspoons garam masala

2 large potatoes, peeled and cut into 1½-inch cubes (*optional*)

1 large tomato, chopped

1 long green chile pepper, seeded and minced

2 tablespoons tomato paste

2 or 3 (8-ounce) packages frozen black-eyed peas, thawed, *or* 1½ to 2 cups dried black-eyed peas, soaked overnight

1½ teaspoons salt, or to taste

¼ cup chopped cilantro

SPINACH AND POTATOES

Aloo Paalak   *vegan*

Clover-like fresh fenugreek leaves and fingers of ginger root.

Fresh fenugreek leaves add a subtle but aromatic and slightly bitter flavor to mild spinach. You can find cubes of frozen fenugreek leaves in the Indian market with about five or six cubes per bag. It is a convenient way to add flavor and nutrition to curries. Fenugreek is said to not only moderate blood sugar, but also to increase mother's milk.

YIELD: 8 SERVINGS

¼ cup canola oil

2 medium onions, finely chopped

3 cloves garlic, minced

2-inch piece ginger

1½ teaspoons ground turmeric, divided

1 teaspoon whole or ground cumin seeds

1½ teaspoons ground coriander seeds

1 teaspoon ground fenugreek seeds (*optional*)

1 teaspoon garam masala, divided

1 chile pepper, seeded and chopped

1 tomato, chopped

1 large bunch fresh fenugreek leaves (*methi*), or 1 (2-inch) frozen cube, thawed (*optional*)

2 large potatoes, peeled and cut into wedges

Canola oil for frying potatoes (*optional*)

1½ teaspoons salt

Ground black pepper to taste

1½ pounds fresh spinach, chopped, *or* 2 (20 ounce) bags frozen chopped spinach, thawed and lightly squeezed

Heat the oil in a large, heavy-bottomed pot and sauté the onions, garlic, and ginger until transparent. Add 1 teaspoon of the turmeric, cumin seeds, coriander seeds, fenugreek seeds, and half the garam masala. Sauté, stirring, until onions start to brown. Add the chile pepper and tomato and sauté for another minute. Set aside.

Rinse the fenugreek thoroughly. Save the leaves and discard the stems. Grind leaves in batches in a food processor (with a little water if you have to). Add the fenugreek to the onion *tardka* and sauté over high heat for a minute. Turn down the heat, cover, and simmer for about 7 minutes.

Meanwhile, dry the potatoes with paper towels. Toss with the ½ teaspoon of turmeric and ½ teaspoon of garam masala. Heat enough oil in a wok or pot and fry the potatoes in one or two batches. Remove them when they are brown and drain on paper towels. (Or cook the wedges in the microwave on high for about five minutes.) Lightly sprinkle with salt and pepper.

Add the spinach and the rest of the salt to the onion mixture. Turn up the heat and sauté, stirring, for about 3 minutes. The dish may be set aside at this point.

Ten minutes before serving, stir in the potatoes and warm over low heat.

HOMEMADE PLAIN YOGURT

The most flavorful yogurt is the most complex—the one that has been made with a jaag *or living starter that has been part of a long series of yogurt making. The health benefits of this great food are well known. Be careful not to burn the milk or let it boil over! All of the utensils used should be very clean.*

In a heavy-bottomed medium pot, bring the milk just to a boil over medium heat, stirring occasionally. Pour into a (preferably glass) serving bowl with a lid. Allow the milk to cool until very warm, but not hot to the touch—about 120°F.

Remove 1 cup of the milk to a bowl and whisk in the yogurt until completely mixed. Stir or whisk into the rest of the milk. Cover with a towel and place in the warmest area of the kitchen away from drafts (I put mine in the unused oven). Allow to sit until thick, usually overnight. (It will thicken in three hours if you halfway immerse your serving bowl in very warm, not hot, water and keep the water warm.) Store in the refrigerator.

YIELD: 8 ½-CUP SERVINGS

1 quart whole or skim milk

⅓ cup plain yogurt (the *jaag*)

At the farm *chula*, nephew Navjot and kids, Jashan and Jai, heat milk for yogurt using cotton sticks for fuel.

RAITA FOR VEGANS

Tofu Raita   *vegan*

Tofu can be prepared Punjabi-style in several ways. It makes a good
raita, *as long as it is thoroughly cooled before serving.*

YIELD: 8 SMALL SERVINGS

½ red onion

½ long chile pepper, seeded

⅓ cup lemon juice

1 scant teaspoon salt

1 scant teaspoon *pani puri or
chaat masala (page 5) or*
ground cumin

1 (14-ounce) package firm tofu,
drained

3 cups halved grape tomatoes

¼ cup sliced mint or cilantro

Grind the onion, chile pepper, lemon juice, salt, and *pani puri* in a food processor. Add the tofu and blend until very smooth. Refrigerate for at least 1 hour. Add the tomatoes and mint or cilantro before serving.

Five forms of chickpeas (from 1 o'clock): Fresh, in pods; Bengal gram (black); dried, unhusked; chickpea flour (*besan*); chickpea lentils.

Hearty Sweet and Sour Chickpeas in a fragrant curry.

Lentils featured in this book. Each is opposite its hulled version except the *chana* (end).

Flavorful *Chana Daal* with *Kaddoo* squash.

The weapons on an elderly Akali Nahung Singh's turban are believed, by this sect, to be the manifestation of *Shakti*, God's creative power.

Our son, Herpaul Singh, tries his hand at snake charming.

Undergoing the pre-wedding *batna* treatment, Cheeku Pannu is "beautified" with yogurt and turmeric.

A magnetic snake charmer and his mongoose visit our house.

Girls of our village carrying bread and buttermilk to workers in the fields.

Crispy Okra and Potatoes.

Refreshing Papaya Salad.

The main dish most Indians associate with Punjab—Greens and Corn Flat Breads.

The delicious food products for which Punjab is well known:
Basmati Rice, Tandoori Chicken, Fresh Produce, Dairy Products, Flat Breads, and Legumes.

Luscious *Mutter Paneer*.

Succulent Double Onion Chicken Curry with cinnamon stick.

Roasted Eggplant and Potatoes on a cloth embroidered by *Bebeji*.

Justly famous breads of Punjab—plain and vegetable-stuffed *Parauntha* with cherry-pepper pickle.

Lacy lotus root gives roasted vegetables an exotic flair.

Carrot Halva, a gorgeous dessert.

Four types of Punjabi fudge—mango, date, chocolate, and chickpea flour.

Decadent *Chum Chum* in pink frou-frou.

Relaxing in the winter sun, *Bebeji* Jagdish Kaur, my greatest teacher.

CHICKPEA AND ONION FLAT BREADS

vegan   Missee Rotee

Chickpeas of all varieties need very little water to grow. In drought years in Punjab, only small, hard chickpeas were able to be grown in my husband's village. Besan, the flour made from chickpeas has a higher protein content than wheat, so it is important for people who eat little or no meat. It is this bread that kept my husband's ancestors alive. You'll love it!

In a large bowl, thoroughly mix all the dry ingredients (chickpea flour through salt). In a small bowl, mix 2 tablespoons of the oil with the onions and pepper flakes. Add the onion mixture to the dry ingredients and add ½ cup warm water.

Oil your hands with the remaining oil or use a dough hook. Work the dough into a uniformly crumbly mixture. Slowly add more water, a spoonful at a time, until the dough begins to stick together. Knead in the bowl to make a dough that works into a smooth, less sticky mass. Cover the dough and refrigerate for several hours or overnight.

With oiled hands, knead the dough again in the bowl. Heat a griddle to medium/high. Form the dough into a log. Cut in half and again until you have divided the dough into 10 or 12 equal balls. Bring your cutting board and rolling pin close to the griddle. Lightly oil your rolling pin and cutting board and roll out one of the dough balls to a disk about 4 to 5 inches wide. Spray the griddle with nonstick spray. Carefully and quickly put the disk on the griddle. When you see that it has begun to cook through, turn with a spatula. Finish by holding each side briefly with tongs over the open gas flame. It may begin to balloon with steam, a sign that all parts have been evenly cooked. Continue with the remaining dough balls.

Serve hot with a pat of butter or *ghee* and lemon or lime-ginger pickle.

YIELD: MAKES 10 TO 12 SMALL BREADS

1½ cups chickpea flour (*besan*)

2¼ cups *chapatti* flour (or 1½ cups whole-wheat flour and ¾ cup all-purpose flour)

½ teaspoon ground turmeric

1 teaspoon toasted whole cumin seeds

2 teaspoons ground, dried pomegranate seeds (*optional*)

2 teaspoons salt

4 tablespoons canola or olive oil

1 cup very finely chopped onion

1 to 3 teaspoons dried red pepper flakes (to taste)

WHOLE-WHEAT CRUMBLE

Chooree   *dairy or vegan*

Occasionally a son-in-law or other honored guest would be served chooree, *whole-wheat crumble on the* thali. *The kids were always hoping for a little for themselves. This is the only dessert my husband remembers eating in the village except for weddings. It is very easy to prepare, and is great for using leftover* phulkas.

YIELD: 1 SERVING

1 *phulka* (whole-wheat flat bread) (page 30)

2 teaspoons melted *ghee* or melted butter, or soy substitute

1 tablespoon *gurd* or brown sugar, crumbled

2 teaspoons sugar

If the *phulka* has dried out, wet it under the faucet, shake it and put it in a tea towel. Microwave on medium for 20 seconds. Tear the bread into the smallest pieces you can manage. Drizzle with the *ghee* and stir in the sugars. Heat in the microwave for 20 seconds or until the sugar has melted. Stir again and serve immediately.

Adorable Kiran and Tripinder would love some *chooree* on their *thali*.

HOT SPICED TEA

dairy or vegan   Masala Cha

There are so many versions of "chai" or spiced, milky tea that I prepare it in a slightly different way almost every time I make it. Sometimes, when I am pressed for time, I just sprinkle a little ground cinnamon and ginger into my cup and heat it in the microwave. At other times, I will throw some ginger peels and a few cardamom pods into the teakettle. But I must confess: the first words I learned in Punjabi were "Na cheenee, na dudh." (No sugar or milk for me.) This version is very warming and well-balanced.

In a medium pot bring the water and spices to a boil. Simmer for 5 minutes. Add the milk and simmer for another 5 minutes. Put the loose tea in a tea "ball" and add to the milk mixture or add the tea bags and simmer for another 1 to 2 minutes. Add the sugar now or serve it separately. Squeeze the tea bags and check the tea for color, it should be a light caramel color; if not, put in another bag or two, depending on how strong you like it. Strain any loose tea and spices as you pour the tea into a cup or pre-warmed teapot. Serve immediately.

YIELD: 8 CUPS

5 cups cold water

1 scant teaspoon cardamom seeds

4 whole cloves

½ cinnamon stick, or ½ teaspoon powdered ginger

¼ teaspoon fennel seeds or ¼ star anise (*optional*)

4 cups whole milk or soy milk

8 teaspoons loose black tea, or 8 to 10 teabags

1 to 3 teaspoons sugar per person (*optional*)

EVENING MEAL

What memories! At the well on the farm, our dear friend Tonia and her brother-in-law Harbir Singh.

GREEN MUNG LENTIL CURRY

dairy or vegan   Moongee Dee Daal

Just as in the village in India, we never tire of this dish. We serve it at least once, sometimes twice a week. As an alternative to making a tardka *by frying the aromatics, you could put all the ingredients at once into a slow cooker, and then reduce the fat even further to one tablespoon. Or make a south Indian version by using the topping with mustard seeds and curry leaves in the chutney recipe on page 90.*

Pick over lentils and wash thoroughly. Put into a medium pot with 7 cups water, the salt, and turmeric and bring to a boil. Cover, reduce heat, and cook for approximately 1 hour and 10 minutes, stirring occasionally. The lentils should begin to open and thicken.

In a separate small pan, fry the onion, garlic, and ginger in the oil until lightly browned. Add the chopped tomato, if using. Stir-fry for a minute and then add to the cooked lentils. Sprinkle with the garam masala before serving if you wish.

YIELD: 5 CUPS

1¼ cups whole green lentils (mung beans)

1 teaspoon salt, or to taste

1 teaspoon ground turmeric

1 medium onion, chopped

3 cloves garlic, minced

1 to 2-inch piece ginger, minced

3 tablespoons canola oil or *ghee*

1 small tomato (*optional*)

1 teaspoon garam masala (*optional*)

HAPPY BIRTHDAY, MAMEEJEE!

Relationships in Punjabi Culture

IT WOULD BE DIFFICULT TO FIND A COUNTRY THAT PUTS MORE STOCK IN RELATIONSHIPS than India. If you speak Punjabi, it is never a mystery knowing how someone is related to you. All you need to hear is the name your parents call a family member. For example, Uncle Gurmit, my mother-in-law's brother, and his wife, Auntie Surindra, are also known as *Mamajee* and *Mameejee*. (*Jee* is an honorific, something like sir or madam.) In addition, every relationship in the Punjabi family has a particular status and is delineated and circumscribed by the name for that relationship. Your *mama* is your mother's brother, his wife is your *mamee*. She is not supposed to love you as much as your *maasee*, your mother's sister. Yet, you give more respect to your *bhua*, your father's sister with whom you may have more disagreements. Are you confused yet? I haven't even gotten started! Every single grandparent, aunt, uncle, cousin, and in-law, to several degrees or generations is treated in a special way, a distinct social hierarchy, somehow known to everyone. It's just absorbed, like the minerals in water, into your very bones.

Folk songs make great use of this code to poke fun or prove a point. One of the songs my husband is famous for singing at parties has the line (roughly translated)—"my uncle (*mama*) accepts me while my auntie (*mamee*) frowns at me!" Thank goodness we could all think out of that box because, besides my mother-in-law, no one has loved us more or been more influential in our lives than our dear Auntie Surindra, *Mameejee*.

When I first went to India, I met my mother-in-law's side of the family first, my husband's *naankay*. As a *bhaabhee*, or wife of a brother or cousin, I had little status. Thank goodness I didn't know that or I would have been even more nervous! In the village, on the father's side, his *daadkay*, it was the custom for the bride to cover her face from the men on the husband's side of the family who are older than he is—which was just about every man in our family, since he was the son of the youngest son. Called *coond*, my mother-in-law practiced it all her life. She covered her face within the family compound, and her entire body when she left the compound, usually to travel to her own village. In an ox-drawn cart or carried in a litter, she was completely enclosed inside a wooden-framed box with heavy curtains. But as soon as she arrived in the territory closer to her own village, off came the curtains and the veil! I thought I would be expected to at least cover my face

A curtained carriage pulled by a bullock is similar to one Bebeji would have used as transport to her village.

from her father-in-law, brothers-in-law, and nephews; but my husband's grandfather on his father's side said that I did not have to cover mine, greatly surprising her.

When I first met my husband, he told me he was following in his *Mamajee Gurmit Singh's* footsteps to attend the University of Michigan master's in engineering program. Although they lived in New Jersey at the time, Uncle and Auntie returned to India to live in Patiala in Punjab. It was there that I met them for the first time. She was beautiful, graceful, and gracious, as she is to this day. I was in awe of her having lavished her father-in-law with loving care during his last months, and at the same time, caring so well for three small children. She became my role model and teacher.

Mama and Mameejee Gurmit and Surindera.

The "Happy Birthday" Menu

So many of the fond memories we have over the years revolve around the food Auntie prepared or taught us to prepare for family gatherings or for the free kitchen at the temple. We would plan well in advance for these occasions, usually the birthdays of our young children, but also holidays. We would decide who would make what dish, enjoying the whole process and cooking up a storm!

Who said you can't have dessert first—and last! It's a birthday party!

> PATIALA MITHEE LUSSEE Sweet Yogurt Drink
> BADAMEE GULAAB Almond and Rose-Flavored Cake with Rosepink Icing
> KADOO KOFTAY Squash Fritters in Tomato Sauce
> TANDOORI MURGA Grilled "Red" Chicken *(page 62)*
> KHOPA NIMBOO CHAVAL Lemon Coconut Rice Pilaf
> ALOO BAINGAN Oven-Crisped Potatoes and Eggplant
> GULAAB JAAMANS Little "Fry Cakes" in Rose-Flavored Syrup

- **Four Days Prior:** Read the recipes from start to finish. Prepare your grocery lists. Buy the nuts, rose flavor, yogurt, buttermilk, coconut, tomatoes, peppers, eggplants, zucchini, chickpea flour, lemons, ginger, cilantro, and spices from the Indian market.

- **Three Days Prior:** Buy the chicken, cake and baking mix, milk powder, and sugar from the supermarket. Skin the chicken and remove the fat.

- **Two Days Prior:** Make the squash fritters and the tomato gravy. Keep separate.

- **One-Day Prior:** Bake the cake and make the *gulaab jamans*. Make the white chocolate "leaves" to decorate the cake. Marinate the chicken, if making.

- **The Day of:**
  AM: Make the pilaf (partially) and the saffron/sugar mixture for the *lussees*. Make the icing for the cake.
  PM: Make the eggplant and potato dish. Grill the chicken. Frost the cake. Clean up.

- **At Serving Time:** Prepare the *lussees* and light the candles on the cake before serving. Boil the water for the rice and finish making it. Reheat the chicken and the eggplant in the oven. Combine the fritters and tomato gravy and heat in the microwave. Reheat the rice. Garnish the dishes. Serve the *gulaab jamans* for dessert.

SWEET YOGURT DRINK

Patiala Mithee Lussee   *dairy*

Auntie and Uncle were living in Patiala when I met them. This is a version of the famous cooling milk drink that most probably was brought there by the Moghuls. I like my version because it is light, and not too sour nor too sweet. If you have a powerful motor on your blender, you do not have to partially crush the ice first.

YIELD: 2 LARGE GLASSES

Small pinch saffron (about 20 threads)

1 tablespoon whole milk

3 tablespoons sugar

½ teaspoon ground cardamom seeds

3 drops vanilla extract *or kewrda or rose flavor*

10 ice cubes

3 cups plain yogurt

2 teaspoons unsalted pistachios, coarsely ground (*optional*)

In a very small, dry pan, heat the saffron for a few seconds over a medium flame. Turn onto a clean sheet of paper. Pick it up between your fingers and crush it until pulverized. Return to the small pan and add the milk and warm it. Pour into a small ramekin or *coli* and steep for a minute. With the back of a spoon, crush any pieces left. Stir in the sugar, cardamom seeds, and vanilla extract. Keep refrigerated up to a day until ready to use.

At serving time,* put the ice cubes between the folds of a tea towel. Partially crush with a heavy pot or hammer and put into the blender. Uncover the sugar mixture and stir it well. Put the yogurt and 2 rounded tablespoons of the sugar mixture into the blender. Blend on "ice crush" until there is little or no noise of the ice cubes. The mixture will be frothy. Pour immediately into two glasses and top each with a teaspoon of pistachio nuts.

---

*If you are making more than two servings still only blend two servings at a time so as not to overwhelm the blender.

ALMOND AND ROSE-FLAVORED CAKE WITH ROSEPINK ICING

egg/dairy   Badamee Gulaab

What is a birthday without a cake? This is a delectable and gorgeous one that I developed after I bought a rose-patterned bundt pan from William-Sonoma. Choose either the glaze or the icing to frost it.

Anticipation! Kiran and Kiki can't wait for me to cut the birthday cake.

Preheat the oven to 350°F. Beat all the cake ingredients until smooth. Pour into a pre-buttered and lightly floured bundt pan (preferably a rose-patterned one). Run your spatula around in a circle at the surface to depress the batter to compensate for it rising too high in the center. Put in the center of the oven. It is done when the cake springs back slightly to the touch or when a toothpick comes out clean, about 40 minutes. Cool for 20 minutes on a rack and then remove cake from the pan. If using the glaze, prick the cake all over with a skewer or fork and pour the syrup over it. If using icing, cool completely before covering with icing.

To make icing: A few hours or less before serving, in a large bowl, mix frosting, food coloring, and rose flavor thoroughly. In a separate bowl, beat the cream until stiff. Fold whipped cream into the frosting with a spatula. Refrigerate.

Just before serving, frost the cake. Use a spoon to press "petals" in the icing. Decorate further, if you like by placing rose petals or roses strategically around the cake. The day before, I like to melt a few bars of white chocolate, tint it green, and then form "leaves" to place around the "roses."

YIELD: 10 TO 12 SLICES

For the cake:

1 package (18.5 ounces) white cake mix

¼ cup water

1 cup buttermilk

3 egg whites, lightly beaten

½ cup ground blanched almonds

½ cup melted *ghee*

1 teaspoon rose flavor

2 teaspoons almond extract

For the Wild Rose Glaze:

½ cup bottled wild-rose syrup

For the Rosepink Icing:

1 can (1 pound) white frosting

Few drops red food coloring

1 teaspoon rose flavor

¾ cup heavy or whipping cream

Optional: Rose petals and white chocolate "leaves"

SQUASH FRITTERS IN TOMATO SAUCE

Kadoo Koftay   *vegan*

Both Mamajee *and his* bhaanja *(Uncle Gurmit Singh and his nephew, my husband) loved to garden. Tomatoes and zucchini were always abundant and we prepared this mouth-watering dish often. It will become a favorite of yours as well.*

YIELD: 8 SERVINGS (18 FRITTERS)

For the fritters:

1 clove garlic, sliced

1-inch piece ginger, sliced

1 small onion

2½ cups (tightly packed) grated green squash like *kudoo* or zucchini (about 1 pound)

Oil for frying

1½ cups chickpea flour *(besan)*

Scant teaspoon baking powder

½ teaspoon dried red pepper flakes

1 teaspoon ground coriander seeds

1 teaspoon ground cumin seeds

1½ teaspoons salt

For the tomato sauce:

3 tablespoons canola oil

1 medium onion, chopped

1 clove garlic, minced

1-inch piece ginger, minced

2 teaspoons ground turmeric

½ teaspoon chili powder

2 teaspoons ground cumin seeds

2 tablespoons ground coriander seeds

½ teaspoon garam masala

½ teaspoon dried fenugreek leaves *(kasoori methi) (optional)*

1 teaspoon salt, or to taste

1 (8-ounce) can tomato sauce or 2 cups chopped fresh tomatoes

2 cups chopped fresh tomatoes (add ½ teaspoon more salt) *or* 1 can (14.5 ounces) diced tomatoes

¼ cup golden raisins

2 cups water

Garnishes: ¼ cup chopped cilantro and ½ teaspoon garam masala

To make the fritters: In a blender or food processor, grind the garlic, ginger, and onion. In a medium bowl, mix the onion mixture with the grated squash. Squeeze the squash as dry as possible, saving the juice for the gravy.

Heat the oil to 350°F. Measure out the chickpea flour into a large bowl and blend in the baking powder, red pepper flakes, coriander seeds, cumin seeds, and salt. Stir in the vegetables. Using two soup spoons, scrape spoonfuls of the vegetable batter into the hot oil. Do not crowd. Turn them once after one side is brown. Drain on paper towels until all are fried. The fritters may be made in larger batches when squash is in season, frozen without the sauce, and then rewarmed as needed.

To make the sauce: In a large saucepan, heat the oil and brown the onion, garlic, and ginger. Add the spices (turmeric through fenugreek leaves) and stir for 1 minute. Add the juice from the squash, if saved. Add the remaining ingredients except the garnishes. Simmer for 15 minutes, covered, and then 5 to 10 minutes uncovered. Check for seasoning. Place the fritters in a serving dish. Pour the sauce over them, sprinkle with the garam masala and cilantro, and serve.

LEMON COCONUT RICE PILAF

vegan   Khopa Nimboo Chaval

Since the Punjabi staple is bread, the only time we made rice was for a party. This beautiful South Indian-style pilaf is definitely dressed in delicious finery.

Rinse the rice until the water runs clear. Cover with clean water and soak the rice for 30 minutes.

Grind the garlic and ginger in a food processor. Heat the oil in a large, heavy-bottomed pot and fry the *kari* leaves. Remove and set aside. Add the mustard seeds to the oil and fry until they pop. Add the onion and brown. Add the ground garlic and ginger, and the turmeric, and sauté for 1 minute. Drain the rice thoroughly and add to the onion mixture. Sauté for 4 minutes, scraping the bottom of the pot with a spatula. At this point, you may turn off the heat and wait until serving time.

About a half hour before serving, bring 5 cups of water to a boil and add to the rice. Add the salt, stir and cover tightly. Simmer on low heat and check after 25 minutes. (If the rice is not fully cooked, fluff with a fork, sprinkle with a few spoons of water, cover tightly and keep on the lowest heat or a warm burner.)

Add the coconut, lemon juice, zest, and toasted cashews. Turn out onto a large, heated platter. Garnish with the reserved *kari* leaves and/or twists of lemon with the peel.

YIELD: 10 1-CUP SERVINGS

2½ cups basmati rice

2 cloves garlic

2-inch piece ginger

⅓ cup canola oil

10 *kari* leaves

1½ tablespoons whole black mustard seeds

1 cup sliced yellow onion

1 teaspoon turmeric

1 tablespoon salt

1 cup dried, unsweetened coconut

Zest and juice of 2 lemons

½ cup chopped toasted cashews (*optional*)

Garnish: slices of lemon

OVEN-CRISPED POTATOES AND EGGPLANT

Aloo Baingan

vegan

This is a dish adapted from one Auntie Surindra has made "famous." Choose shiny, firm eggplants. If you broil the eggplant separately from the potatoes, you will get a better result. Heat them together in the oven, not in the microwave, before serving time. The baking time will vary depending on the width of the eggplant or potato slices.

YIELD: 8 1-CUP SERVINGS

For the eggplant:

¼ cup salt

4 to 5 (about 2½ pounds) Chinese (long) eggplants *or* 2 large Italian variety eggplants (up to 3 pounds)

½ cup canola oil

2½ tablespoons green mango powder

1 tablespoon ground cumin seeds

2 teaspoons garam masala

1½ teaspoons salt, or to taste

Pinch black salt (*optional*)

For the potatoes:

2 to 3 large (about 2 pounds) russet potatoes

1 large red onion

1¼ teaspoons salt

3 tablespoons canola oil

¼ teaspoon ground turmeric

1 teaspoon ground cumin

1 teaspoon green mango powder

⅛ teaspoon ground cayenne pepper, or to taste (*optional*)

Garnishes: Leaf lettuce and roasted red pepper slices

To prepare eggplant: To remove the bitterness of the eggplants, first dissolve the ¼ cup salt in 1 cup hot water in the bottom of a large bowl. Add another cup of cool water. Cut the eggplants into slices ½- to ⅓-inch thick, discarding the blossom end and bottom slice. Put the eggplant slices into the salt water. You may need to weigh the slices down with another bowl as you add enough cool water to cover. Set aside for 10 minutes.

Grease a broiler pan (best) or cookie sheet. Drain the eggplants and dry them on paper towels. Put them into a large bowl. Mix the oil with the remaining ingredients in a small container. Drizzle the seasoned oil over the eggplant slices as you toss them. You may have to scrape the spices from the bowl or redistribute them from one slice to another to ensure that each slice is evenly coated on both sides. Fan out half the slices on the pan.*

Turn on the broiler. Place the rack 6 inches from the heat and put the pan underneath. Check every 2 minutes and turn over the slices. They should be dry and somewhat browned when removed. Repeat with the other slices. Place all the slices on the pan and set aside.

To prepare the potatoes: Preheat the oven to 400°F. Cut the potatoes into ¼-inch thick slices. Soak in cold water and set aside for about 15 minutes to remove excess starch.

Brush or spray oil on a large pizza pan or cookie sheet. Slice the onion lengthwise into ⅓-inch thick slices. Spread the slices out on the pan and then brush or spray with oil and toss with ¼ teaspoon salt. Mound in the center of the pan.

In a medium bowl, mix the oil and spices and the rest of the salt. Rinse the potato slices and dry with paper towels. Toss the potatoes in the seasoned oil until lightly coated on all sides. Spread them around the mound of onions. Bake for 20 minutes. Stir the onions and turn the potatoes. Bake until fairly crispy on some edges, about 20 more minutes. Check for salt and sprinkle on more if needed. Set aside.

To serve: Reheat the vegetables in a hot oven until crisp. Line the outer edge of a warm platter with lettuce leaves. Mound the potatoes in the center of the platter. Scatter some onion slices in and around the mound of potatoes. Arrange the eggplant slices around the potato mound and tuck in the red pepper slices around the eggplant. Scatter the remaining onion slices across the eggplant slices. Serve immediately while hot.

Gorgeous eggplants fresh from the farm.

*Alternatively you may spray the slices with baking spray. Sprinkle half the spices evenly across the slices on each tray. Turn the slices over, spray them and sprinkle with the rest of the spice mixture.

LITTLE "FRY CAKES"
IN ROSE-FLAVORED SYRUP

Gulaab Jaamans   *dairy*

When we had just moved from India to New Jersey, our new friend Geeta Desai taught Auntie Surindera this recipe. It was empowering to learn to make these little cakes that, up until then, we had only tasted from the hand of the halvaee, *the sweetmaker in India. We have made them countless times since.*

YIELD: 16 BALLS / 8 SERVINGS

For the syrup:

3 cups water

3 cups sugar

6 green cardamom pods

¼ to ½ teaspoon rose flavor

For the "fry cakes":

1 scant cup Bisquick® baking mix

1 cup dry milk (1 envelope)

⅓ cup whole milk

3 to 4 cups canola oil for frying

Choose a medium pot that will hold both the cakes and the syrup. Boil water, sugar, and cardamom in the pot for 20 minutes to the light syrup stage (215°F). Remove from heat and stir in the rose flavor. Allow to cool while making the cakes.

Thoroughly mix the baking mix and dry milk together. Slowly add only enough milk to make a very stiff dough, the stiffer the better. Allow to rest for 10 minutes.

Oil your hands and knead the dough into a large ball. You will have to oil your hands more than once as you proceed. Knead gently until the dough is smooth. Divide the ball into two equal balls and roll the balls into logs. Cut each log into eight equal pieces. Oil your hands again and roll each piece into a smooth ball in the palm of your hand.

Heat the oil in a wok to 320°F over medium/high heat. Put one ball into the oil to test it. Fry for about 6 minutes. It should begin to color to a dark, medium brown, but not turn black. Remove with a slotted spoon and check inside to see if the ball was thoroughly cooked and adjust the heat and/or timing before proceeding. Add only enough of the balls to the oil so that they turn freely as they brown. Fry for about 6 minutes or until the balls are evenly colored. Remove the balls with a slotted spoon and put in the pan with the syrup. Be careful not to touch the syrup with the spoon that will go back into the oil.

Repeat the ball cooking process with the remaining dough. Before the second batch of balls is ready to go into the syrup, remove the first batch to a serving bowl, and then place the second batch into the pot of syrup. (The second batch will then soak up the syrup much better this way.) After 10 minutes, all of the syrup and balls can be put into the serving bowl. Each ball will swell to about 2 inches.

This dish may be served warm or at room temperature. If covered tightly in the refrigerator, it will last for several days. Warm before serving.

BOYS' NIGHT IN

Sikh athletes in games and sports

College chums, Jagwant and
Sarban Singh, in deep discussion.

THE BOYS WERE ALL SWEATY AND DISHEVELED AFTER their Mohindra College field hockey team had soundly beat the opponent. Uncle Gurcharan Singh, my mother-in-law's brother, was only a teenager then, but as the captain of the team he had already been invited by their patron, the fabulous Maharaja Bhupinder Singh, to dine at the palace in Patiala. Of course, for that very formal occasion he was dressed in his finest tweed jacket, embroidered *kameez* and *churidar pajama*, his turban impeccably tied. But this time they were led directly into the *lussee khana* or kitchen by His Highness's aide-de camp, Mehar Singh, who was also a fan of the team. With their clothes dusty and long hair falling from topknots covered only with small cloths, they were a straggly sight.

Laughing and chatting as they drank a cooling glass of buttermilk, they looked up in collective shock as a formally dressed maharaja walked through the door. Immediately, His Highness bellowed, "What is going on here?" Everyone blanched, including Mehar Singh; but he bravely spoke up. "I invited them for a glass of *lussee*." No one, not even Mehar Singh knew what would happen next. There was a pause of seconds—but it could have been hours. "Why just for *lussee*!" said His Highness expansively, "Why not for dinner!" He turned and left. Mehar Singh distributed some of the delicious *pakoras* that were being made by the cooks. But they were eaten in dead silence.

During his lifetime, His Highness was among the top cricket players in the world, so now, fittingly, the extraordinary Motibagh Palace is home to the Indian National Sports Museum. Many Sikh athletes are honored there, like Milkha Singh, also known as the Flying Sikh, who won many medals at international games in the 200-meter run and the 400-meter run. A 93-year-old runner, Fauja Singh, is endorsed by Adidas and has run marathons in New York and London. Karamjit Sandhu, a female athlete, won a gold medal at the Asian Games. She set two records that remained unbroken for ten years. The field hockey player Balbir Singh has been on three gold-medal-winning teams and he won the medals in three Olympics in a row.

Whether it is the pure buffalo milk, the whole-wheat bread, or the closeness to the soil, boys and girls grow tall and strong in Punjab. In olden times and now when children are being awakened to their heritage, they play a game of martial art called *gatka* with sticks or swords, a cross between fencing and karate. In the villages, like my husband's where balls were a luxury, they play a game called *kabuddee*, a very physical form of tag.

Sikhs only began to get organized and play competitively when the sixth teacher, Guru Hargobind, organized wrestling competitions and introduced martial arts. Guru Gobind Singh, the tenth teacher, took this concept farther when he created *Hola Mahallah*, a holiday where Sikhs could demonstrate their martial skills in simulated battles. The philosophy is that building a healthy body is integral to a balanced spiritual life. Today, the tradition continues with Sikhs known worldwide for their prowess in field hockey, soccer, cricket, tennis, and golf.

Our dear friend, Harvinder Singh Dhaliwal, founded and is the chairman of the Sikh Sports Association of the U.S.A., an organization devoted to promoting the healthy mind/body connection among the youth of today. His work in India and here continues the legacy of service and of the character-building, health benefits, and good fun of sports.

The "Boys' Night In" Menu

Hearty, stick-to-the ribs food can be both healthy and easy to prepare. When groups of boys or girls get together to watch sports on TV, they can entertain themselves by rustling up the great food on this menu. Plenty of protein, calcium, omega oils, and even vitamins C and A, among others, will ensure a good performance when it is their turn to catch the ball! Add some store-bought naans for those really hungry athletes.

Appetizer: *MUCHCHEE PAKORA* Fried Fish Fritters
ADRAK CHUTNEY Red Ginger Chutney

Main Course: *KEEMA YA TOFU MUTTER* Ground Meat or Tofu with Peas
MASALA ALOO Spicy Smashed Potatoes
BOONDEE RAITA Yogurt Salad with Chickpea Crunchies

Dessert: GATCHAK Crunchy Nut Brittle

- **Two to Three Days Prior:** Read the recipes from start to finish. Prepare your grocery lists. Buy the ghee, spices, melon seeds, nuts, kewrda flavor, cilantro, scallions, ginger, lemons, peppers, garlic chili sauce, chickpea flour, rice flour, and *boondi* from the Indian market. Make the nut brittle if not making it with "the boys" on the day of the party.

- **One-Day Prior:** Buy the ground meat or tofu, fish, dried *ancho* peppers, and other ingredients needed from the supermarket. Wash, peel, and seed the vegetables. Store in plastic bags. Make the red ginger chutney.

- **The Day of:**
AM: Make the yogurt salad except for adding the *boondi*. Marinate the fish. Refrigerate both. Decide on the flavoring and chop the nuts for the brittle, if making.
PM: Make the *keema*. Make the smashed potatoes and keep warm in a slow cooker. Clean up.

- **At Serving Time:** Fry the fish and serve with the chutney. Heat the *keema* and serve with the hot potatoes and yogurt salad. Make the nut brittle if you haven't already.

My husband and his cousin-brothers lived together and attended Khalsa school, Bhatinda, together. They had a boys' night in every night.

FRIED FISH FRITTERS

fish   Muchchee Pakora

Every wedding I attended in Ludhiana or Chandigarh served fish fritters as a very special appetizer. But I never had them in my husband's village, which was far from the rivers. Fish is not so rare in most places in North America, so enjoy this delectable recipe whenever you like! These are best eaten immediately after frying.

Rinse the fish and pat dry with paper towels, especially if using frozen fish. The fish may need to be cut into equally thick pieces of about 2 inches by 3 inches if not using the whole smelt or shrimp. Mix the lemon juice with the turmeric and garam masala and marinate the fish in it for at least 30 minutes.

If using the ancho chile pepper, place in ³/₄ cup of boiling water. Soak the ground ancho chile pepper for 10 minutes. (Then use this water in place of the ³/₄ cup warm water.)

Heat the oil in a wok until hot, but not smoking, about 350°F. Make a batter of the chickpea flour, rice flour, warm water (plus ancho chile pepper if using), salt, onion, green chile pepper, coriander seeds, and cumin seeds.

Fold the fish pieces into the batter. Fry one piece to check for seasoning. Put 4 to 6 pieces of the fish (depending on the size of the wok) into the hot oil. Fry about 5 minutes until light brown, turning 2 to 3 times. Leftover batter may be made into fritters, *pakoras*, but do not give them to vegetarians since fish was in the same oil.

Drain the fish fritters on paper towels and serve immediately or keep warm in a 200°F oven. Serve with the Red Ginger Chutney *(page 146)*.

YIELD: 30 PIECES (2 INCH X 3 INCH)

2 pounds catfish or tilapia fillets, smelts, or fresh shelled shrimp

Juice of 1 lemon

1 teaspoon ground turmeric

1 teaspoon garam masala

For the pakora batter:*

1 dried ancho chile pepper or other dried, smoked pepper, seeded and ground (*optional*)

Canola oil for frying

1 cup chickpea flour

¹/₂ cup rice flour

³/₄ cup lukewarm water

1¹/₂ teaspoons salt

¹/₄ cup finely chopped onion (*optional*)

2 tablespoons green chile pepper, finely chopped or ¹/₄ teaspoon ground cayenne pepper

1 teaspoon crushed coriander seeds

¹/₄ teaspoon carom seeds (*ajwain*) (*optional*)

¹/₂ teaspoon whole or ground cumin seeds

Garnishes: lemon slices and cilantro leaves

*To make **plain** *pakoras* for the Curry of Vegetable on page 156 or for snacking, replace the rice flour with ¹/₂ cup chickpea flour. Working in batches, cut or scrape "pieces" of batter from a spatula with the dull side of a table knife into hot oil to make squiggles of 1¹/₂ inches for the vegetable dish, or 2¹/₂ inches for snacking. Fry until fairly dark brown and drain on paper towels. Use the same day or freeze.

RED GINGER CHUTNEY

Adrak Chutney *vegan*

This chutney is an unusual creation of mine, developed when we returned from New Mexico with ancho chiles—roasted and dried red poblano peppers, beloved of Native Americans. Mild and smoky, would they make this an Indo-Indian recipe?

YIELD: 1 CUP

2 large dried red ancho chile peppers, seeded

⅓ cup chopped ginger

Juice of 1 lemon

1 cup chopped fresh or jarred roasted red bell pepper, seeded

1 cup chopped sweet onion (like Vidalia)*

1 teaspoon salt

½ teaspoon sugar

1 tablespoon garlic chili sauce

½ teaspoon toasted fennel seeds (*optional*)

Rinse the ancho chile peppers and break into pieces. Bring a cup of water to a boil and soak the pieces in it for a few minutes until somewhat softened. Discard most of the water except a few spoonfuls. Put the reserved water and ancho chile peppers into a blender with the ginger and lemon juice. Purée and then push through a fine mesh sieve. Discard the solids.

Combine the bell pepper, onion, salt, sugar, garlic chili sauce, and toasted fennel seeds in a food processor and purée. Add the ancho chile mixture and mix well. Refrigerate until serving time.

*Red onion will give the chutney a pink color.

GROUND MEAT OR TOFU WITH PEAS

meat or vegan   Keema Ya Tofu Mutter

Punjabi boys away from home learn to make this dish if they make nothing else. Whether you like it thick to serve with naan or pita, or add some water to serve it like a gravy over mashed potatoes, this dish is always comforting.

In a large, heavy-bottomed pot, brown the onions, garlic, and ginger in the hot oil. If using ground meat, add it now and brown. Drain most of the fat. Add the chile peppers. Add the spices (turmeric through garam masala) and stir-fry for 1 minute. If using tofu, add now.

Add the chopped tomato, tomato sauce, salt, and water; cover and cook on very low heat for 10 minutes. Add the peas, cover, and cook for 10 more minutes. Pour into a serving dish. Stir in most of the cilantro, leaving a few leaves for garnish.

YIELD: 8 ³/₄-CUP SERVINGS

2 medium onions, chopped

3 cloves garlic, minced

2-inch piece ginger, minced

4 tablespoons canola oil

2¹/₂ pounds ground beef, lamb, turkey, or firm tofu*

3 green chile peppers, seeded and thinly sliced

2 teaspoons ground turmeric

2 teaspoons whole or ground cumin seeds

2 teaspoons ground coriander seeds

¹/₂ teaspoon fennel seeds (*optional*)

2 teaspoons garam masala

2 medium tomatoes, chopped

1 (15-ounce) can tomato sauce

2¹/₂ teaspoons salt

¹/₂ cup cold water (*optional*)

3 cups green peas

¹/₂ cup cilantro leaves and nice stems, sliced

*If using tofu, first drain it and crumble on several layers of paper towel. Add it after you brown the spices.

SPICY SMASHED POTATOES

Masala Aloo   *dairy*

Who doesn't love mashed potatoes? They are comfort food par excellence! The peel of the potato contains the most vitamins, so leave them on if they are thin and clear of blemishes. Leftovers can be stuffed into a parauntha *(page 19) or a* samosa *(page 59).*

YIELD: 10 GENEROUS SERVINGS

5 pounds russet potatoes

5 cloves garlic

4 tablespoons unsalted butter

1 medium onion, chopped

1 teaspoon ground cumin seeds

½ teaspoon ground cayenne pepper

1 teaspoon paprika

½ teaspoon ground white or black pepper

½ to ¾ cup whole milk

2 teaspoons salt, or to taste

Clean the potatoes and trim off any bad spots. Peel them if preferred. Cut into equal-size pieces. Bring a pot of water to boil and add the potatoes and garlic cloves. Cook until a knife can be inserted easily into the largest piece of potato. Do not over cook. Drain.

Meanwhile melt the butter over a low flame in a small saucepan. Add the onion and sauté until transparent, but not brown. Add the cumin seeds and sauté two more minutes. Add the cayenne pepper, paprika, and black pepper. Remove from heat.

Put the potatoes and garlic in a heatproof serving dish and mash. Add the onion mixture; fluff with a fork while adding the milk and salt to taste. Serve hot. Or keep warm in a slow cooker until serving time.

Any athlete would love this bowl of Keema Mutter and Masala Aloo.

YOGURT SALAD
WITH CHICKPEA CRUNCHIES

dairy   Boondee Raita

My American friends go crazy over this traditional raita. *It tastes like it contains whipped cream, even if you use non-fat yogurt. If preparing this a few hours early, add the salt, cilantro,* boondee, *and* chaat masala *just before serving.*

Beat the yogurt with the water until smooth. Reserving a few green scallion slices, a few cumin seeds, and the *chaat masala* for the garnish, combine all the other ingredients. Garnish with reserved scallions and a little cumin and/or *chaat masala* and *boondee* sprinkled on top.

YIELD: 8 ½-CUP SERVINGS

4 cups (32-ounces) plain yogurt

¼ cup cold water

½ red onion, minced

1 to 2 tablespoons green chile peppers, minced

4 scallions, minced, including some green

½ red bell pepper, minced

1 small tomato, seeded and chopped (*optional*)

¼ teaspoon ground cayenne pepper

1 teaspoon whole or ground cumin seeds, toasted

1½ teaspoons salt

½ cup sliced cilantro leaves

1 cup *boondee** plus 1 tablespoon for garnish

½ teaspoon *chaat masala* (*optional*) (*page 5*)

Founder of the Sikh Sports Association and friend, Harvinder Singh Dhaliwal.

*Boondee are tiny, fried balls of chickpea flour and spices. You can find them packaged at the Indian grocery store.

CRUNCHY NUT BRITTLE

Gatchak dairy or vegan

Timing is everything in this recipe! Once you decide what nuts and flavoring to use, chop the nuts, and measure all the ingredients ahead of time. This recipe is very quick and easy. And there is nothing like the flavor of homemade candy! The nuts make this a very healthful way to enjoy a dessert.

YIELD: 20 2-INCH SQUARES

Please note: The variety of nuts and seeds listed is just a suggestion. You can use a total of 1¾ cups of raw, unsalted chopped nuts and seeds of one or more varieties in this recipe.

½ cup pistachios

¼ cup cashews *or* sesame seeds

¼ cup almonds

¼ cup melon seeds (*magaz*) *or* pine nuts

¼ cup peanuts *or* pumpkin seeds

¼ cup walnuts *or* pecans

3 tablespoons *ghee or* coconut oil

1½ cups white sugar

2 tablespoons water

¼ to ½ teaspoon ground cardamom seeds

Pinch of salt

Flavorings:

1 teaspoon *kewrda* flavor *or*
2 teaspoons lemon juice *or*
2 teaspoons fennel seeds

Coarsely chop the pistachios and the larger nuts by hand, each separately to control the size of the pieces. Mix all the nuts and seeds (fennel seeds included, if using) together and roast in a toaster oven or in a dry frying pan over medium heat for a minute or until fragrant. Be careful not to burn!

Grease a rimless metal cookie sheet and a rolling pin with 1 of the tablespoons of ghee. Put the sugar, 2 tablespoons of the *ghee* and the water into a heavy saucepan. Have your chosen flavoring ready. Begin heating the sugar over medium-high heat. As it begins to melt into a syrup, keep swirling or stirring constantly. This mixture burns within seconds, so make sure the mixture heats evenly. You may have to add a tablespoon or two more water and stir if your sugar does not melt evenly. The mixture will begin to caramelize into a medium brown color. Remove from the burner and quickly stir in the flavoring and nuts/seeds. Immediately pour onto the prepared cookie sheet and spread out into the thinnest layer you can manage. Cut into 2-inch pieces. Or wait until it hardens and break into pieces. Store in an airtight container to maintain crunchiness.

INDEPENDENCE DAY

A tale of two villages during Partition

My husband and I enjoy the first India Day parade in New York City.

IN THE UNITED STATES, SYNONYMOUS WITH THE FLAG-WAVING PARADES OF THE Fourth of July is Independence Day. Hearts fill with pride as we watch our children marching down the center of our diverse town in bands and troops—children of Christians, Jews, Muslims, Hindus, and Sikhs cooperating to bring joy to the whole town. My husband will celebrate 50 years of these celebrations in this great country. The best of times!

We have also marched down Fifth Avenue in New York City on a beautiful 15th day of August dressed in our most colorful *kurta/pajama,* scarf, and turban on India's Independence Day. However, it was difficult to feel the same unadulterated pride. My husband had been too close to the horror of those days of the Partition in 1947 to forget. For us it is a tale of two villages, echoing as much quiet heroism on the one hand, and violence on the other as Dickens' *Tale of Two Cities*—in the worst of times.

Partition happened at the same time that India gained her freedom from England. Pakistan split off, based upon where the majority of Muslims lived. That summer, the heat was so oppressive that my husband's parents went with many of the family on his mother's side to the Himalayan hills. The family owned extensive lands in the Bahawalnagar area of west Punjab, populated mostly by Muslims, as well as land in a smaller village in east Punjab—land that would go to India.

My husband's maternal uncle was supervising on the larger farm when he heard on the radio that rioting and killing had begun. He got his gun and called for his Muslim servant to bring him a camel. In order to mount the camel, Uncle handed him the gun. As soon as the servant passed the gun up, Uncle saw an immediate realization come over the man's face. Uncle rode off for east Punjab through the

Both headmen of their respective villages, grandfathers Nanaji and Babaji on the day Parmpal left for the U.S.

fields, avoiding the roads. He left everything the family owned, never to return, while trains filled with the mutilated bodies of both Muslims and Hindus were arriving in towns on both sides. A half-million would be slaughtered.

Word of the growing carnage had also arrived in my husband's village. Standing high up in his fortified compound, the *heveli*, peeking through the brick fretwork, even at nine years of age, my husband felt a crush of fear as palpable as the oppressive heat. The Muslims of the village had left the morning before for a refugee camp, but despairing, returned in the afternoon and had gathered in the house across the street. That night, horrible, high-pitched screams were heard as a few of their men took swords to their women and children. As the sun rose, the Muslim men began yelling taunts from the house. He peeked through the lattice as several Sikhs stood on the roof of the two-story house across the street and began shooting the Muslim men a few at a time as they came through the door to the courtyard, swords held high, shouting, "*Allah hu Akbar!*" Grandfather and one paternal uncle stood above the gate of the *heveli* and frantically yelled to stop the killing, but to no avail. It took an hour.

Before the aborted exodus, *Babaji* had given shelter to a much-needed blacksmith and his family. He hid them in the storage area inside the compound, away from prying eyes. *Babaji* fed them for months until it was safe for them to return to their home.

From Peshawar to Delhi the madness and violence spread like a conflagration. In my mother-in-law's village, her cousin Mangal Singh had persuaded all of the Muslims to take shelter in his own house. He and his son, Joginder Singh, rifles in hand, deterred any violence until the frenzy was past and safe passage was assured. Not one drop of blood was shed. Two villages, two outcomes.

The "Independence Day" Menu

When you see the many ingredients in Punjabi recipes, do not succumb to fear or despair. The techniques for these dishes are simple and forgiving, and you may use some commercially prepared products. Most of the work can be done prior to the party, and then you can enlist a partner to grill the dishes. Your guests, including the vegetarians, will want to set off fireworks in honor of this meal!

Several types of pakora (fritters) are found in several of the menus in this book. However, each of the recipes is very different in texture and taste. I've included such a variety to give you an example of the breadth of Punjabi cuisine. As noted in the recipe headings, several types may be purchased ready-made. Yet, just as with masalas, you will find it is well worth the effort to prepare them from scratch when you taste the difference!

Appetizer:	*TANDOORI GUNDAY* Grilled Onions on Croutons
Main Course:	*MURGH MASALADAR* Spicy Grilled Chicken on a Can
	PAKORIAN DEE SUBZE Curry of Vegetables with Chickpea Fritters *or*
	ALOO MUTTER Curry of Vegetables with Potatoes (*var.*)
	METHI PARAUNTHA Layered Flat Breads with Fenugreek
	SHAKRAGUNDAY Stuffed Sweet Potatoes Two Ways
	ANAINAS MARUBBA Pineapple Chutney
Dessert:	*KULFEE* Nutty Frozen Dessert

- **One Week or More Prior:** Read the recipes from start to finish. Prepare your grocery lists. Buy the flavor extracts, spices, *chapatti* flour, *amchoor*, commercial spice mixtures—*garam masala*, *chaat masala*, and *tandoori* chicken *masalas* (if not making your own), *pakoras* or the ingredients to make them, *gurd*, dried grated coconut, nuts, malt vinegar, *ghee*, *paneer*, frozen fenugreek, ginger and other necessary dairy products from the Indian market.

- **Five Days Prior:** Measure and chop the nuts for the various recipes. Make the *kulfee* and freeze it. Make the *pakoras*, if you have not purchased them.

- **Four Days Prior:** Have on hand instant potato flakes and a long, green chile pepper. Make the breads, wrap and freeze them.

- **Three Days Prior:** Buy the chicken, peas, cilantro, sweet onions, potatoes, sweet potatoes, lemons/limes, pineapple, cranberries, cherry tomatoes, chilies, olive oil, and light sour cream. Don't forget small paper bowls for the curry if eating outdoors.

- **Two Days Prior:** Make the spice mixtures (if making your own). Make the pineapple chutney. Refrigerate.

- **One-Day Prior:** Make the gravy for the curried vegetable dish. Skin the chicken and marinate in the refrigerator. Make oil/spice for the croutons.

- **The Day of:**
  AM: Buy the French bread. Make the sweet potatoes; wrap in foil. Thaw the paraunthas. Soak the wooden skewers.
  PM: Finish the curried vegetable dish. Slice the onions and make the onion skewers. Start the grill. Clean up. Begin grilling the chicken(s). Soak the *pakoras*.

- **At Serving Time:** Slice the bread and grill the onions while the chickens rest. Serve them and then finish heating the sweet potatoes on the grill. Heat the breads and the curry. Garnish the dishes.

His eyes tell the story of what he saw in his village during Partition.

GRILLED ONIONS ON CROUTONS

Tandoori Gunday   *vegan*

There are typical Punjabi flavors in this recipe, but the presentation is Italian-style like bruschetta. My husband loves the grilled onions! This is a way to feature them.

YIELD: 8 SERVINGS

3 large garlic cloves

1 cup olive oil

2 teaspoons green mango powder

1½ teaspoons toasted cumin seeds, ground

1 teaspoon *chaat masala (page 5)*

1 teaspoon garam masala

½ teaspoon black pepper

1½ teaspoons salt

2½ pounds Vidalia onions

1 quart (12 to 14 ounces) cherry tomatoes

2 loaves French bread

1 lemon

1½ cups sliced cilantro

Soak 16 wooden skewers in warm water for several hours. Peel the garlic cloves and crush well with the flat side of a broad knife. Put into a jar with the olive oil. In a small bowl, mix the spices and salt and set aside.

Begin heating the grill. Peel the onions and cut into ½-inch thick horizontal slices. Using two skewers parallel to each other to pierce the **side** of the onion slices, skewer as many slices of onion as you can fit; continue making skewers until all the onions are used. Place the tomatoes on separate skewers allowing some space in between each tomato.

Brush the onions and tomatoes on all sides with the garlic oil and sprinkle with the spice mixture. Grill on a medium fire for approximately 5 minutes on each side. The tomatoes may finish before the onions, so be careful to remove them to a bowl before they soften too much and fall off the skewers.

Slice the bread into 1-inch thick slices. Brush both sides of the slices with the garlic olive oil and toast on the grill.

When the onions are finished, allow them to cool for a few minutes, and then push the onions into the bowl with the tomatoes. Cut the onion slices into quarters. Squeeze the lemon juice over all. Taste for seasoning and adjust. Toss with the cilantro and serve on top of the croutons.

SPICY GRILLED CHICKEN ON A CAN

meat/dairy   Murgh Masaladar

When I was recovering from surgery, I watched lots of Food Network TV and decided to copy the barbecuing on a can technique, Punjabi-style. I don't remember what show it was on, but I do remember they used a can of beer; I use a can of ginger ale.

Two days before serving: Rinse the skinned chicken and squeeze the lime juice over and inside it. Sprinkle with salt and pepper inside and out and set aside in the refrigerator in a large zip-top plastic bag.

One day before serving: In the food processor, grind the onion, garlic, and ginger into uniform small bits, but **not** to a paste. In a wok or skillet, stir-fry the onion mixture in the hot oil for 1 minute. Cover and reduce the heat. Cook for 5 minutes, stirring and scraping once per minute or so. Uncover, turn the heat to medium and stir vigorously until fairly brown but not burned, about 6 more minutes.

Measure the seeds into a spice grinder and grind until a fine powder. Add the coconut and grind again. In a large zip-top bag, mix the cooked onions, *tandoori masala*, sour cream, salt, cayenne pepper, and coconut-spice mixture. Rub inside the chicken and pat the mixture all over the chicken. Refrigerate overnight.

Day of serving: Remove the shelf from the grill if you have one because it will knock the chicken over when you close the grill. Preheat the grill to 350°F. You will be using indirect heat, so either push the coals to one side, or, if using gas, turn on only part of the burners so the chicken will fit in the "off" section.

Open the can of ginger ale and punch a few more holes in the top. Pour out a little of the liquid. Put the can in a deep bowl, and set the chicken over it with the can going into the cavity of the chicken. Pat the chicken all over with the marinade. Cover the ends of the legs and wings with aluminum foil. Place the chicken on the can on the grill, splaying the legs for balance. Cover, and grill for an hour and 15 minutes or until the thigh reaches 160°F.

Grip the can with tongs and place the chicken on a platter on its back. Rest the chicken under foil for 10 minutes before carving (the temperature should increase to 165°F). Sprinkle with *chaat masala* before serving.

YIELD: 4 TO 6 SERVINGS

1 whole chicken (about 3 pounds), skinned

1 lime

salt and pepper to taste

1 large onion

4 cloves garlic

2-inch piece ginger

⅓ cup canola oil

2 tablespoons white poppy seeds

2 teaspoons whole cumin seeds

1 teaspoon whole coriander seeds

Pinch of whole cardamom seeds

¼ cup unsweetened finely grated coconut

1 tablespoon *tandoori* chicken *masala (page 62)*

½ cup light sour cream

1½ teaspoons salt

¼ teaspoon ground cayenne pepper

1 can ginger ale

Garnish: *Chaat masala (page 5)*

CURRY OF VEGETABLES WITH CHICKPEA FRITTERS

Pakorian Dee Subze

vegan

Plain pakorian, chickpea fritter.

Many of you are familiar with aloo mutter or *curried potatoes with peas, the Punjabi standby that is always a hit with the entire family (see variation on page 157). Did you know you may substitute* pakoras *for the potatoes? In the Indian market I saw a box of small, hard* pakoras *that I fondly remember eating in a curry in the village forty years ago. So I had to reproduce that delicious dish in my own kitchen. Of course there was no tomato paste then, so the women used many more tomatoes cooked slowly down into the sauce.*

You may buy the pakoras *or make them yourself using the entire "batter" recipe on page 145. If making this dish with the* pakoras, *it is always somewhat "soupy." With potatoes, it can be thicker, if you like it that way.*

YIELD: 10 1-CUP SERVINGS

¼ cup vegetable oil

2 medium onions, chopped

3 cloves garlic, minced

2-inch piece ginger, grated

2 teaspoons ground turmeric

1½ teaspoons whole or ground cumin seeds

1 tablespoon crushed coriander seeds

1 teaspoon ground fenugreek seeds (*optional*)

1 medium/large tomato, chopped

1 or 2 long green chile peppers, seeded and finely sliced

1½ teaspoons salt, or to taste

In a large, heavy-bottomed pot, heat the oil and sauté the onions, garlic, and ginger over medium heat until lightly browned, stirring frequently. Add the spices and brown for 1 more minute. For a smooth gravy, purée this *tardka* in the blender. (The *tardka* may be refrigerated at this point for a day or two.)

Return the *tardka* to the pot (and reheat if it has been refrigerated) and add the tomato, chile pepper, and salt, stirring constantly for another few minutes. Stir in the tomato paste, 1 teaspoon of garam masala, and three cups of water. Simmer over low heat for 10 minutes, stirring occasionally.

Soak the *pakoras* in 4 cups warm water for 3 to 8 minutes, depending on their hardness and then lightly squeeze out and discard the water. Add the *pakoras* and peas, plus 2½ cups water. Taste for salt and heat through. Before serving, sprinkle with the last teaspoon of *garam masala* and the cilantro leaves.

Variation: To make **Curry of Vegetables with Potatoes (*Aloo Mutter*)** use 4 cups potatoes, peeled and cut in 1¼-inch cubes, in place of the *pakoras* for this more familiar version of the dish. Add the potatoes with the tomato paste and increase the simmer time to 30 minutes. Add more water if you like a "soupier" dish.

⅓ cup tomato paste

2 teaspoons garam masala

3½ cups small, hard chickpea-flour *pakoras*

3 cups frozen peas, thawed

½ cup cilantro leaves and stems, finely chopped, plus ¼ cup leaves for garnish

Our fortress-like family compound, the *haveli*, circa 1963.

LAYERED FLAT BREADS WITH FENUGREEK

Methi Parauntha   *vegan*

I love this bread for three reasons: everything goes in at once; the ingredients make it a meal in itself—especially good for brunch with yogurt and lemon pickle; and it can be made ahead. Oh, and one more reason—it is delicious! If fresh fenugreek is not available (it looks like very large clover leaves), you can buy it frozen. One or two thawed cubes will do.

YIELD: 12 BREADS

3 cups *chapatti* flour

⅓ cup instant potato flakes

1 cup chopped fresh fenugreek leaves

1 tablespoon long green chile pepper, minced

1 tablespoon minced ginger

1½ teaspoons salt

1½ teaspoons coriander seeds, toasted and ground

⅛ cup melted *ghee* or canola oil, for brushing

In a large bowl, mix all ingredients except the *ghee* or oil, and then gradually add 1¼ cups water. Knead the dough until no longer sticky. Allow the dough to rest covered in the refrigerator for an hour or overnight.

Divide dough into quarters, then make three equal-size balls from each quarter. Roll the balls in loose flour and then flatten. Roll out on a lightly floured board to 5½- by 6½-inch disks.

Preheat a griddle to 360°F or until a drop of water sizzles. Brush or spray with oil. Lift one of the breads with a spatula and flip onto the griddle. Cook one side for 2 minutes, then flip. Brush with *ghee* or oil. Grill for 1 more minute, then flip and oil the other side. Continue to flip until bread is cooked and starts to swell when pressed with the spatula. Remove from heat and continue to cook the remaining breads. Serve immediately if possible, or keep warm covered in a tea towel.

Once cool, the breads can be individually wrapped in plastic wrap then bundled in foil and frozen. Reheat easily by quickly wetting under the faucet one at a time, and heating in a 400°F toaster oven, or spread on the racks of a larger oven or on the grill.

Variation: Mint leaves may be used in place of the fenugreek leaves.

STUFFED SWEET POTATOES TWO WAYS

In India these are sold roasted on the street by vendors, just like chestnuts are in the U.S. Sweet potatoes are such a healthful food. Either of these variations would be great anytime, but especially on the holiday table.

Scrub the sweet potatoes and remove any blemishes. Make a slit horizontally down the side of each from end to end as a guide for where you will cut through later. Microwave on high for approximately 5 to 8 minutes or until they are cooked. Do not overcook. When the potatoes are cool to the touch, using a very sharp knife, finish cutting through them horizontally making two even halves.

For the walnut topping: Score the flesh of the potato halves lightly with a fork. Mix the dry spices, sugar, and a ¼ teaspoon salt in a small dish. Brush the yams on all sides with some of the melted *ghee*. Sprinkle on the spice mixture. Pierce a sheet of heavy aluminum foil and place on a hot grill or on a broiler pan; place the yams on the aluminum foil and either grill, covered, or broil to finish caramelizing and heating them through. Melt a table-spoon of the *ghee* or butter in a small saucepan and toast the walnut pieces in it. Sprinkle with ¼ teaspoon salt and then sprinkle evenly on the potatoes.

For the pineapple chutney topping: Scoop out the potato flesh from the halves leaving at least a quarter inch inside along the peel. Mash the flesh until smooth and then add the *ghee* and chutney. Spoon into the shells. Pierce a sheet of heavy aluminum foil and place on a hot grill. Put the potatoes on the aluminum foil and close the cover or place under the broiler to heat them through.

YIELD: 10 SERVINGS

5 nicely shaped, unblemished sweet potatoes (about 10 ounces each) plus 2 more for extra filling (*optional*)

For Sweet and Spicy Walnut Topping:

1 tablespoon *chaat masala (page 5)*

1 teaspoon ground cinnamon

½ teaspoon garam masala

1 tablespoon *gurd* or brown sugar

½ teaspoon salt

3 tablespoons melted *ghee* or butter

½ cup chopped walnuts

For Pineapple Chutney Topping:

2 tablespoons *ghee* or butter

1 cup pineapple chutney *(page 160)*

Choose one or the other, both toppings are delectable on these colorful, healthful treats.

PINEAPPLE CHUTNEY

Anainas Marubba   *vegan*

This is a recipe I developed for a barbecue. I wanted something colorful, yet both sweet and more acidic than most chutneys. Pineapple seemed a perfect choice. If the pineapple you've chosen is not very sweet, you may wish to add more sugar.

YIELD: 4 CUPS

¼ cup canola oil

½ cup minced onion

3-inch piece ginger, grated

1 chile pepper, seeded and minced
   (*optional*)

½ teaspoon salt

6 cups ½-inch cubes fresh
   pineapple*

¾ cup dried cranberries or dried
   cherries

¼ cup malt or cider vinegar

¾ cup dark brown sugar

1 teaspoon garam masala

Heat the oil and sauté the onion until transparent. Add the ginger and chile pepper and sauté for another minute. Add the salt, pineapple, cranberries, vinegar, sugar, and garam masala. Bring to a boil and cook over medium/high heat for five minutes; then keep stirring and cooking until the liquid is evaporated. Cool. Store in the refrigerator.

Son Paul and wife Nancy enjoy an unusual way to see the Rose Garden in Chandigarh.

* If your pineapple isn't large enough to give you 6 cups, you can use some of the core or supplement with canned (the canned pineapple should be added after the mixture has boiled).

NUTTY FROZEN DESSERT

In Bhatinda, the kulfeewala *balanced a long stick across his shoulders, a bucket of* kulfee *on one end and a bucket of* falooda *noodles and syrup on the other. His calls were as welcome as the bells on the ice cream truck, or as this treat that Auntie Surindera made for us while we were sitting around her pool on a hot day.*

Grind the nuts finely in a food processor. Decide on the flavorings you wish to use—all, or one or two. In a large bowl, mix together all the ingredients. Freeze in individual frozen treat molds, inserting a stick when mixture is half frozen. Or freeze in custard cups.

YIELD: 24 TRADITIONAL ¼-CUP MOLDS OR 12 ½-CUP SERVINGS

2 tablespoons unsalted pistachios

1 pint heavy cream

1 (14-ounce) can sweetened condensed milk

1 (14-ounce) can evaporated milk

Pinch of ground cardamom seeds

5 drops rose extract (*optional*)

½ teaspoon almond or pistachio extract (*optional*)

5 drops kewdra extract (*optional*)

"POLISHED!"

An amusing story featuring a learning experience

MY NAME MAY BE FAMOUS IN PUNJAB BY NOW. IT IS NOT BECAUSE I WAS GIVEN A TOTALLY Indian-sounding nickname, "Ronnie," at birth (in the early forties, not the sixties!) by my Irish/German-American mother and Hungarian-American father. Sounded out phonetically, "Rani" Veda, means Queen of Holy Knowledge in Sanskrit. Quite auspicious, really, but not at all relevant to this story.

The town of Bhatinda in Punjab, where we had moved into a rented house, was already well-known as a railway junction and for its "Wild West" attitude. But no, my fame was not tied to the town. It was a day in 1966 when my husband and *Bebeji*, my mother-in-law, left me alone for the first time since we had arrived in India.

It seemed like a good idea at the time.

I surveyed the spare rooms—a nicked dining set of indeterminate wood, the finish long gone and the planks and spools dried gray from the desert climate. The high-ceilinged plaster walls had some peeling paint, pale green, I think. But clearly I remember the dessicated doorjambs, the only architectural touch in the room. What to do?

I looked around for something oily to use to polish some life back into these sorry specimens. Now mind you, even I knew that there would be no furniture polish in the house or even in the market. Manufactured products were few indeed. In those days one could only find Binaca® toothpaste, and most people chewed on a stick from the *kicker* tree to clean their teeth. So searching, I found a metal can—like a gas can—which held a whitish, oily substance. I found a rag and began to polish.

Polished for hours, the thirsty wood soaked up the oily substance; and with my "elbow grease," the table, chairs and even the doorjambs began to gleam. Surely I would be in *Bebeji's* good graces forever, I thought.

Then they came home, and immediately I knew that something was wrong. My mother-in-law sniffed the air and looked at the table. She blanched and then flushed. "She didn't know," my husband said in Punjabi. "I didn't know what?" I thought. "Where did you find this woman!" was all she said, over and over. I knew she wanted to say more than that, and may have later. But mercifully, I didn't have any of that vocabulary yet.

I had used enough *desi ghee,* real clarified butter, to feed half a village for a year! I had never even heard of it! As precious as gold, the medicine for all ills, I had wasted this elixir on a rental-house doorjamb! No one could be this dumb. Come to think of it, the *ghee* was fra-

A decorative butter churn.

grant like butter, but it wasn't yellow. I asked why not, trying to give some justification to what I realized from my mother-in-law's demeanor must have been the *faux pas* of the century. Butter from cows is yellow, yes. This was clarified butter from water buffaloes. "Oh!"

So, mind you, even though I had taught myself to read before kindergarten, devoured an entire set of the Book of Knowledge (no less) before sixth grade, and graduated from the University of Michigan with a double major—in my mother-in-law's eyes I didn't know diddly. I learned about *ghee* and many other things Punjabi, a little too late, perhaps, to ever redeem myself in her eyes. But the story lives on.

It really is healthy to laugh!

The "Polished" Menu

This is a menu featuring—what else? Precious ghee, of course! Ghee can make things shiny, crispy, flaky—definitely fragrant. Roghan means to polish, and the ghee in this menu does all that and more. If you've broken a bone or just given birth, your family will treat you to an extra spoonful. If your son-in-law or father-in-law is visiting, make sure you top his portion with at least a spoonful. It's the Punjabi way. And now you know!

In the category of "unbelievable coincidence," I just received an advertisement in the mail claiming, "Rebuild your bones with butter!" It goes on to state that unpasteurized ghee or "oil of butter" from grass-fed cows "could end our hip-fracture pandemic."

Appetizer:	*RANI DEE GOOTHLEE* The Queen's "Purse"
Main Course:	*ROGHAN JOSH* Classic "Polished" Lamb Curry
	SABE CHUTNEY Apple Chutney
	ALOO PHULLIAN Green Beans and Potatoes
	MASOOR PEELEETORI METHI Red Lentils with Summer Squash and Fenugreek
	ROGHANEE ROTEE Broiled Whole-Wheat Flat Breads with Cream
Dessert:	*PISTA SHAHI* The King's Pistachio Cookies

- **One Week Prior:** Read the recipes from beginning to end. Decide whether you wish to purchase commercially prepared *ghee* or make it yourself. Purchase the lentils, fenugreek, nuts, apricots, raisins, butter, and spices from the Indian market. Make *ghee* from a pound of butter *(see page 7)*. Prepare the fenugreek leaves and refrigerate or buy the frozen at the market.

- **Three to Four Days Prior:** Buy the rest of the items from the supermarket. If you buy a leg of lamb, ask the butcher to grind enough to make the purses. Have him cut the rest into cubes for the *roghan josh*.

- **Two Days Prior:** Make the meat filling for the purses.

- **One Day Prior:** Bake the cookies. Make the apple chutney. Prepare the dough for the *rotees*. Refrigerate.

- **The Day of:**
AM: Prepare the green beans. Make the lentil dish.
PM: Bake the purses. Make the meat dish.

- **At Serving Time:** Serve the purses with drinks. Warm the meat and vegetable dishes in the microwave as you and your friends make the breads. Serve the cookies with ice cream, if you like.

THE QUEEN'S PURSE

Rani Dee Goothlee

meat/dairy

Favors from the Rani (sweets or jewels presented by the queen) would not come wrapped in paper, but in beautiful cloth pouches tied with silk cord. This was the inspiration for this dish. You will need a muffin tin and fresh chives that are long enough to tie into a knot. Otherwise use thin ribbon.

A gift of *ladoo* sweets in a *goothlee*, much like one the *rani* (queen) would present to her guests.

YIELD: 8 PIECES

2 tablespoons golden raisins

1 cup dried apricots

1 teaspoon whole cumin seeds

1½ teaspoons whole coriander seeds

2 tablespoons dried unsweetened, grated coconut

3 tablespoons canola oil

1 medium yellow onion, minced

1½-inch piece ginger, minced

2 cloves garlic, minced

½ pound very lean ground meat— ground leg of lamb, ground sirloin (but not hamburger)

¼ teaspoon ground cinnamon

Bring 1 cup of water to a boil and add the raisins and apricots. Remove from heat and set aside to plump (about 20 minutes).

Toast the cumin seeds, coriander seeds, and coconut in a dry frying pan or toaster oven for a minute, until fragrant, and then grind in a spice grinder.

Heat the oil in a large skillet and saute the onion, ginger, and garlic until golden. Add the meat and sauté until browned. Pour off all but a few spoonfuls of fat. Add the toasted spices plus the ground cinnamon and cardamom and sauté for 1 more minute. Coarsely chop the apricots and pistachios and add to the meat. Add the salt and raisins with the soaking water. Stir-fry until dry.

Preheat the oven to 400°F. Unwrap the phyllo dough and cover with a damp towel while you work with it. Brush 1 sheet with melted butter by holding down the sheet with a finger and brushing away from you. Place another sheet on top and brush again. Add a third sheet, brush with melted butter and then sprinkle evenly with a pinch or two of salt. Add two more sheets for a total of five, brushing each with melted butter.

Cut the layered dough into 8 squares of about 5 to 7 inches, depending on the size of your muffin cups. (You will be cutting the squares to fit the bottom and up the sides of the cups—with enough dough to gather and twist.) Put the squares into the muffin cups. Place a few spoonfuls of the meat mixture in each "purse." Gather up the sides and slightly twist. Bake for about 15 minutes.

Microwave the whole chives until just tender. Tie one around each purse like a string or make bows with thin ribbon. Serve hot or warm with chutney or in a little pool of ketchup thinned with a $\frac{1}{2}$ teaspoon of corn syrup (for the kids).

¼ teaspoon ground cardamom seeds

¼ cup unsalted pistachios

1½ teaspoons salt, plus more for sprinkling on the dough

8-ounce package phyllo dough

¼ cup melted *ghee* or unsalted butter

8 fresh whole chives (*optional*)

CLASSIC "POLISHED" LAMB CURRY

Roghan Josh

meat/dairy

I tasted this dish for the first time on a houseboat in Kashmir, which was moored on the lovely Jhelum River, one of the five rivers that run through Punjab. Our host was the courtly Habib, who was so very hospitable to us and to others. I remember how proud he was of the gifts that people had sent him in appreciation of his service.

The name of this famous Kashmiri recipe means "red-polished meat," referring to the shiny red coating on the meat. No onion or garlic is used, as was the custom among the pundits or Brahmins of Kashmir. The cooking technique is similar to the one used by the Milanese to make risotto.

YIELD: 8 ½-CUP SERVINGS

1¾ cups plain yogurt

1½ teaspoons ground ginger

1 teaspoon asafoetida or garlic powder

3 pounds boneless red meat, preferably lamb or goat, trimmed of fat and cut into cubes

2 tablespoons canola oil

2 teaspoons whole coriander seeds

1 teaspoon whole black peppercorns

2½ teaspoons whole black cumin seeds*

2-inch piece ginger, grated

1½ tablespoons paprika

½ teaspoon ground cayenne pepper (*optional*)

2 teaspoons salt

Garnish: ¼ cup cilantro leaves

Mix the yogurt with the ground ginger and asafoetida in a large bowl. Add the meat and toss to coat.

Begin heating the oil in a heavy-bottomed pot or Dutch oven with tight-fitting lid. (Do not use a non-stick coated pan since then the browning may not take place.) Add the meat. Stir occasionally at first with a wooden spoon until the liquid dries up, somewhat browning the meat. Add a ¼ cup water and stir again. Try to scrape the fond or brown bits into the "gravy" and then stir again until there is no more liquid.

Heat a small pan and toast the coriander seeds and peppercorns for 1 minute. Add the cumin seeds and cook for 1 more minute, being careful not to burn them. Grind in a spice grinder. Mix with the grated ginger, paprika, cayenne pepper, and a ¼ cup water and then add to the meat. Stir frequently, scraping up the fond, until the water is absorbed.

Mix the salt with another ½ cup of water and repeat the process. Turn the heat to low, cover, and heat for another 15 minutes, until the meat is very tender and "polished" with sauce. Serve with the cilantro as garnish.

* Black cumin seeds or *shah zeera* are smaller, darker, and have a more menthol flavor than ordinary white cumin seeds. They are also more expensive. But you may substitute ordinary white cumin seeds.

APPLE CHUTNEY

vegan or dairy   Sabe Chutney

I developed this recipe when we were on an R.V. road trip to the Canadian Maritimes. Our campsite was near a very old apple tree covered with small, sour, yet ripe apples, perfect for chutney. I used ingredients on hand and shared it with some fellow travelers. They loved it, and a star was born.

In a medium wok, sauté the onion in the oil or *ghee* until transparent. Add the garlic and ginger and sauté for a minute. Add the apples and sauté until the apples are still firm but cooked. Add the sugars, raisins, lime juice, nuts, salt, and spices of your choice. Cover and cook over low heat, stirring occasionally, until heated through. Serve warm or at room temperature. Refrigerate leftovers.

YIELD: 3 CUPS

1 medium onion, finely chopped

1 tablespoon canola oil or *ghee*

3 cloves garlic, minced

2-inch piece ginger, minced

6 cups peeled ½-inch-thick sour apple slices, cubed

1 tablespoon *gurd* or dark brown sugar

¼ cup sugar, or more if apples are very sour

⅓ cup golden raisins

Juice of 1 lime

½ cup unsalted cashews, coarsely chopped

½ cup unsalted almonds, coarsely chopped

½ teaspoon salt

¼ teaspoon freshly ground black pepper

¼ teaspoon fennel seeds (*optional*)

¼ teaspoon ground cardamom seeds (*optional*)

Could you guess that granddaughter Jessica Kaur likes apples?

GREEN BEANS AND POTATOES

Aloo Phullian   *vegan*

The sun-dried tomatoes add a sweet-sour sparkle to make this a Punjabi/Italian fusion dish that can be made quickly at the last minute. Your family will polish it off!

YIELD: 8 SERVINGS

3 tablespoons canola oil or *ghee*

1 medium onion, finely chopped

2 cloves garlic, minced

1 teaspoon ground turmeric

1 teaspoon ground cumin seeds

1 teaspoon ground coriander seeds

¼ teaspoon ground cayenne pepper (*optional*)

3 medium/large red potatoes, (peeled only if skin is rough) cut into 1½-inch cubes

1½ teaspoons salt

1 pound green beans, trimmed

10 slivered sun-dried tomatoes (*optional*)

Garnishes: 1 teaspoon garam masala and sliced cilantro

Heat the oil in a large skillet and add the onion and garlic. Sauté until golden. Add the spices and sauté for 1 to 2 minutes. Add the potatoes and salt and sauté for a few minutes. Add the trimmed green beans and sun-dried tomatoes. Sauté for a few minutes more and then cover and simmer on low heat for 10 minutes. (You may need to add a tablespoon or two of water if you do not have a very tight-fitting lid.) Check the potatoes—they should be cooked but not mushy and the beans should be tender but still green. Serve immediately sprinkled with cilantro and the garam masala.

Note: If you wish to make this dish ahead, blanch the cut beans in boiling water for thirty seconds and shock in ice water. This step will preserve the bright color of the beans if they are to be reheated.

RED LENTILS WITH SUMMER SQUASH AND FENUGREEK

vegan   Masoor Peeleetori Methi

This is a very light vegetarian dish that balances heavier preparations on the menu. I substitute edible (not ornamental) pumpkin (called petha *in Punjabi or* calabasa *in Spanish) for the squash when it is available.*

Pick over the lentils and rinse. In a medium saucepan, bring the water and salt to a boil and add the lentils. Cover and cook, stirring occasionally, for 15 minutes. Set aside.

Cut the roots from the fenugreek and soak the leaves and stems in a large pan of cold water. Swish several times to release any sand. Lift the fenugreek to a colander and rinse again. Allow to drain, and then pluck the leaves and discard all the stems. Chop the leaves, place in a glass bowl with 1 cup of water, cover, and microwave for five minutes on high.

Meanwhile peel the squash and cut into 1-inch cubes (you should have about 4 cups). (If using pumpkin, first microwave on high for 8 minutes before peeling and cubing.) Place the lentils and squash in a large saucepan. Cover and simmer over low heat until the squash is cooked, about 15 minutes. Mash slightly.

Heat the oil in a large wok and add the onion. Sauté until transparent and then add the garlic and ginger. Add the spices and sauté until the onions are golden. Add the green chile pepper, stir and sauté for another minute. Add the fenugreek and stir-fry for a few minutes. Stir in the squash mixture. Lower the heat. Cover and cook for 5 more minutes before serving. (This dish freezes well.)

YIELD: 6 CUPS

½ cup red lentils

2 cups water

2 teaspoons salt

2 bunches fresh fenugreek leaves (*methi*) or two frozen cubes, thawed

2 pounds yellow summer squash or edible pumpkin

¼ cup canola oil

1 medium onion, chopped

3 cloves garlic, minced

2-inch piece ginger, grated

1 rounded teaspoon ground turmeric

1 teaspoon whole or ground cumin seeds

2 teaspoons ground coriander seeds

1 green chile pepper, sliced

BROILED WHOLE-WHEAT FLAT BREADS WITH CREAM

Roghanee Rotee

dairy

This rotee *is a little more festive because of the touch of cream. It is softer than* tandoori rotee *(page 64) and fragrant with* kewrda *flavor. Some breads may actually swell open and can be used like pita for sandwiches. Do **not** use chapatti flour in this recipe.*

YIELD: 8 BREADS (8-INCH)

1³/₄ cups whole-wheat flour

1³/₄ cups all-purpose flour

1 teaspoon salt

1 cup whole milk

4 drops *kewrda* flavor plus 2 drops for the cream (*optional*)

¹/₂ cup warm water plus a few tablespoons more, if needed

1 teaspoon plus 2 tablespoons heavy cream

Whisk together the flours and salt in a large bowl. Make a well in the center and add the milk and 4 drops of *kewrda*. Stir in one direction with a fork in the center going outward, gradually adding the warm water. The dough will be fairly hard. Knead in a tablespoon or so more warm water. Keep kneading until the dough is elastic and no longer sticks to the sides of the bowl. Spread a teaspoon of the cream over the ball of dough and let it rest, covered, for at least 30 minutes, but no more than an hour. If longer than that it may be refrigerated for up to two days.

If the dough has been refrigerated, let it come to room temperature for 30 minutes. Begin heating a griddle over medium to medium-high heat and turn on the broiler or toaster oven. Put the 2 tablespoons cream plus two drops *kewrda* flavor into a small bowl.

Divide the dough into eight equal balls. Roll them between your palms until they are totally smooth. Dip a ball of dough in loose flour and flatten it with your palm. Very lightly flour a board and rolling pin and begin rolling the ball into a disk 7 to 8 inches in diameter. Put the disk on the griddle and heat for about 1¹/₂ minutes or until the bottom begins to bake and little "hills" rise in the surface. Remove and brush the uncooked side with some of the flavored cream. Put the *rotee* under the broiler on the second rack. Broil for about 2 to 3 minutes or until the top of the bread is brown and bubbly in spots. Repeat process with remaining balls of dough. These are best eaten immediately.

THE KING'S PISTACHIO COOKIES

dairy
Pista Shahi

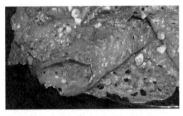

A tray of The King's Pistachio Cookies.

Babe Paley is supposed to have said, "You can never be too rich nor too thin!" But when I began making this cookie, it was to be a base for the Roses and Rubies Mousse (page 77), which I envisioned would make an elegant ice-cream sandwich. But the cookies, in combination with the mousse, were altogether so rich that it didn't work. Each is great on its own though.

Preheat the oven to 375°F. In a heavy saucepan over low heat, stir the syrup, butter, brown sugar, salt, and cardamom seeds until the butter is melted. Remove from the heat and stir in the nuts and flour.

Line baking sheets with parchment paper (the parchment paper will help to release these sticky cookies quickly). Place a scant tablespoonful of the batter on the baking sheets for each cookie, spacing them at least 3 inches apart. (It is very important that you leave 3 inches between the cookies, otherwise they will spread into each other. In fact, it may be better at first to put only 4 cookies on a sheet at a time, and bake only one sheet at a time until you have some experience.) Bake for 5 minutes until lightly browned. Too little time and they will be sticky; too long and they will burn. Stay nearby.

Remove the baking sheet from the oven and immediately put the parchment paper on a cool, flat surface. If you wish to curl the cookies, you must work very quickly. As soon as they are cool enough to touch, but still quite warm, hang them, one at a time, over a rolling pin to begin to curve them, then roll them loosely around the handle of the rolling pin for a tighter curl.

Store carefully. These cookies are fragile, and in heat or humidity they will stick together. They are best stored in an airtight container such as a large plastic sweater box. If you must layer them, carefully place waxed paper between the layers.

YIELD: 2 DOZEN 3½-INCH COOKIES

1 cup light corn syrup

1 stick (8 tablespoons) unsalted butter

1 cup firmly packed light brown sugar

¼ teaspoon sea salt

1 teaspoon ground cardamom seeds

1 cup unsalted pistachios, finely chopped

1 cup plus 2 tablespoons all-purpose flour

Parchment paper

SUMMER FUN

The first Sikh temple and summer camps in New Jersey

THE MOONLIGHT PLAYED SILVER ACROSS THE CHILDREN CURLED IN THEIR SLEEPING bags. I had told stories and sung songs and lullabies until I was exhausted. Finally everyone, all fifty campers, was asleep. I stretched out, contented, on the *durbar* hall floor. We were finally able to enjoy the large air-conditioned room that was usually filled with worshippers. It was quite a change from the first camp for Sikh children we'd held years earlier in New Jersey. At that time we slept on the basement floor of the old building our small community had purchased. Then I had swept it of pesky black caterpillar-like creatures, scrubbed down the two showers, and cleaned out the cupboards in the small kitchen. But by morning, all those critters were back. The campers had almost as much memorable "Ewww!" factor as if they had been outdoors! It was so much better now in the new hall.

Most of the children who attended in those days were the only Sikhs in their schools. Not feeling totally accepted is a problem for many children for one reason or another, but add an identity crisis, and you get the picture. That is why my husband and I felt it was so important to give the kids a fun bonding experience as Sikh youth. That is why, in addition to the week of classes in Punjabi, Sikh Religion and History, and *Shabad Kirtan* Sacred Music, we made sure the campers had a full day of pure fun. Over the years we took them to a forest for a hike and picnic, Great Adventure, Medieval Times, a water park, horseback riding, and a play. Several weeks went into the planning and lining up of the volunteers, buying the food, and preparing the history and religion lessons. But the whole process brought me much happiness. It helped that I was off work during the summer. And it was well worth the effort, since the kids gained so much confidence by being together. In fact, just recently I spoke to one of the former campers who told me how much the experience meant to him, since he felt lonely in his school and felt "normal" at camp.

Once a flagpole was erected by the *sewadars*, we had a rousing opening ceremony around it each morning. We would also always have a special ceremony at the close of the camp. There would be readings from the holy book, the *Guru Granth Sahib*, and then the children would perform a program for their parents: singing hymns, reciting the names of the ten gurus, and retelling facts from Sikh history—what they had learned during the camp. Everyone participated and we were all so proud of them! Even the smallest, shyest children

Daughter, Sheila Kaur, eagerly accepts an award from Gianiji Darshan Singh of the Gurudwara, Bridgewater, N.J.

could feel important by giving out napkins to the congregation before the *prashaad* was distributed.

Afterwards we ate *langar,* the free community meal the volunteers had prepared. Since no meat, fish, or eggs were allowed in the *guruduwara,* the Sikh temple where we held our camp, I had to be creative in developing kid-friendly menus. Some of the children were used to vegetarian Punjabi food, but some were used to eating chicken nuggets and fries. Most of the kids liked oatmeal, cereal, or grilled *besan* toasts for breakfast. We had grilled cheese, macaroni and cheese, spaghetti, and other American fare available for lunch. For supper the kids had red beans and rice, chickpeas and *poorees* or other kid-friendly Punjabi dishes. Nobody went hungry, because there was always good ol' peanut butter and jelly for the most finicky!

The "Summer Fun" Menu

Although we served vegetarian recipes for the gurudwara *camps, this menu gives you a choice of either a vegetarian or meat kebab for the main dish. If you prepare the onion/ginger/garlic mixture called a tardka earlier, your assistant can grill the eggplants just before you put on the kebabs. Then finish the eggplant dish on the stove while the kebabs are grilling. Clean the grill and then make the naan outside on the grill as your guests watch. And if you can, eat the meal outdoors: it always tastes better there, doesn't it?*

The thundeye *is a great recipe for both kids and adults. Punjabi mothers will make a variation of this drink for their children, especially during exams. It has all the elements of the ayurvedic recipe for brain food. The almonds, melon seeds, and poppy seeds are thought to boost intelligence.*

Appetizer: *PANEER SALADE* Fresh Cheese and Tomato "Sandwiches"

Main Course: *BOTEE KEBABS* Lamb and/or Vegetable Kebabs
SONT Syrupy Ginger-Mango Chutney
BHARTHA Roasted Eggplant Purée
TANDOORI NAAN Grilled White Flat Breads

Dessert: *THUNDEYE* Cooling Milkshake

- **Three Days Prior**: Read the recipes from start to finish. Prepare your grocery lists. Make the *paneer* and refrigerate, if making your own.

- **Two Days Prior**: Buy the *gurd,* dried ginger and dried mango powders, the spices, white poppy seeds, melon seeds, nuts, rose petal spread or rose flavor, cilantro, eggplants, red and yellow onions, peppers, and ginger from the Indian market.

- **One-Day Prior**: Buy the remaining necessities at the supermarket. Wash, peel, and seed the vegetables. Store in plastic bags. Grind the spices for the milkshake and marinate the lamb. Refrigerate all.

- **The Day of:**
AM: Prepare the chutney. Make the *tardka* for the eggplants.
PM: Make the dough for the *naans.* Skewer the kebabs and refrigerate until ready to grill. Thaw the peas and pearl onions. Clean up.

- **At Serving Time:** Make the cheese "sandwiches" and plate and serve them. Preheat the grill and grill the eggplants. Finish the eggplant dish. Let the meat kebabs come to room temperature for 15 minutes. Begin rolling the *naans.* Grill the kebabs. Cover and let rest while grilling the *naans.* Garnish the dishes.

FRESH CHEESE AND TOMATO "SANDWICHES"

Paneer Salade   *dairy*

This recipe is a capricious riff on the Italian caprese salad. You may use two large balls of fresh mozzarella in place of the lemon-flavored cheese if you are short of time. But if you are adventurous, make your own cheese according to the recipe below.

YIELD: 8 TO 12 SANDWICHES

For the fresh lemon-flavored cheese:

6 cups whole milk

2 cups heavy cream

½ cup fresh lemon juice

1 teaspoon ground cumin seeds *or* 1½ teaspoons *chaat masala* (page 5)

1 tablespoon sliced fresh mint or 1 teaspoon dried mint

1 teaspoon salt

Grated peel of 1 lemon

For the salad:

Basil leaves or mixed baby greens/lettuce

1 red onion

2 yellow bell peppers

8 medium **ripe** tomatoes

1 to 2 teaspoons lemon pepper seasoning *or* 1 to 2 teaspoons *chaat masala*

At least a day before serving:

Over low heat, bring milk and cream to a slow simmer, stirring occasionally. Remove from heat and add the lemon juice. Stir for a few minutes until the milk is well curdled and separated from the whey.

Line a colander with a cloth napkin over a large bowl. Drain the milk mixture for 15 minutes. (You can use the liquid whey—high in protein—that drains into the bowl to cook the lentils or in a soup.) Squeeze the curds dry and then knead the drained cheese in a bowl with the spices, salt, and lemon peel. Line a large plate with several folds of newspaper. Unfold a large cloth napkin on top and put the cheese in the middle. Fold the napkin around the cheese. Top with more newspaper and then a large, heavy can. Refrigerate for several hours or overnight.

When ready to serve the salad: Rinse the basil leaves and pat dry. Scatter them on a platter. Cut the onion into the thinnest slices and scatter over the basil leaves. Cut the peppers into strips and scatter on the platter.

Slice the top off the tomatoes with a bread (serrated) knife and reserve. Slice the tomatoes into ½-inch-thick slices. Cut the cheese into slices matching the tomato slices. Put one slice of cheese on top of half of the tomato slices and top with the other tomato slices. Place these "sandwiches" on the platter. Cut the reserved tomato tops into cubes and scatter among the peppers. Sprinkle all with lemon pepper or *chaat masala* and serve a tomato "sandwich" plus some of the vegetables to each guest.

LAMB AND/OR VEGETABLE KEBABS

meat/dairy or vegan   Botee Kebabs

Botee *means "bone," because these delectable pieces of meat strung on the skewer look like they are still on the bone. You may use cherry tomatoes or pieces of marinated zucchini as well as the onions and peppers for your vegetarian guests. Be sure to soak the wooden skewers for at least an hour before using them.*

Toast the poppy seeds and cumin seeds in a dry pan. Grind in a spice grinder. Grind the garlic and ginger in a food processor. Add the hung yogurt or sour cream, salt, garam masala, cayenne pepper, and ground poppy and cumin seeds. Marinate the lamb cubes in the yogurt mixture overnight in the refrigerator in a plastic zip-top bag.

Cut each red or green pepper into eight square pieces, removing the pith and the seeds. Alternate the meat cubes with the onion and pepper pieces on skewers.

Grill or broil for 2 minutes on one side, then brush with *ghee*, turn, and broil for at least 2 more minutes per side. (Well-done kebabs should be broiled for 3 minutes per side.) Place on a platter, garnish, and serve immediately.

For vegan kebabs: Grind the spice mixture, garlic, and ginger and mix with a quarter cup olive oil. Let the mixture rest for an hour. Thread pieces of fresh zucchini, alternating with red or green bell peppers and pearl onions (frozen and thawed) on skewers. Brush with the oil mixture. Sprinkle with sea salt and freshly ground pepper and grill until browned on the edges, but not mushy.

YIELD: 8 TO 10 LONG KEBABS

3 teaspoons white poppy seeds

1 teaspoon ground cumin seeds

3 cloves garlic

2-inch piece ginger

1 cup hung yogurt *(page 6)* or light sour cream

2 teaspoons salt

1½ teaspoons garam masala

½ teaspoon ground cayenne pepper

2½ to 3 pounds lamb from leg, cut into 1½-inch cubes

2 large red or green bell peppers

1 (1 lb.) bag frozen pearl onions, thawed

3 tablespoons *ghee*

Garnishes: 2 teaspoons *chaat masala (page 5)*; ½ cup sliced cilantro; lemon wedges; red onion slices

SYRUPY GINGER-MANGO CHUTNEY

Sont   *vegan*

Sont is dried ginger powder, the only form of ginger we could commonly find in this country until a few years ago. This easy recipe can be made quickly for unexpected guests and tastes a little like tamarind chutney, but has a thinner consistency. The mango powder adds a sweet/sour tang to the heat of the ginger. But if you want it hotter, add a half teaspoon of cayenne pepper.

YIELD: 1½ CUPS

1 cup cold water

½ cup *gurd* or dark brown sugar

1 cup sugar

5 teaspoons dried green mango powder (*amchoor*)

2 teaspoons ground ginger

½ teaspoon cumin seeds

½ teaspoon salt

2 teaspoons paprika

Bring the water, sugars, green mango powder, and ginger to boil in a medium pan. Boil for about 8 minutes or until it becomes a thin syrup.

Toast the cumin seeds in a dry pan and grind (or use ground cumin). Add to the sugar syrup along with the salt and paprika. Cool. This chutney may be stored in the refrigerator for a month.

ROASTED EGGPLANT PURÉE

vegan — Bhartha

Bebeji always made bhartha *with peas, but cousin Birinder prefers it with extra sliced onion. Whichever way you like it, you will love the smoky eggplant taste. The plastic wrap idea came from Alton Brown of Good Eats.*

Preheat the oven or grill to 400°F. Wash and prick the eggplants and place on an oiled baking sheet or grill (indirect heat). Roast for 40 minutes or until soft, turning every 10 to 15 minutes. Remove the eggplants from the oven or grill and allow to cool. Wrap each eggplant in plastic wrap except for green end, cut the green end off and squeeze the flesh into a colander in the sink. Drain for ten minutes. Discard the peel and plastic wrap. (This step may be done the day before and the eggplant pulp refrigerated.)

Meanwhile in a large skillet, sauté the chopped onion in the oil until transparent. Add the garlic and sauté for a few minutes. Add the ginger, stirring. Add the spices and sauté for a few minutes. Add the tomatoes and chile pepper and sauté for a few more minutes.

Add the eggplant pulp and the peas or onion slices. Stir occasionally while cooking for 5 minutes on medium heat. Lower heat, cover tightly, and simmer for another 45 minutes, stirring occasionally. This dish may be refrigerated until serving time and then reheated and garnished. After placing in a serving dish, sprinkle with garam masala and cilantro.

YIELD: 10 ½-CUP SERVINGS

2 medium/large eggplants

1 large red onion, chopped

⅛ cup canola oil

4 cloves garlic, minced

1½-inch piece ginger, finely grated

1½ teaspoons ground cumin seeds

1½ teaspoons ground coriander seeds

¼ teaspoon ground cayenne pepper

3 Roma tomatoes, chopped

1 green chile pepper, seeded and chopped

1½ teaspoons salt

1 cup thawed green peas *or* 1 cup sliced red onion

Garnishes: 1 teaspoon *garam masala (page 5)*; ¼ cup chopped cilantro

GRILLED WHITE FLAT BREADS

Tandoori Naan   *dairy*

*I know that only a tandoor will give me exactly what I want—
a bread that is chewy on the bottom, tender in the middle, and
charred on the top. But this comes very, very close and you can
make it at home!*

*The dough may be wrapped in plastic and refrigerated for a
day or two. But then it will take longer to warm to room
temperature and to rise. Best made on the barbecue grill.*

YIELD: 8 BREADS

1 teaspoon active dry yeast

2 teaspoons sugar

1/2 cup warm water

4 cups all-purpose flour, plus more
for dusting

1 1/2 teaspoons salt

1/2 teaspoon baking powder

2/3 cup hung yogurt *(page 6)* or
Greek yogurt

2 tablespoons melted *ghee or
butter or* canola oil

Coarse cornmeal, if using oven

In a small bowl, stir the yeast and sugar with a 1/2 cup of
warm water until dissolved. Set aside until foamy, about
5 to 10 minutes depending on room temperature.

In a large bowl fluff the flour, salt, and baking powder
with a fork. Then with a wooden spoon, make a well in
the flour. Pour the yeast mixture and yogurt in the center
all at once, and begin stirring in one direction from the
center out, trying to incorporate all the flour.

Oil your hand and begin kneading the dough until elastic—about 5 minutes. The motion is to scrape the dough
from the bottom and sides of the bowl and fold it as you
turn the bowl with your other hand in one direction.
When you are finished, the dough should be in a very
smooth ball and leave your hand and the bowl. Remove
dough from bowl, wash and dry the bowl, and replace the
ball of dough. Roll the dough in some oil or *ghee* and cover with a cloth. Leave in a warm place for 1 1/2 to 3 hours
(depending on room temperature), until the dough is light.

With a dough scraper (if you have it), divide the dough in
half. Take those halves and divide each into four equal
parts. You will have eight balls. Oil your hands with a little oil and roll each ball between your palms until
smooth. Flatten the balls in some loose flour and lightly
flour a flat surface. With a rolling pin, roll out circles of
dough as flat as possible. Put a few of them on a cookie
sheet sprayed with oil or on the clean counter or table.
Cover with clean, slightly damp towel(s) and let rest for 5
minutes as you roll out a few more. Then stretch the
naan into a teardrop shape about 8 inches wide at the
top and 7 inches long.

Three ways to grill the breads:

On the barbecue grill: Preheat the grill to 450°F. Put the stretched breads on indirect heat and close the lid for a minute. Open the lid and move them to direct heat until that side is brown and the top bubbly. Repeat with the other side. Remove from heat and brush with *ghee* or butter. Eat immediately (best) or wrap in a clean tea-towel.

On the griddle: Preheat the griddle to medium-high. Place a *naan* that you have stretched on the griddle. When bubbles form on the top, turn it over. Keep turning until the bread is cooked through and browned in spots. Remove from heat and brush with *ghee* or butter. Continue with remaining dough circles.

In the oven: Remove the racks. Preheat the oven and a baking stone or tiles lining the bottom of the oven to 500°F (will take 30 minutes). Sprinkle the baking stone with coarse cornmeal. Place the *naan* on the stone (you may have room to bake only two at a time). Place in oven and bake until bottoms are cooked (2 to 3 minutes). Turn over and repeat. Remove from the oven with tongs and wrap in a clean towel. Repeat with the other *naans*. If the *naans* have not browned, replace the top rack of the oven, turn on the broiler, turn the *naan* over and broil on the top shelf for less than a minute to ensure it is browned. Keep warm in a clean towel until all are done. Brush with *ghee*. Serve immediately.

Children dressed as the Punj Pyare
in a Baisakhi Day parade.

COOLING MILKSHAKE

Thundeye   *dairy*

Once when we went to our local Indian neighborhood in New Jersey, I tried this drink made with ice cream and nuts. After a little research, I found that in Punjab it is made with lots of cold water and some milk—a cooling blend of nuts, seeds, and flavors. Students drink it for its "brain-boosting" powers before exams, and others for its cooling properties during the Hindu festival of Holi, an ecstatic time when people toss powdered colors at each other, and when intoxicants are sometimes added. If you cannot find the melon seeds, use 2 tablespoons pine nuts or more almonds in their place.

YIELD: 9 8-OUNCE DRINKS

1 teaspoon ground cardamom seeds

1 teaspoon anise or fennel seeds

1 teaspoon black peppercorns

¾ cup sugar

1 cup cold water

3 tablespoons rose petal spread or ¼ teaspoon rose flavor

2 tablespoons blanched almonds

2 tablespoons white poppy seeds

2 tablespoons skinned melon seeds (*optional*)

24 ice cubes

3 cups whole milk

9 scoops vanilla ice cream

Put the cardamom seeds, anise seeds, and peppercorns in a small pan with the sugar and water. Bring to a boil and boil for six minutes to make a thin syrup. Allow to cool and then stir in the rose petal spread. Set aside for 1 hour.

Grind the almonds, poppy seeds, and melon seeds in a spice grinder. Soak in a cup of hot water for 1 hour.

When you are ready to serve the drinks, strain the syrup through a fine strainer and discard the solids.

To make three drinks at a time, smash 6 ice cubes in a folded tea towel. Put them into a blender with a well-stirred ¼ cup of the almond mixture, 1 cup of milk, a scant ¼ cup of syrup, and 3 scoops of ice cream. Blend on "ice-crush." Pour into 3 glasses. Repeat two more times.

SHIKAAR!

A vignette about hunting in Punjab, the sport of kings

THE MUSLIM INVADERS CAME TO INDIA TO conquer, and they did! Their style of dress, poetry, painting, and cooking lives on in so many wonderful ways throughout northern India. The Hindu and Sikh maharajas emulated the Moghul emperors' lifestyle choices—multiple wives, court activities—as well as their forms of recreation and art.

The sensual, jewel-like paintings of the Kangra period have always enchanted me. Magnificently celebrating the joys of the chase—of the couch as well as the hunt, they depict beautiful women in diaphanous silks competing for attention with exuberant tigers and deer leaping across gorgeous landscapes. Hunting was considered a royal pastime by the emperors and the maharajas in most of the world at that time. The gentry, be it in India or England, owned the lands and all of the animals living on their land.

His Highness, dressed in plus-fours, on a shoot in the mountains.

To give you an idea of why, even today, it is the sport of kings: the typical cost of participating in the opening of grouse season in Scotland, "The Glorious 12th" (of August), is £10,000 per day! Elaborate rituals surround the hunt—still seen here in the U.S. when the horsy set rides to the hounds. Jackie Onassis used to come out to Bedminster, New Jersey, very close to where our Sikh temple is located, to gallop across the meadows, bugles blaring and hounds barking!

But traveling across the moors in a Land Rover or tailgating with a picnic basket, even if that basket were to contain smoked salmon and champagne, has nothing on the fabulous hunting trips of the Maharaja of Patiala. Our dear friend Jasbir Kalouria related to us the eyewitness accounts of his father who was an aide-de-camp to His Highness.

On the day of the hunt, cooks were sent ahead to prepare elaborate feasts in so many tents that it looked like an entire village. Special vans made by Rolls Royce opened and locked together, back-to-back. Inside, His Highness Bhupinder Singh and honored

Waiting by a tent while on *shikaar*, a young valet relaxes until called by the maharaja.

Bapuji, Harcharan Singh, my husband's father, around the time of his marriage.

guests would dine on gold service and linens, with crystal chandeliers above. There is a famous incident when the Duke of Windsor brought his wife, Wallis, and his hunting dogs all the way to Patiala to enjoy some sport. Even the elaborate housing for His Highness' animals astounded him: doghouses built of marble, like miniature palaces. When the Duke of Windsor returned to England after one of these hunts, he told his fellow royals, "We may be kings, but they know how to live like kings!"

My father-in-law also enjoyed gathering his friends on his extensive land to hunt partridges and *heeran*, white-tailed deer, although his entourage was certainly not as elaborate. They would set out before daylight far from the village with oiled rifles and servants in tow. Dressed just like the maharajas in plus-fours, woolen trousers that were gathered four inches under the knee, they competed with each other to bag a prized black stag. When my father-in-law brought one back to the village, everyone admired his prowess and enjoyed a great feast. No one was more proud than his only child.

The "Shikaar" Menu

Serve these dishes to your guests and they will feel like royalty! It's a great menu if you wish to impress guests who are vegetarian or non-vegetarian because the rice and squash are substantial enough to be grand entrees. The colors and flavors work well together so that it's "picture perfect" as well as memorably delicious. If you are making the entire meal yourself over several days, you may need two refrigerators to hold the dishes. Or better yet, make this a group project for your first Indian Gourmet Club dinner!

Appetizer: *SALADE CHAILWALI* Mixed Greens with Walnuts and Red Peppers

Main Course: *KHOUMANEE PISTA SHIKAAR* Apricot and Pistachio-Stuffed Game or Pork Loin
(Alternate Main Dish) *BHARIA PAYTHA* Apricot and Pistachio-Stuffed Acorn Squash
KHOUMANEE PISTA MARUBBA Apricot and Pistachio Chutney
SUBZE BIRIYANI Fancy Vegetable-Rice Bake
KAYSAR SAAS Saffron and Nut Cream Sauce
PEELEE DAAL TE PAALAK Yellow Mung Lentils with Spinach *(page 72, variation)*
RANI RAITA Yogurt Salad with Fruit and Nuts
POOREE Puffed Whole-Wheat Breads *(page 109)*

Dessert: *SHAHEE TOOKREE* Royal Bread Pudding

Next Day: KAYSAR MUCHCHEE Saffron Cod

- **Four Days Prior:** Read the recipes from start to finish. Prepare your grocery lists. Buy the spices, dried apricots, nuts, whole milk powder, pumpkin, lentils, and *kewrda* flavor from the Indian market. Make the apricot chutney.

- **Three Days Prior:** Complete your food shopping at the supermarket. Chop and measure the nuts. Cut up the bread for the stuffing.

- **Two Days Prior:** Make the lentils, except for the spinach. Make the stuffing for the meat. Refrigerate all.

- **One-Day Prior:** Bake the *biriyani,* cool and refrigerate. You can make and bake the dessert now or the next day. Brine the roast. Refrigerate all.

- **The Day of:**
  AM: Make the *saas.* Make the *raita.* Make the dessert if you haven't already.
  PM: Bake the roast. Make the salad. Remove the rice from the refrigerator. Clean up.

- **At Serving Time:** Remove the roast (and the pudding) from the oven. Heat the lentils, adding the spinach, and warm the rice and the *saas.* Mix and dress the salad. Garnish the dishes.

MIXED GREENS WITH WALNUTS AND RED PEPPERS

dairy   Salade Chailwali

Chail is a town in the Himalayan foothills made famous by His Highness, Bhupinder Singh. During our travels, as we drove farther into the mountains, we saw great bunches of red peppers hanging to dry from the rooftops in the valleys, their vibrant red beautifully accenting the autumnal colors of the great chinar *trees.*

In a 450°F toaster oven, roast both of the whole red bell peppers, turning several times until charred all over. Cool in a paper bag. Remove the skin and put one of the peppers into a blender with the buttermilk, salt, and pepper and purée until smooth.

Cut the other roasted pepper into strips and toss with the lettuce, walnuts, and onion. Serve with the buttermilk dressing.

YIELD: 8 SERVINGS

For the dressing:

1 red bell pepper

1½ cups buttermilk

½ teaspoon salt

½ teaspoon freshly ground black pepper

For the salad:

1 sweet red pepper

8 cups spring mix lettuces (mesclun), rinsed and drained

1½ cups walnut pieces, toasted

½ medium red onion, finely sliced

Patiala princes on *shikaar* in the Himalayan foothills.

APRICOT AND PISTACHIO-STUFFED GAME OR PORK LOIN

Khoumanee Pista Shikaar   *meat*

Shikaar *means the hunt or the meat from the hunt. If you have access to venison, boar, quail, or Cornish hens, the apricot stuffing would be great with any one of them. As a non-hunter, I use a boneless loin of pork here, but follow your own dietary preferences for a flavorful dish that looks great on the platter, especially if fanned out with saffron* saas (page 190) *drizzled down the center and around it.*

The use of salt and spices to preserve and bring moisture into meat is a very old technique in Punjab. What's new here is using refrigeration, sugar, and water.

YIELD: 8 TO 10 SERVINGS

3½-pound boneless loin of pork or venison, or 4 skinned Cornish hens, or 8 quail

2 tablespoons canola oil

Salt, pepper, and garlic salt or powder, to taste

Garnish: Butter or Boston lettuce cups with a spoonful of chutney in each.

For the brine:

1 cup brown sugar

1 cup salt

1 cup very hot or boiling water

1 tablespoon garam masala

For the stuffing:

2 cups day-old bread, torn into ½-inch pieces

Approximately ½ cup chicken or vegetable broth

1 cup apricot and pistachio chutney *(page 187)*

Make the brine: Dissolve the sugar and salt in the cup of very hot or boiling water. Add the garam masala. Cool. Put the brining mixture in a large zip-top plastic bag or bowl big enough to hold the meat. Place the meat in the bag, add enough cool water to cover, and refrigerate for 8 hours or overnight.

Make the stuffing: Toss the bread with as much broth as you need to moisten the pieces but not make them soggy. Mix in the chutney.

Rinse the brined roast and allow it to come to room temperature for 30 minutes. Preheat the oven to 375°F (450°F if roasting quail).

With a metal skewer or bread knife, make a hole through the center of one end of the loin about halfway through and then try to meet the hole through the other end. With your hand or a dowel, stretch the hole open evenly as much as you can to make a cavity for the stuffing. Fill the cavity with the stuffing from both ends. (If you are using Cornish hens or quail, simply wash out their cavities, dry and then stuff.)

Heat the oil in a roasting pan or Dutch oven large enough to accommodate the meat. Brown the meat on all sides and season to taste. Roast the meat, covered, for 45 to 55 minutes (30 minutes for quail, turning once). The temperature of the meat (not the stuffing) should reach 135°F. Remove from the oven and allow to rest, covered, for

10 minutes. The meat will cook further as it sits and the juices will redistribute. If serving cold the next day, allow it to cool and then wrap tightly and refrigerate.

At serving time, slice the pork or venison roast into 1-inch-thick rounds. (The Cornish hens and quail should be served whole.) Garnish the platter with small lettuce leaves filled with a spoonful of chutney, one for each guest.

The Shikaar menu of stuffed pork loin, biriyani, and apricot chutney.

APRICOT AND PISTACHIO-STUFFED ACORN SQUASH

Bharia Paytha *vegan*

So many people are now vegetarians for ethical or health reasons that it is important to have delicious alternatives to serving meat— especially if it is pork or game.

YIELD: 8 MAIN-DISH SERVINGS

6 acorn squash, halved with seeds removed

Salt and pepper to taste

1 tablespoon oil or butter

2 cups day-old bread, torn into ½-inch pieces

Approximately ½ cup vegetable broth

1 cup apricot and pistachio chutney (page 187)

Pomegranate seeds (*optional*)

Preheat oven to 350°F. Place squash halves on rimmed cookie sheets or a roasting pan. Season with salt and pepper and place in the oven. Pour a little water in the bottom of the pan—up to a half an inch. Cover the squash with foil or a lid and bake for about 1 hour, or until fork tender.

Scoop out the pulp entirely from four squash halves and mash in a bowl with the butter. Toss the bread with as much broth as you need to moisten the pieces but not make them soggy. Mix in the chutney. Mix the stuffing with the mashed pulp.

Score the remaining squash halves and then divide the filling among them. Return to the oven and broil for a few minutes until the stuffing is cooked and brown on top. Sprinkle with pomegranate seeds and serve.

APRICOT AND PISTACHIO CHUTNEY

vegan   Khoumanee Pista Marubba

All kinds of fruits were brought to India by the first Moghul emperors through the Khyber Pass at great expense. A whole melon or even a fresh piece of fruit was considered a luxurious gift for very special guests. Dried fruit was also precious.

This is technically not a chutney, which is made of fresh ingredients, but rather a marubba, *a spicy jam. Great on sandwiches! If you can find unsulfured fruit, use it.*

On a large cutting board, chop the apricots with a sharp, heavy knife into ¼ to ½-inch dice. In a medium pan put 1 cup water and the apricots, sugar, salt, vinegar, and spices and bring to a boil. Cook and stir until the water is absorbed. Turn down the heat to low and add another ½ cup of water. Cover and simmer for 15 minutes. Remove the cardamom pods and cinnamon stick. Add the pistachios. Store in the refrigerator.

YIELD: 3 CUPS

1 pound (about 2¼ cups) dried apricots

½ cup *gurd* or brown sugar

½ teaspoon salt

1 tablespoon malt vinegar or cider vinegar

4 whole black cardamom pods

1 (2½-inch) cinnamon stick

1 tablespoon grated fresh ginger

½ cup chopped pistachios

FANCY VEGETABLE-RICE BAKE

Subze Biriyani   *dairy*

Redolent of spices and nuts, this royal dish is a specialty of the Muslims of Punjab, but is usually made with meat. Since my mother-in-law was a vegetarian, we never mixed meat in our vegetable or rice dishes. This vegetarian version can double as a main course. The flavor improves if made a day ahead, refrigerated, and then reheated.

YIELD: 8 TO 10 SERVINGS

For the vegetable mixture:

¼ cup coarsely chopped cashews plus 1 tablespoon for garnish

¼ cup coarsely chopped almonds plus 1 tablespoon for garnish

¼ cup canola oil or *ghee*

2 cups diced (1-inch cubes) fresh white mushrooms

1 medium yellow onion, chopped

2 cloves garlic

1-inch piece ginger

¼ teaspoon ground turmeric

1 cup diced (1-inch cubes) potato or cauliflower florets

1½ cups diced (1-inch cubes) edible pumpkin (*calabasa*) or carrots

¼ teaspoon dried red pepper flakes

½ cup plain yogurt

1 teaspoon salt

2 tablespoons golden raisins

For the rice:

2 cups basmati rice

1 medium yellow onion, chopped

2 tablespoons *ghee*

1 cinnamon stick

6 cloves

6 whole green cardamom pods

Rinse the rice several times and soak in water for 30 minutes while you prepare the vegetable mixture.

To make vegetable mixture: Toast the cashews and almonds in a dry pan until fragrant. Set aside. Heat a large wok and add the *ghee*. Fry the mushroom cubes over high heat until brown. Set aside. In the same pan in the remaining *ghee*, fry the onions until golden. Grind the garlic and ginger; add them and the turmeric to the onions and fry for a few minutes. Add the potato or cauliflower and pumpkin or carrot and stir-fry for about 4 minutes. Stir in the red pepper flakes, yogurt, and salt, cover, and cook over low heat for 2 minutes. Mix in the raisins, nuts, and mushrooms. Set aside.

To make the rice: Drain the rice well. In a large saucepan, brown the chopped onion in the *ghee*. Add the whole spices and fry for 1 minute. Add the well-drained rice and stir-fry for a minute or two. Add the mace and salt. Add 3½ cups of boiling water. Cover the pot and simmer for just 15 minutes. Remove whole spices, stir, cover, and set aside.

To make the sauce: In a small, dry pan heat the saffron for 1 minute. Pulverize between your fingers, then put back into the small pan and heat with the cream until dissolved. Stir in the remaining sauce ingredients. Set aside.

Preheat the oven to 350°F.

To assemble the dish: Grease a 10x10-inch baking/serving dish with lid with non-stick spray. Taste the rice for seasoning. Taste the vegetables for seasoning. Spread a layer of half of the rice in the casserole, then add a layer of all of the vegetables, and top with the remaining rice. Carefully pour the sauce completely over the surface of the rice. Cover the dish tightly with aluminum foil, and then put on the lid as tightly as possible so the rice will finish steaming in the oven. Bake for 30 minutes in an electric oven or for 40 minutes in a gas oven. This dish may be served immediately but it improves if cooled, refrigerated, and reheated the next day.

2 whole black cardamom pods

2 bay leaves

2 pinches mace or freshly grated nutmeg

2½ teaspoons salt

For the sauce:

½ teaspoon saffron threads

½ cup heavy or light cream

¾ cup whole milk

¼ cup plain yogurt

¼ teaspoon salt

1 teaspoon *kewrda* flavor (*optional*)

SAFFRON AND NUT CREAM SAUCE

Kaysar Saas   *dairy*

Cream sauces and the use of nuts and dried fruit were a part of the royal chef's repertoire, a legacy of the great cuisine brought to Punjab by their Moghul conquerors. This one, fragrant with precious saffron, is adapted from a recipe by Devika Teja, and may be served on the meat, squash, or rice dishes in this menu.

YIELD: 2 CUPS

Pinch of saffron

1 tablespoon boiling water

⅓ cup chopped unsalted pistachios

⅓ cup blanched unsalted almonds

1 tablespoon *ghee*

½ teaspoon ground cardamom seeds

1 teaspoon salt

2 cups half and half

In a small, dry pan heat the saffron for 1 minute. Pulverize between your fingers, and then put it into a small ramekin with the boiling water.

Grind the pistachios and almonds together. In a medium saucepan, melt the *ghee* and add the nut mixture. Heat but do not brown the nuts. Stir in the cardamom, salt, and saffron mixture and then the half and half. Stir constantly over medium heat until the sauce thickens enough to coat a spoon, but do not allow to boil. Remove from the heat and pour into a gravy boat. Cover with plastic wrap and allow to rest for 20 minutes before serving. This sauce can be refrigerated and then reheated.

YOGURT SALAD WITH FRUIT AND NUTS

dairy   Rani Raita

In the past, walnuts, apples, and grapes were brought long distances from the cooler mountain areas, so only the very rich could afford them. These three were the only fruits my husband remembers tasting when he was a child in the village. By the way, nuts are considered "fruits" in Punjab. This raita is especially enjoyed by children. If they prefer it less spicy, just remove their portion before adding the masala.

Toast the walnuts; cool and chop coarsely. Reserve a spoonful for the garnish.

Beat the yogurt with a whisk until smooth. Add the salt, sugar, and spices and beat again. Add the grapes, apple, and toasted walnuts. Refrigerate if not serving immediately. At serving time, sprinkle the yogurt with the reserved nuts.

YIELD: 8 ³/₄-CUP SERVINGS

½ cup walnuts

4 cups (32 ounces) plain yogurt

½ teaspoon salt (*optional*)

1½ tablespoons sugar

½ teaspoon toasted cumin seeds, ground

½ teaspoon *chaat masala (page 5)* or *pani puri masala*

1 cup halved seedless grapes

1 large apple, cored and diced into ½-inch cubes

ROYAL BREAD PUDDING

Shahee Tookree _dairy_

My Dad was a prince of a man and his favorite dessert was a simple bread pudding with vanilla flavor. This royally rich version of bread pudding, however, is exotic with saffron, nuts, and kewrda _flavor. It is still a very practical dessert since it is easy to prepare and travels well to parties._

YIELD: 9 SERVINGS

1½ loaves day-old semolina or French bread

1¼ cups whole milk

2 pinches saffron

¼ teaspoon ground cardamom seeds

¾ cup sugar

½ cup heavy cream

½ cup whole milk powder (_mava_)

Few drops _kewrda_ or 1 teaspoon vanilla extract

¼ cup _ghee_

1½ tablespoons coarsely chopped unsalted almonds

1½ tablespoons coarsely chopped unsalted pistachios

Cut the crusts off the bread and slice into 1-inch-thick slices. Set aside. Carefully heat the milk in a medium pan almost to boiling. Crush the saffron and add to the hot milk. Add the cardamom and sugar, stirring until sugar dissolves. Add the heavy cream. Remove from the heat and whisk in the milk powder and _kewdra_ or vanilla extract.

Preheat the oven to 350°F. Melt the _ghee_ and pour evenly to coat a 10x10-inch ovenproof glass casserole. Put the bread slices in the _ghee_ and quickly turn them once to distribute the _ghee_ evenly on both sides of the bread and set them on a cookie sheet. Put them in the oven until they are lightly brown on both sides. (You may need to turn the slices to ensure they brown evenly.) Remove from the oven.

Neatly overlap the slices in the 10x10-inch casserole. Pour the milk mixture over the bread. Allow the bread to rest for 5 minutes, absorbing the milk. Turn the slices over and allow to rest another 5 minutes or until most of the milk is absorbed.

Bake in the oven for 15 minutes. Sprinkle the nuts on the bread. Return to the oven for 5 or more minutes, until the pudding is fairly firm. Remove from oven. Serve warm or cold.

NEXT-DAY
SAFFRON COD

fish   Kaysar Muchchee

If you have leftover kaysar saas *(Saffron and Nut Cream Sauce), this is an elegant use for it. Actually, this fish dish could also replace the meat as the main course for this menu.*

Preheat the broiler. Dry the rinsed cod between paper towels, especially if it has been thawed. Salt and pepper both sides. Place the fish on an oiled broiling tray and spread the *kaysar saas* over the fish. Sprinkle with coconut. Broil until the sauce and coconut browns and the fish flakes. Do not overcook.

YIELD: 1 SERVING

5-ounce portion boneless cod, with skin if possible, rinsed

Salt and pepper to taste

1½ tablespoons cold *kaysar saas* *(page 190)*

1½ tablespoons grated, unsweetened coconut *(optional)*

REFRESHING TWIST

The problems and advantages of having two cultures

Sitting between me and Bebeji on a rope bed in the center of the courtyard, Maiji is serene as she catches the warmth of the sun.

AS WE SAT IN THE WINTER SUN IN THE COURT-yard of the village where my mother-in-law grew up, I listened to a story that rivaled any fairy tale. Across from me, lounging on a rope bed was *Maiji*, my mother-in-law's paternal aunt. Her face was a lined, weathered map of the ages. Her presence magnetic, an intriguing mixture of confidence and contentment—or was it resignation? At nearly ninety years old, she was amazingly agile and witty. Her father had saved her, I heard. She had been buried alive after she was born and frantically dug up by her father just in time. "What?" I asked, rather rudely. What could possibly make a grandmother do such a horrible thing? It was her grandmother who had put a sweet in her mouth, buried her, and told her to "go back and send a brother!" I learned that most girls need dowries when they grow up even though the practice has been outlawed since 1961. Boys bring dowries to the family. Girls were a liability for that reason. What was unusual was that her father had saved her. Usually the fathers did not "wake up" in time or were convinced of the utility of such a practice. Punjab has one of the highest ratios of boys to girls on earth. In the old days it was infanticide of girls. Today, although against the law since 1994, it is the practice of selective abortion after ultrasound that keeps the ratio high. And the bias against women continues in the practice of bride abandonment and, less often, bride burning, which are the result of greedy families who are never satisfied with just one dowry.

When we returned from India, I had an opportunity to understand how cultural blindness is not confined to one country or region. The first time we took *Bebeji* to the beach at Sandy Hook, I noticed horror on her face. She was traumatized by the nearly naked bodies of teenagers canoodling in the sand—in public. I realized how we had become used to such goings on. We barely pay attention. It dawned on me then that all cultures have their traps. One's own culture seems more attractive of course, but every one has dangerous downsides. All of us become too comfortable with what we grow up with; cruelty or arrogance and even degradation may be accepted as normal—if it is part of daily life. Having some objectivity about social mores is a great asset. So I feel very lucky to have had a firm grounding in two cultures—American and Indian. An opportunity to look within as I raised children—how I approached a problem, what I used to solve it, and what I took away in the learning experience.

Yet my own children as well as the children I taught at the temple were sometimes painfully caught in the clash of two worlds. So many of them felt that they did not fully belong to either the Indian community or to the American culture. Like children everywhere, many thought they needed to "fit in" to have friends. And their parents, like parents everywhere, were more comfortable replicating their own childhood patterns. For all of us, especially immigrants, the "mother country" may become frozen in time, an idealized snapshot of another era. Yet out of the clash of cultures in the new world, the "now," a unique perspective may develop; the ability to listen to one's inner conscience and inner truth rather than slavishly follow tradition or fashion. The power of a human being to actually choose the best in each situation—what a refreshing twist!

The "Refreshing Twist" Menu

Cooking from a double perspective enriches everyone. Here is a menu that revels in fusion, either because of the method by which it is made, or by mixing the standard flavors of two or more countries.

"Fusion" was the buzzword when we took Uncle Gurmit and Auntie Surindera to the Tabla restaurant in New York City not long after it opened. We thrilled to the dishes of Chef Floyd Cardoz, originally of Goa and Bombay, who masterfully combines the spices of India with European ingredients and techniques.

The symbiotic relationship of the British Raj to India also produced lasting culinary effects in both India and Britain. The British may have colonized India two centuries ago; but certainly the Indians have conquered the palates of the British in this century.

I invite you to make your own fusion dishes. It's great to get the creative juices flowing and it is rewarding on so many sensual levels.

Appetizer: *MATTHIAN* Homemade Savory Crackers
               ARDOO CHA Ginger-Peachy Iced Tea

Main Course: *MURGA PUDEENA* Minted Roast Chicken
               KHATEE MITHEE BUNDGOBI Sweet and Sour Cabbage with Carrots
               ALOO DUM Smartly Spiced Potatoes in Yogurt Sauce

Dessert: *CHAI RABAREE* Tea-Flavored Creamy Dessert

- **Four or More Days Prior:** Read each recipe from beginning to end. Make sure you have all the spices, ginger, *gurd*, *chapatti* flour, tamarind paste, poppy seeds, malt vinegar, almonds, garlic, and onions on hand. If not, buy them from the Indian market.

- **Two Days Prior:** Buy the remaining ingredients from the supermarket. Bake the crackers and store in an airtight container.

- **One-Day Prior:** Brine the chicken and refrigerate. Make the dessert and refrigerate. Make the garam masala *(page 4)* for the potatoes.

- **The Day of:**
  AM: Turn on the exhaust fan and make the cabbage dish. Make the tea. Chop the herbs for the garnishes and the chicken stuffing. Slice the lemons.
  PM: Make the potatoes. Two and a half hours before serving the chicken, remove it from the refrigerator and rinse. Set aside for 30 minutes for it to come to room temperature while you prepare the stuffing. Stuff and roast the chicken. Clean up. Arrange the crackers. Set up the glasses for tea. Put the superfine sugar in a pretty bowl.

- **At Serving Time:** Reheat the vegetables. Make the gravy while the chicken rests.

HOMEMADE SAVORY CRACKERS

Matthian   *dairy*

Whenever we sponsored an akhand paath, *a continuous reading of the holy book (the* Guru Granth Sahib*), my mother-in-law would fry up an enormous batch of crackers so that the volunteers reading for one or two hours during the night would have something to snack on with a cup of tea before they started. During the day and evening we always had a vegetarian meal ready for them when they finished. These crackers are rich, but baked, not fried.*

YIELD: 32 2½-INCH PIECES

2 cups *chapatti* flour

1 teaspoon salt

1 teaspoon coarsely ground black pepper

1 teaspoon carom seeds (*ajwain*) or caraway seeds

2 teaspoons dried fenugreek (*methi*) leaves or fresh or dried dill

1½ sticks (12 tablespoons) unsalted cold butter or *ghee*

Set out a medium bowl filled with ice and a cup of water.

Combine the flour, salt, pepper, carom seeds, and fenugreek in a large bowl. Cut in the cold butter using a pastry cutter or two knives until it is like coarse meal. One tablespoon at a time, sprinkle the ice water on the flour mixture, fluffing it with a fork after each addition until it sticks loosely together (about 7 tablespoons). Do not over mix. Gingerly form the dough into a ball and cover with plastic wrap. Refrigerate for 20 minutes.

Preheat the oven to 450°F. Working quickly, lightly flour a flat surface and your rolling pin. Roll out the dough about ⅛ inch thick. Using a pizza or ravioli cutter or a 2½-inch-wide glass, cut out squares or circles. Place them on a baking sheet an inch apart and bake until light brown, about 10 minutes.

GINGER-PEACHY ICED TEA

vegan   Ardoo Cha

The British left citified Punjabis with an afternoon tea drinking habit—but it must be drunk boiling hot. Adding ice and peach flavor are the American-style twists to the masala cha *we drank there. I created this recipe for our daughter Sheila's baby shower and like it because the ginger and the peach flavor come through even if no additional sugar is added. It's strong enough to hold up to ice. In American parlance, "ginger-peachy" means "Everything is perfect!" P.S. She had twin boys!*

Bring the water to a boil in a large saucepan. Remove from the heat and steep all the teabags in the water, covered tightly, for 6 minutes. Squeeze the teabags and discard. Cool the tea in the refrigerator.

Extract the juice of the ginger by grating it on a microplane or other very fine grater over a bowl. Remove the pulp into a clean cloth napkin or handkerchief and squeeze over the bowl to extract more of the juice. Add the ginger juice to the tea. Stir the peach slices with their juice into a pitcher of the cooled tea.

Fill a glass with ice and a few peach slices. Pour the cooled tea over the ice. Add a slice of lemon and/or a sprig of mint. Guests may stir in their own sugar.

YIELD: 8 TO 10 TALL GLASSES

8 cups cold water

6 orange-pekoe teabags

8 peach-flavored teabags

3-inch piece ginger

4 very ripe fresh peaches* or 1 (15-ounce) can sliced peaches in juice

8 lemon slices (*optional*)

8 mint sprigs (*optional*)

2 to 3 teaspoons per person superfine sugar (*optional*)

*If using fresh peaches, bring six cups of water to a boil. Blanch the peaches in the boiling water for 30 seconds. Remove the peaches, cool immediately in a large bowl filled with ice water, peel, and slice.

MINTED ROAST CHICKEN

Murga Pudeena *meat*

There are three layers of flavor in this delectable dish which uses brining, a modern technique for bringing more flavor and juiciness directly into the meat. Usually poultry is prepared in India without the sugar and the skin; but by stuffing aromatics under the skin, I've added another twist. The third layer is more traditional—salt and spices sprinkled on the outside before roasting. All together now, give three cheers for a grand presentation, fragrant and meltingly tender!

YIELD: 8 SERVINGS

6½ to 7-pound roaster or capon chicken or two 4½-pound chickens

For brining:

1 cup dark brown sugar (*gurd*)

2 to 4 small dried red chile peppers

3 whole black cardamom pods

4 whole cloves

1 tablespoon black peppercorns

1 cinnamon stick

1 star anise

¾ cup kosher salt, plus more as needed

For stuffing under skin:

1 or 2 lemons, or ¼ cup lemon pickle *(page 55)*

1-inch piece ginger

2 cloves garlic

½ cup finely sliced mint leaves

½ cup finely sliced cilantro leaves

3 tablespoons softened *ghee* or olive oil

¼ teaspoon salt (leave out if using lemon pickle)

To brine: The day before serving the chicken, put the *gurd* in a medium pot with a few cups of water and the spices and bring to a boil, dissolving the sugar. Stir the salt into the solution until it dissolves. Cool completely in the refrigerator. Rinse the chicken thoroughly. Put into a container large enough to immerse the chicken, but small enough to fit in the fridge or into a cooler. Mix a quart of cold water into the cooled brine and pour it over the chicken. Weigh the chicken down with a heavy pot or plate. Add enough water to cover the chicken completely. Refrigerate for four hours or overnight or put in a cooler for four hours with plenty of ice packs inside the container. (Be sure to wash the ice packs and the cooler with a soap solution when you finish.)

To stuff: Preheat the oven to 375°F. Squeeze the juice of half a lemon into a food processor and adding a quarter of the peel or use the preserved lemon pickle. Add the ginger and garlic and grind. Add the mint and cilantro leaves. Mix in the softened *ghee* or oil and salt.

Drain and rinse the chicken. With your hand, carefully loosen the skin on the breast and around the legs and thighs, moving from under the breast to the leg, then around the thighs to the back. You may need to carefully use kitchen scissors or a small knife to loosen the skin, but try not to break it. Starting under the back of the thigh, push the stuffing in under the loosened skin over the entire body back to front until all is used up, patting it evenly. Put the other lemon half into the cavity.

To roast: In a small bowl mix the garam masala with the melted *ghee*. Place the chicken on a rack and brush with the *ghee* mixture. Sprinkle with kosher salt and freshly ground pepper and loosely tent with foil. Roast for 40 minutes. Brush again with the remaining *ghee* mixture. Uncover, and increase the oven temperature to 425°F. Roast for another 30 minutes until the skin is browned or until the breast registers 170°F and the leg joint is loose. Remove from the oven.

Allow chicken to rest for 15 minutes before carving. The scrapings from the pan and the juices may be strained, brightened with a little lemon juice, warmed, and served in a gravy boat or over the carved chicken.

For roasting:

1 teaspoon garam masala

2 tablespoons melted *ghee* or olive oil

1 tablespoon kosher salt

1 teaspoon ground black pepper

SWEET AND SOUR CABBAGE WITH CARROTS

Khatee Mithee Bundgobi

vegan

I modified this recipe from one my friend Narinder Bhatia sent to me and it is unusual because of the absence of onions and garlic, those most popular members of the Punjabi trinity of aromatics. Its flavors best resonate with Chinese dishes for a delectable fusion. Once you have the ingredients lined up, and I recommend you do this before you start, it cooks very quickly.

YIELD: 8 SERVINGS

1 large green or savoy cabbage

¼ cup canola oil

1½ teaspoons whole black mustard seeds

2 tablespoons ginger slices, cut into fine "matchsticks"

1½ teaspoons turmeric

2 teaspoons ground coriander seeds

½ teaspoon freshly ground black pepper

2 pinches ground cayenne pepper (*optional*)

2½ teaspoons garam masala

1½ teaspoons salt

2 large carrots, peeled and coarsely grated

1 to 2 teaspoons malt or cider vinegar

½ cup *Laxmi*® jarred tamarind concentrate (Do not use dark concentrate.)*

2 to 3 tablespoons *gurd**, brown sugar, or honey (not vegan)

Trim and core the cabbage and finely slice it. Heat a large wok and then heat the oil. Add the mustard seeds and stir until they begin to pop. Immediately add the slivered ginger and stir-fry for 1 minute and then add the rest of the spices and the salt.

Add half the cabbage and stir-fry over medium-high heat until it begins to wilt. Then continue to add additional cabbage until it is all wilted. Stir-fry for another 3 minutes, then lower the heat, add the carrots and vinegar and cover and simmer for 5 minutes. Add the tamarind and sweetener of your choice and stir-fry again for 4 minutes. At this point you should taste for the balance of sweet, sour, salty, and hot and make adjustments as you like. Also check for the way you like your vegetables—tender/crisp or well-cooked and continue cooking or remove from the stove as necessary and serve.

*See *imlee* and *gurd* in the food glossary.

SMARTLY SPICED POTATOES IN YOGURT SAUCE

dairy   Aloo Dum

The royal technique of cooking in a tightly sealed pot called dum puhkt *or "sealed breath" was imported to Punjab from elsewhere in India. The potatoes were first fried in* ghee *and then cooked in a pot with a lid sealed tight with dough and set over a slow fire. Live coals were placed on the flat lid. In my estimation, the extra step of frying the potatoes adds little (except to your waistline), so I left it out. And a good ovenproof pot with tight-fitting lid eliminates the need for dough, but develops enough steam to cook them. The fragrance from freshly ground spices makes this dish unforgettable, so do try to grind your own!*

Bring a large pot of water to a boil. Add the potatoes and boil for about 15 minutes. Make sure the potatoes are just cooked by inserting a fork that enters somewhat easily, but the potatoes should not burst or become mushy. Drain and set aside to cool.

To make the dry spice mixture: Remove the seeds from the black cardamom pods by smashing in a towel with a rolling pin. Have the spices lined up, measured, and in order on a sheet of paper. Toast them in a dry frying pan in this order: peppercorns, black cardamom seeds, green cardamom seeds, cloves, coriander seeds, and cumin seeds, and grind in a spice or coffee grinder. Add the nutmeg and set aside.

To make the paste mixture: In a small dry skillet, toast the almonds and finely grind. Set aside. Then toast the coconut and poppy seeds the same way until fragrant. Allow to cool and then finely grind in a spice grinder. Set aside. In a food processor, grind the garlic and ginger. Add the dry spice mixture, the almonds, and 2 to 4 tablespoons of water and grind to a paste. Combine the paste with the ground coconut and poppy seeds and set aside.

Preheat the oven to 425°F.

YIELD: 8 SERVINGS

3 pounds (24) small new potatoes, about the same size

For the dry spice mixture:*

2 black cardamom pods

10 black peppercorns

¼ teaspoon green cardamom seeds

6 whole cloves

2 tablespoons whole coriander seeds

2 teaspoons whole cumin seeds

2 pinches freshly grated nutmeg

For the paste mixture:

2 tablespoons almonds

3 tablespoons unsweetened coconut

2 teaspoons white poppy seeds

5 cloves garlic, sliced

1-inch piece ginger, sliced

(continued on next page)

SMARTLY SPICED
POTATOES IN YOGURT SAUCE *(continued)*

For the sauce:

½ cup minced yellow onion

2 tablespoons *ghee*

½ teaspoon ground turmeric

¼ teaspoon ground cayenne
   pepper

2 teaspoons salt

1¼ cups plain yogurt

Garnishes: Sliced almonds; 2
   tablespoons sliced cilantro

To make the sauce: Sauté the onions in the *ghee* in a medium, ovenproof heavy-bottomed pot with a tight fitting lid. Add the turmeric, cayenne pepper, and salt. Cook for a few seconds, and then add the spice paste. Beat the yogurt with a fork until smooth. Add half to the pot, cooking and stirring to reduce the liquid for 5 minutes. Remove from the heat and stir in the rest of the yogurt.

Peel the cooked potatoes. Prick them all over, but do not break them and add to the pot and coat carefully with the sauce. Cover the dish very tightly. (You may wish to cover with foil and then with the lid to make a tighter seal.) Put into the 425°F oven and "steam" this dish for 20 minutes. Remove from oven and allow to rest for 10 minutes, still covered, before putting the potatoes in a heated serving dish and garnishing with the sliced almonds and cilantro.

---

* You may substitute 2 tablespoons commercially prepared garam masala for the first six spices listed for the dry spice mixture on page 201.

TEA-FLAVORED CREAMY DESSERT

dairy   Chai Rabaree

In Punjab, where milk is abundant and refrigeration scarce, cooks preserve the milk by slowly reducing it until it is thick and grainy while adding the sugar. My recipe is a smooth riff on that plain dessert. Desserts are called "sweet dish" pronounced "swedish" all over Punjab. It took me several weeks before I realized that they were not talking about some exotic import from Europe!

In a small bowl, soak the gelatin in a few spoonfuls of the milk. Set aside.

In a large, heavy pot, bring the rest of the milk and the cream to a boil (being careful it does not boil over). Lower the heat and add the teabags and the *masala*. Simmer until reduced by half.

Remove the teabags and add the sweetened condensed milk. Bring to a boil, stirring. Mix a few spoonfuls of the hot milk mixture with the gelatin to completely dissolve it, and then stir it into the pot.

Pour the pudding into ramekins or a pretty bowl and cool completely for three hours. Garnish before serving.

YIELD: 8 ½-CUP SERVINGS

2 packets Knox gelatin*

1 quart whole milk

2 cups heavy cream

2 black tea bags

½ teaspoon powdered tea
    *masala***

1 (14-ounce) can sweetened con-
    densed milk

Optional garnishes: whipped
    cream rosettes; ground
    cinnamon

*Some religions restrict or forbid the use of gelatin. If you can't use gelatin, cook the milk mixture in the microwave for another 6 minutes. Cut an 8-ounce package of reduced-fat cream cheese into small cubes. Put into a blender and cover with some hot milk mixture. Blend until smooth. Mix it into the rest.

**If you do not have a commercial tea *masala*, it can be made by boiling a cup of water in a small pan with a knob of sliced ginger, a few fennel seeds, cloves, peppercorns, and a ¼ teaspoon green cardamom seeds until the liquid is reduced to ¼ cup; strain, discard solids and then add this liquid to the milk mixture.

FAST!

Hospitality is in our blood

THERE ARE ALL KINDS OF LEGACIES. MOST PEOPLE THINK OF LEAVING MONEY OR material goods to their children. I hope that *Bebeji* and I will have left our love of family and friends and especially our sense of hospitality. We both loved to entertain guests. And it was a good thing! The staff at the high school where I worked as a counselor used to marvel at the number of houseguests we enjoyed, sometimes for months at a time. We had eleven places to sleep and many times they were all taken. That meant we learned to do things quickly (not always my forte) and imperfectly (not something my mother-in-law was always comfortable with). But we managed. Actually, we became a good team over the years even though our styles were very different. Maybe because of that!

Learning to be hospitable under all conditions in the U.S. was comparatively easy for her. She was used to a much more difficult time caring for guests—a constant occurrence, since she married into a household in Bhatinda, an important railway junction. In those days there were no hotels, nor any tradition of restaurants outside the largest cities. Travelers stopped at the homes of relatives or the relatives of relatives or friends of friends. This was probably due to the influence of the caste system and the fear of *jooth* or uncleanliness. And although *Babaji*, her father-in-law, made it clear that he did not wish to welcome travelers after nine at night, sometimes it was unavoidable. There were no phones, no stoves, and no refrigerators. So when guests would show up at any time of the day or night expecting a simple meal and a bed, it meant starting a fire on the *chula*, the hollow brick stove covered with mud and cow dung (considered purifying), to make a quick potato *subze*, kneading the dough, and rolling out a few fresh *phulkas*. Crouching on her haunches, with one hand she would feed the dry cotton sticks used for fuel to the bottom of the stove, and with the other she would adjust her heavy shawl from the cold. There were no handles on the lids of the pots. They were covered with a flat brass plate, difficult to pick up with tongs, but good for holding hot coals when a dish needed to be "baked." The rules of cleanliness determined that the one who prepared the food did not taste it, so *Bebeji* was very, very good at guessing how much spice or salt went into a dish; it was always perfectly seasoned. In Bhatinda, most travelers stayed overnight and spread their own bedrolls that they had carried with them on the train onto all-purpose cots, *munjas*, with heavy, woven jute rope stretched and tied across—surprisingly comfortable.

Beegee **Surjit Kaur Auntie** and *Bhanji* **Mohinder Kaur**, two of Bebeji's angels in her last days.

Guests in India were not expected to pitch in. But in the U.S., we did welcome any help we could get from our guests. I learned to prepare some dishes from them. When *Beegee* Surjit Kaur Auntie came, she always made the best *phulkas*, paper thin and delicate. No one was her match. She would also sew Punjabi suits for us, especially when *Bebeji* was having more physical difficulties and had to use the oxygen machine. *Bhanji* Mohinder Kaur was our angel who came all the way from California to care for and give companionship to *Bebeji* in her last years. Women who lived with us over the years became like our mothers and sisters, and many young people—eighteen at last count—became like our own children.

Now my children are continuing the legacy. Raji and her husband David are known for their good food and hospitality. Our son, Paul, and his wife, Nancy, hosted a grand *sangeet* at their house for his sister Sheila's wedding. And Jonathan, Sheila's husband, is an accomplished cook. It is comforting to know that even though all of them lead busy lives, they still extend the warmth of family hospitality.

The "Fast!" Menu

When unexpected guests call, it's nice to be able to make food without too much fuss. Fast—yes, but delicious and healthful, too. Fast food does not have to be found in cardboard. You can rustle up a magnificent meal for a hungry crowd with some help from the supermarket and some practice. Some of the dishes in this menu are what I would call Indian-American fusion. My favorite chef, Floyd Cardoz of Tabla restaurant in Manhattan, is the master of Indian-French fusion—an inspiration!

Babaji's granddaughter-in-law, graceful Surjit Kaur, boils tea on the chula much as Bebeji did before she left for the U.S.

Appetizer:	*SUBZE SHORBA* Squash Soup with Chutney Swirl
Main Course:	*RAMAAS CUTLAS* Broiled Salmon Strips
	MUTTER PANEER Curried Peas with Cheese
	LAAL QUILLA SALADE Red Fort Salad
	MASALA DOUBLE ROTEE Indian-Style Garlic Bread
Dessert:	*AMB BURFEE* Mango Fudge

- **Stock Up!** Having a pantry replenished regularly with certain staples always goes a long way toward being prepared for emergencies. Dried lentils, canned beans, beets, mandarin oranges, tomatoes, soup, mango purée, jarred chutney, whole-wheat flour, *tandoori* paste, and dry milk should be on the shelf. Frozen peas, salmon strips, nuts, and fried paneer should be in the freezer. Fresh lemons, onions, garlic, ginger, potatoes, and cilantro are also wonderful staples. Restock the spices when running low. A few things, like pitas or *naans,* can always be quickly picked up at the corner market. But it is difficult to buy exotic spices at the last minute.

  Read the recipes from start to finish before you need to make them at the last minute. Prepare your emergency grocery lists.

- **One-Day Prior (if given notice):** Buy the lettuce, grape tomatoes, beets, orange, onion, soup, nuts, salmon strips, garlic bread, chutney, and cream from the supermarket. Make the salad dressing and refrigerate.

- **The Day of:**
  AM: Make the mango fudge. Marinate the salmon.
  PM: Make the peas and cheese. Make the salad. Sprinkle the spices on the bread.

- **At Serving Time:** Heat the soup. Grill the salmon and heat the garlic bread in a warm oven. Garnish the dishes.

SQUASH SOUP WITH CHUTNEY SWIRL

Subze Shorba _vegan_

This, I believe, is the fastest recipe in the book. It could not be easier! I love garlic pickle masala in cream of tomato soup, too. You could replace it with achar masala _(page 24)._

YIELD: 8 CUPS

2 quart-size cartons squash soup or 4 smaller cartons

1 to 2 teaspoons garlic pickle _masala*_ or 1 teaspoon ground cumin

Garnishes: mint chutney; a swirl of sour cream or plain yogurt mixed with chopped cilantro

Mix the soup and the _masala_ in a medium saucepan and warm over medium heat until steaming. Pour into individual teacups and swirl in some mint chutney or sour cream.

*This is a red color and comes in cellophane packets at the Indian markets.

BROILED SALMON STRIPS

fish/dairy   Ramaas Cutlas

*This is a fast take on the old standby—*tandoori-*style. This recipe can easily be halved, or I make fish salad for lunch with the leftovers. We eat salmon at least once a week these days. But you may substitute other firm-fleshed fish. It's so good, and good for you.*

Rinse the fish and pat dry with paper towels. Depending on the type of fish, cut it into portions or use fillets. Sprinkle the lemon juice on the fish. Mix the salt, yogurt, *achar masala* or *tandoori* paste, and ginger and spread lightly on the fish. Marinate for at least 10 minutes.

Cover the broiler tray with foil. Preheat the oven and broiler tray on the broil setting. Spray the foil and the fish (skin-side up if not skinless) with non-stick spray and broil the fish for 4 to 6 minutes depending on the thickness of the filets. Turn and sprinkle with the green onions. Return to the broiler for 2 to 3 more minutes. Do not over cook.

YIELD: 8 SERVINGS

2½ pounds boneless salmon, or filets of tilapia or flounder

Juice of 2 lemons

1 teaspoon sea salt

⅓ cup plain yogurt

2 tablespoons *achar masala (page 24)** or jarred *tandoori* paste

2 teaspoons grated ginger

Garnish: 2 scallions, finely sliced

Kiratpur at the headwaters of the Sutlej, one of the five rivers of Punjab and Bebeji's last resting place.

* Use half the amount or less if using a commercial pickling spice blend.

CURRIED PEAS WITH CHEESE

Mutter Paneer   *dairy*

Mutter Paneer *is our son-in-law David's favorite Indian dish. It is one that can be made very quickly for guests—if you have fried up the paneer in advance and have it in the freezer. If you prefer not to fry the cheese, that is also perfectly acceptable. In India, this dish was reserved for very important guests. Traditionally, there is no one more important than your son-in-law!*

To make the cheese at home, follow the recipe on page 216. Or you may purchase ready-made paneer at the Indian market.

YIELD: 8 ½-CUP SERVINGS

2 medium yellow onions, chopped

¼ cup canola oil

3 cloves garlic, minced

1½-inch piece ginger, minced or grated

1½ teaspoons ground turmeric

1 tablespoon ground coriander seeds

2 teaspoons whole or ground cumin seeds

1 teaspoon garam masala

2 medium tomatoes, chopped

1 can (8 ounces) tomato sauce (*optional*)

1 bag (24 ounces) frozen peas, partially thawed

2 teaspoons salt

2 cups *paneer* cubes (¾-inch)

¼ cup cilantro, sliced

In a large skillet, sauté the onions in the oil until transparent. Add the garlic and sauté for 1 more minute and then add the ginger. Add the turmeric, coriander seeds, cumin seeds, and 1 teaspoon garam masala and sauté for a few minutes, until the onions are lightly browned. Add the tomatoes, tomato sauce, and 1 cup of water. Cook over medium heat, stirring, until the oil rises to the top, then add the peas. Simmer, covered, for 15 minutes or until the peas are barely cooked.

Add the *paneer* and another cup of water and stir carefully. Simmer, uncovered, for another 10 minutes. (This dish should have a nice gravy and the peas should be green.)

Serve sprinkled with a pinch more garam masala and the cilantro.

Note: If you do not have all the spices, substitute 2 tablespoons curry powder for the turmeric, coriander seeds, and cumin seeds.

RED FORT SALAD

Laal Quilla Salade

The most famous red sandstone fort is in New Delhi, but Bhatinda has its own brick fortress built in an unusual crenulated (wavy) style. It has been there in some form or other for well over a thousand years.

This beautiful salad, with the addition of halved boiled eggs would make a great light lunch. I've used a palette of shades of red just as they are used together in the lovely Moghul paintings to denote festivity and life.

Crisp and full of flavor, the Red Fort Salad will protect your health.

For the dressing:

1 teaspoon honey

2 tablespoons raspberry vinegar

1 teaspoon minced garlic

¼ cup olive oil

½ teaspoon salt

Black pepper, to taste

YIELD: 8 SERVINGS / ⅓ CUP DRESSING

2 cups diced beets (about 1 medium), or 1 (15-ounce) can beets, drained and diced

2 cups sliced Roma tomatoes or grape tomatoes

2 oranges, peeled and segmented, or 1 (11-ounce) can mandarin oranges, drained

1 small red onion, thinly sliced

1 bunch red radishes, sliced

2 cups finely sliced radicchio or red cabbage

1 large head red leaf lettuce, torn

To make the dressing: Mix the honey into the vinegar in a small bowl and then add the rest of the ingredients.

If using fresh beets, microwave for 5 minutes and then peel and dice. Toss all of the salad ingredients with the dressing and serve immediately.

INDIAN-STYLE GARLIC BREAD

Masala Double Rotee   *dairy*

Our grandkids love garlic bread. You may buy the loaves already buttered and just put some spices between the pieces, or like me, you can make your own.

YIELD: 8 SERVINGS

1 stick (8 tablespoons) butter

3 cloves garlic, minced

1 teaspoon paprika

1 teaspoon ground cumin seeds

2 large loaves French or Italian bread

Preheat the oven to 300°F. In a small saucepan melt the butter and lightly fry the garlic in it. Add the paprika and cumin seeds. Cut the loaves of bread diagonally partially through into at least 1½-inch-thick slices, but do not slice all the way through to the bottom of the bread. Place the loaf of bread on a piece of aluminum foil big enough to cover the whole loaf. Bring up the sides of the aluminum foil. Brush inside each slice of the bread with the butter mixture and then cover the loaf completely with the aluminum foil. Heat in the oven for 10 minutes.

More than 1,000 years old! The crenulated walls and a gate leading into the fort in Bhatinda.

MANGO FUDGE

dairy

Amb Burfee

This recipe (and my method) is worth the price of this book! Just make it once, after having made burfee *the long, difficult (and prone to burning) way, and you will be thrilled with the ease of preparation. Pre-measure the nuts so they can be added quickly. Try to use whole milk powder; it tastes so much better. And if you like your* burfee *very sweet, like many Punjabis, add an additional* ⅓ *cup of sugar.*

Spray or grease an 8x8-inch glass baking pan and set aside. Place the sugar, mango pulp, cream, *ghee*, and milk powder in a 2-quart microwavable (preferably glass) casserole or bowl. Heat on high for 1 minute and then stir well. Continue heating for 4 more minutes, stirring halfway through the cooking time.

Remove the mixture from the microwave. Add the ¼ cup pistachios. Make sure they are very thoroughly mixed in. Turn the mixture out into the greased baking pan, and pat it smooth. Cool in the refrigerator for at least two hours.

Before serving, touch with edible silver foil. Cut five lines each way so you have 25 squares. Or, if you wish, make 25 little balls, flatten slightly and press a whole pistachio in the center. Store in the refrigerator.

YIELD: 25 PIECES

⅔ cup sugar

1 cup canned, sweetened mango pulp (Ratna® brand, if possible)

⅔ cup heavy cream

⅓ cup *ghee*, softened

4¾ cups whole (*mava*) or skim milk powder, lumps crushed*

¼ cup chopped, unsalted pistachios, plus more for garnish (*optional*)

Edible silver foil (*optional*)

* I use an entire 14-ounce bag of Deep® Pure Milk-*Mava* Powder.

VEGETARIAN HEAVEN

The touching story of *Bebeji's* passing

CERTAINLY COOKING IS AN ART MORE EPHEMERAL THAN PAINTING, EVEN THOUGH some meals are as colorful and well-composed as a Matisse. No matter how many hours of creative labor are lavished on a flavorful meal, it is eaten—literally destroyed in the end. So a meditation on the impermanence of all things material is the special privilege of the cook. There is no need for the spiritual student to sit at the feet of a Buddhist monk who makes the intricate designs in sand only to sweep them away, nor a need to sit all night at the cremation grounds. Prepare a wonderful dinner; listen to the sizzle of the onions in the pan; sit and savor the aroma, the colors, flavors, and textures. A meal is to be enjoyed by all the senses and then transformed into our own body and blood, a miracle, really.

What does survive? Is it the experience of planning and preparation? Is it the memory of the sensations? Can we use the whole process of eating as a lesson in the real work of transformation from the mundane to the spiritual? These were some of the questions that I would ponder as my mother-in-law and I worked side by side in the kitchen. She was larger than life—a character who etched herself in memory. Actually it was she who could recall in great detail all of the information about any person in the family or circle of friends. She loved to talk because she spent so many years in silence. She filled the house with her presence. And it felt totally empty when she left.

Where does an immensely powerful figure go? One minute here and the next? *Bebeji* and I talked of the end several times during the last year of her life. In her twenties, she had had a terrible bout of pleurisy. She remembered being so ill that she saw the *Panj Pyare*, five Sikhs dressed in white with blue turbans who

The serene *gurudwara* at Kiratpur, near where Bebeji's ashes were strewn in the river.

A solemn procession of village women.

212

came for her with a *rath,* a chariot. She refused to go with them because she had a young son who needed her. She laughed when I said that because we're in the U.S., next time they will come in a pink Cadillac!

Bebeji had soldiered on with partially calcified lungs for years. When tethered to an oxygen machine, she began to slow down. My study of past-life regression with the great Roger Woolger, and of the Tibetan Book of the Dead taught me that we need to keep the mind and emotions steady and fixed on God at the end. Of course the Sikh gurus said the same, to remember God through the mantra *Waheguru!,* How great God is!. "When the time comes, *Bebeji,* look for the light," I told her, "and don't look back." She didn't respond then, but weeks later I overheard her talking to one of her friends, "I'm not going to try to see what everyone does after I've died, I'm going to go straight into the light!"

There was no doubt in my mind that she did. For as her niece Raj, who came all the way from California, Auntie Surindera, and I sang *Jaap Sahib—God has no country, no color, no caste—*at the top of our lungs around her bed, *Bebeji* left this world. It was incredible, but I definitely felt an energy, like electricity, go spiraling through my body. Could it have been her soul?

Unbeknownst to me, *Bebeji* had instructed Mohinder Bhan, her faithful relative, to remove the oxygen just before she passed. Her nephew Avi, the physician who pronounced her, was there all the way from Colorado. Our daughter Raji bathed her body, while Auntie dressed her in the white suit she had sewn for herself and had set aside for this occasion years before in a place known only to Auntie. Her feet were then covered in her husband's socks, saved since his death in 1951. Everyone played the part *Bebeji* had assigned. She was in charge even after her death. It should not have come as a surprise when her niece, Satinder, phoned to say that *Bebeji* wanted her ashes to be strewn at Kiratpur in the headwaters of the Sutlej River, near the Himalayas. She had never mentioned that to us. We made the pilgrimage in December of 1995. What does survive, indeed!

The "Vegetarian Heaven" Menu

Years ago the only foods a vegetarian could expect in a restaurant were a grilled cheese sandwich and house salad. Nowadays, the variety of ethnic foods found all over this country have made it easier to find a tasty vegetarian or vegan meal when ordering out.

Teenagers are much more conscious of what they eat for a variety of reasons. While only 2 to 3 percent of adults are vegetarian in the U.S., a Harris Poll found that 10 percent of girls 13 to 18 are vegetarians. Thirty percent of college students polled by Aramark, the catering company, said that it was very important for them to have vegetarian choices in the cafeteria.

Call me biased, but Punjabi vegetarian food is so tasty and healthfully balanced with protein that very few would miss the meat. The enticing dishes in this menu will make you and your guests converts!

Appetizer:	*ALOO TIKEE* Potato Patties
	IMLEE CHUTNEY Tamarind Date Chutney
Main Course:	*PAALAK PANEER* Spinach with Cheese
	CHANA DAAL KUDOO Yellow Chickpea Lentils with Long Squash
	LUSSON ROTEE Broiled Whole-Wheat Breads with Garlic
Dessert:	*SOOJEE PRASHAAD* Semolina Halva with Nuts and Raisins

- **One Week or More Prior:** Read the recipes from beginning to end. Purchase the *kudoo* (squash) and other food you need from the Indian market. Cut and fry the *paneer* and freeze it.

  Make the *imlee* chutney and refrigerate it. Peel and cut the *kudoo*. Blanch the pieces in boiling water for 10 seconds. Plunge in ice water, drain, and spread in a single layer to freeze. Bag and store in the freezer. (No need to do this if using a very fresh squash within the week of serving it.)

- **Two Days Prior:** Make the *prashaad*. Refrigerate.

- **One Day Prior:** Thaw the *kudoo* (squash). Make the *chana daal* and refrigerate.

  Make the dough for the *rotee* and refrigerate.

- **The Day of:**

  AM: Cook the potatoes for the *tikee*. Make the spinach and cheese dish. Measure the spices for the *tikee*, and then chop the onions and ginger and thaw the peas.

  PM: Make the *tikees*. Bring the chutney and *prashaad* to room temperature. Clean up.

- **At Serving Time:** Serve the *tikees* and the chutney. Warm the spinach and the lentil dishes. At dinnertime, call the whole family together to make the *rotee*.

POTATO PATTIES

Aloo Tikee   *vegan*

The woman who has had the greatest influence on me besides Bebeji *is her sister-in-law, Auntie Surindera. We followed her to New Jersey where Auntie taught me the recipe for these patties, a healthier alternative to deep-fried pakoras or samosas. They are so good that one of my students will not come to a cooking class unless I make them part of the menu!*

8 medium Yukon Gold potatoes

½ medium onion, finely chopped

2 teaspoons grated ginger

2 teaspoons salt

2 teaspoons lemon juice

2 tablespoons finely sliced cilantro

1 tablespoon coriander seeds

1 rounded teaspoon whole cumin seeds

½ teaspoon ground cayenne pepper, or to taste

2 teaspoons ground dried pomegranate seeds, or 1 more teaspoon lemon juice

½ teaspoon garam masala (*optional*)

½ cup frozen green peas, thawed, cooked slightly, and well-drained

1 cup Bisquick ™ or all-purpose flour

½ cup unsweetened dried coconut (*optional*)*

In a large pot, boil the potatoes in their skins in water to cover until barely tender. Cool, peel, and mash. Add the onion, ginger, salt, lemon juice, and cilantro.

Lightly toast the coriander and cumin seeds in a dry pan. Grind in a clean coffee or spice grinder. Add to the potatoes along with the rest of the spices. Mix lightly but thoroughly, preferably with your hands so as not to crush the ingredients.

Add the peas, mixing them in uniformly with your hands.

Preheat a non-stick griddle to 400°F or a pan until very hot. Take a ball of potato mixture, flatten it in a small dish of Bisquick® or flour, coating it on both sides and making a 3-inch disk about ¾-inch thick. Make as many patties as will fit on the griddle without crowding.

Oil or spray the griddle or pan. Fry the patties for 3 minutes or until brown and crisp on the bottom. Just before turning, brush or spray the patties with oil. Turn and fry for 2 more minutes until uniformly brown. Re-oil the griddle with each new batch. Serve patties hot with Tamarind Date Chutney *(page 215)* or ketchup.

---

*The water content of potatoes varies. If your first patty does not hold together, mix the dried, grated coconut into the remainder of the potatoes and allow to rest for 15 minutes before making the rest of the patties.

TAMARIND DATE CHUTNEY

vegan   Imlee Chutney

Although there are decent chutneys now available in the refrigerated section of Indian markets, nothing beats homemade taste. Unrefined sugar is much more flavorful than the processed stuff that is labeled brown sugar in the U.S. It is called jaggery *in Hindi,* gurd *in Punjabi and I use it in all my recipes that call for brown sugar.*

Grind the dates in the food processor with a tablespoon of water to make a smooth paste. Heat the dates, ginger, and *gurd* in a saucepan with 1½ cups water. Boil, stirring occasionally, until thick and syrupy. This will take 5 to 15 minutes depending on the dryness of the dates.

Add the spices, salt, and tamarind, stirring until the tamarind is hot. Remove from the heat and add the lemon juice. Add the sugar in increments, stirring thoroughly until dissolved after each addition and then tasting for sweetness. Cool and refrigerate. More water may be added if a thinner preparation is required.

YIELD: 2 CUPS

½ cup (about 6) pitted dates, stems removed and cut into chunks

1 tablespoon grated ginger

½ cup unrefined sugar (*gurd*) or dark brown sugar

¼ teaspoon garam masala or ground cumin seeds

½ teaspoon ground cayenne pepper (*optional*)

½ teaspoon salt

½ cup Tamcon® brand tamarind concentrate, or 1 (14-ounce) jar Laxmi® brand tamarind concentrate*

1 tablespoon lemon juice

5 tablespoons sugar, or more to taste

*See *imlee* in the food glossary.

SPINACH WITH CHEESE

Paalak Paneer   *dairy*

Luscious paalak paneer, an all-time Punjabi favorite.

My all-time favorite vegetarian dish, and I am not alone! This recipe from Bebeji's hands to yours is luscious and lightly spiced. Some Punjabi cooks don't use tomato or cumin in a variation of this recipe and they purée the spinach before adding the cheese, but we love it this way, making it taste very different from saag (page 52). Add cayenne pepper to taste if you wish a hotter product. Suit yourself!

YIELD: 10 SERVINGS (6 CUPS)

- 4 cups (32 ounces) ricotta cheese or freshly drained curds
- 3 tablespoons vegetable oil plus more for frying
- 1 large onion, finely chopped
- 2 or 3 cloves garlic, minced
- 2-inch piece ginger, minced
- 1 rounded teaspoon ground turmeric
- 1 teaspoon whole or ground cumin seeds
- 1 teaspoon crushed or ground coriander seeds
- 2 teaspoons salt, or more to taste
- 1 (6- to 8-inch) green chile pepper, seeded and minced
- 1 teaspoon dried fenugreek leaves (*methi*) or ½ teaspoon ground fenugreek seeds (*optional*)
- 1 large tomato, chopped (*optional*)

Shortcut: A 7-ounce package of *paneer* from the dairy case of your Indian market, cut into cubes and fried, can substitute for the homemade cheese and you can skip the first step of this recipe.

To make the *paneer* cheese**: Drain the ricotta in a colander lined with a cloth napkin for several hours in the sink. Cover a counter with a large piece of plastic wrap. Place several layers of folded newspaper on the plastic. On a large enough tea towel or cotton cheesecloth spread the ricotta 6x9x1 inch and smoothly fold the tea towel or cloth over it so as not to allow the cheese to escape or to make wrinkles in the cheese after pressing. Put several more layers of newspaper on top and then a cutting board on top of that. Put a heavy weight on top of the board (a pot filled with water works well) and press the cheese overnight. Cut the cheese into 1-inch squares. You may use as is, or fry the squares in batches in hot oil until lightly brown on all sides. Remove and drain on paper towels.

To make the vegetable: Heat a large wok and add the 3 tablespoons oil. Add the onion, garlic, and ginger and sauté until lightly brown. Add the spices and salt and cook for about 1 minute. Add one at a time the chile pepper, fenugreek, tomato, and tomato sauce, stir-frying for a few seconds after each addition. Cook over medium heat for a few minutes, until the oil rises to the surface, then add the spinach. Sauté for 2 or 3 minutes, then lower heat to simmer and cook, covered, for 30 minutes if using frozen spinach, 15 minutes if using fresh spinach. Stir occasionally, check for moisture, and add ½ cup water if needed.

Ten minutes before serving add the *paneer* and garam masala, carefully folding them into the spinach. Cover and cook over the lowest heat. Top each serving with a little melted *ghee* if desired.

1 (15-ounce) can tomato sauce (*optional*)

1 (1 pound, 8 ounce) package frozen chopped spinach, thawed, or 30-ounce fresh spinach*

1 teaspoon garam masala

3 tablespoons *ghee*, melted (*optional*)

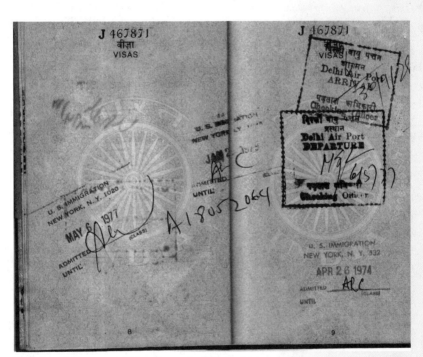

No one would have guessed from her earlier, veiled existence—Bebeji's well-traveled passport.

* If using fresh spinach, soak, rinse, drain, remove all tough stems and tear into smaller pieces. Put into a large container in the microwave and heat on high until wilted down enough to add to the sauté pan or wok.

** *Paneer*, the most common Indian form of cheese, may be made ahead and frozen; so to save time (and oil) I always make two or three times the recipe. Soak about 2½ cups frozen, fried *paneer* in warm water and drain before using it in this recipe.

YELLOW CHICKPEA LENTILS
WITH LONG SQUASH

Chana Daal Kudoo   *vegan*

Bebeji *taught me to make this very popular combination from Punjab, also known as* "tardka daal" *when made minus the squash.* Chana daal *is very high in protein and is great for those who favor carb-reducing diets. Did I mention it is full of flavor?*

YIELD: 8 ½-CUP SERVINGS

1¼ cups *chana daal* (yellow hulled chickpea lentils), picked over and rinsed well

4 to 5 cups cold water

1 teaspoon ground turmeric

2 teaspoons salt, or to taste

2 to 4 small red chile peppers (*optional*)

2 cups (approximately 1 pound) kudoo* (light green squash), peeled and chopped into 1½-inch dice

For the *tardka*:

3 tablespoons vegetable oil,

1 medium onion, chopped

2 cloves garlic, minced

2-inch piece ginger, minced

Pinch of toasted cumin seeds (*optional*)

1 small tomato, chopped (*optional*)

1 green chile pepper, seeded and chopped

½ teaspoon garam masala (*optional*)

Put the *chana daal* and water in a large pot. Bring to a rolling boil and skim the foam and discard. Add the turmeric, salt, and chile peppers. Cover and cook over medium-low heat for 15 minutes. Add squash and continue to cook for 45 more minutes, stirring occasionally.

To make the *tardka*: Heat a medium pot and add the oil. Add the onion and sauté until transparent. Add the garlic, ginger, and cumin, and stir-fry until the onions are lightly browned. Add the tomato and some chopped green chili pepper and fry for two or three more minutes.

Pour the *daal* mixture into a serving dish and top with the *tardka*. Stir. Sprinkle with garam masala and serve.

---

*Kudoo is also called *dudhi*. Use bottle squash or zucchini if this light green squash is not available.

BROILED WHOLE-WHEAT BREADS WITH GARLIC

dairy   Lusson Rotee

This is a nutritious bread with lots of flavor. Resting the dough several times in the process helps the gluten to relax and makes it easier to roll into a large bread. If you can make it on the outdoor grill, it's even better!

In a small bowl, dissolve the yeast and sugar in the 2 tablespoons warm water. Set aside until foamy.

In a medium bowl, whisk the ¾ cup warm water, yogurt, and salt. In a large bowl, whisk the two flours and baking powder. Make a well in the center of the flour and pour in both the yeast and yogurt mixtures. Stir with a wooden spoon or dough hook until thoroughly mixed.

Grease your hand and begin to knead the dough until it is elastic and leaves your hand and the bowl. Knead in earnest for at least six more minutes. Oil the ball of dough and cover the bowl with a tea towel. Leave it in a warm place for two hours or until the dough has doubled in size. This will depend on the warmth of the room.

In a small pan, sauté the garlic in two tablespoons of the *ghee* until it just begins to brown. Set aside.

Divide the dough into nine equal, smooth balls. Let the balls rest while you begin heating one or more iron griddles, the charcoal or gas grill, or a heavy skillet over medium-high heat. Flatten a ball between your palms and then pat it and stretch it to 7 inches in diameter. Cover with a damp tea towel and let it rest for five minutes while you flatten another round. Stretch them again, if needed. Slap onto the hot griddle, grill, or skillet and cook one side for about a minute or until little "hills" begin to form on the uncooked side. Flip and bake the other side for 2 minutes. Flip again and cook for 2 more minutes. Repeat if the bread is not quite done or if you like it more browned. Place on a rack and brush with the melted *ghee* with garlic.

Roll out two more breads and cover while the first two are being grilled. Repeat until all are grilled. They may be served immediately or kept warm for a few minutes wrapped in a tea towel.

YIELD: 9 7-INCH BREADS

1 packet active dry yeast

1 tablespoon sugar

2 tablespoons plus ¾ cup warm water

½ cup plain yogurt

2 teaspoons salt

2 cups all-purpose flour

2 cups whole-wheat flour (not *chapatti* flour)

½ teaspoon baking powder

3 tablespoons minced garlic

3 tablespoons melted *ghee*

SEMOLINA HALVA WITH NUTS AND RAISINS

Soojee Prashaad   *dairy*

A plate of *Soojee Prashaad.*

Our grandchildren, Natasha Kaur, Jessica Kaur, Sophia Kaur, and Samantha Kaur, love to make prashaad *with me early Sunday morning after a sleepover. We then go to our prayer room upstairs and the girls help Grandpa say the prayers. Soon the twin boys, Ethan Singh and Jacob Singh, will be able to join them.*

Beloved of children everywhere in India, prashaad *means "God's grace." When it is prepared while singing or reciting hymns by someone who has bathed, covered his or her head, and removed their shoes, it becomes sacred, or* kraa prashaad. *This is the holy "communion" of the Sikhs, distributed to each participant regardless of religious affiliation.*

YIELD: 10 TO 12 ½-CUP SERVINGS

1 stick (8 tablespoons) unsalted butter

1 cup farina/semolina (Regular, not instant Cream of Wheat ™ is fine.)

5 cups boiling water

1 cup sugar

¼ teaspoon ground cardamom seeds (*optional*)

½ cup golden raisins (*optional*)

½ cup almonds or pistachios, chopped (*optional*)

Melt the butter in a large, heavy-bottomed pot over medium heat. Be careful not to burn it. Add the semolina and keep stirring and scraping (a flat wooden spatula or wide wooden spoon is best) until the semolina is uniformly medium brown. Stand back to avoid being splashed as you carefully add the boiling water, two cups at a time, stirring until almost all the water is absorbed and the halva is thick after each addition. Add the sugar with the last cup of water, the cardamom, and raisins. Stir and scrape vigorously until the spoon can make a path at the bottom of the pot. Stir in most of the nuts, if using. Turn the halva into a pretty bowl and sprinkle with the remaining nuts. Serve hot or warm.

Note: You will need to devote approximately 40 minutes to making this dish. Have all the ingredients measured before you begin. At each stage it is important to scrape the halva constantly off the entire bottom of the pan to avoid burning. It need not be prepared in a religious manner, although prayers from any tradition will be just as efficacious.

GLOSSARY OF PUNJABI FOOD TERMINOLOGY

Please note: The first word is a Punjabi transliteration, the second an English translation.

Adrak **/ Ginger root:** A rhizome, not a root, fresh ginger is one of the "trinity" of aromatics used in Punjabi cooking. The others are onions and garlic. Try to find a smoothed skinned, fresh piece. If grating it, notch the place you wish to stop, peel it to that spot and then grate, holding the entire knob in your hand. The peels may be put into a pot of tea, but some cooks scrape the peel off using the side of a spoon. Store ginger, unwrapped, in the refrigerator. Ginger is warming, and has many health benefits including anti-inflammatory, and anti-nausea properties. (*See also Sont /* Dried ground ginger)

Ajwain **/ Carom seed:** These seeds look a little like slightly fatter caraway seeds but taste more like thyme, adding flavor to all kinds of fried snacks and savory dishes and helping to digest them as well. Like caraway, they have a strong flavor that is not appreciated by everyone on first go. Our daughters drank *ajwain* tea to relieve gastric problems during pregnancy and to relieve colic in their breast-fed babies—by boiling the seeds in water, straining, and drinking with a little lemon and sugar.

Amchoor **/ Green mango powder:** The most important method used to give a sweet/sour taste to Punjabi food is adding *amchoor*. Green or unripe mango slices are dried and usually ground into a powder, although sometimes used whole in stews. Substitute with lemon juice in a pinch. *Amchoor* can be bought at Indian markets.

Anardhana **/ Pomegranate seeds:** An important way to add sweet/sour flavor to Indian food, especially in Punjab. They are usually dried and ground at home but you can also buy a packet already ground. Pay attention to the manufacturing date as you would with all pre-ground spice mixtures. Sieve and discard the larger (white) pieces.

Ayurveda **/ ancient Hindu science of medicine:** Food is respected in India. "*Annam Brahmin*— Food is god." Like God, food sustains us and can heal us. The tastes of bitter, sweet, hot, cool, and salty are important to balance the three temperaments—wind, fire, and earth, and should be present in each meal. (Sweet does not mean sugar, however. Lentils and milk are "sweet.") Each spice has medicinal as well as balancing and, of course, flavoring qualities.

Besan **/ Chickpea flour:** A flour made from ground, hulled chickpeas and used to make fried snacks like *pakoras,* or in a batter to fry fish or vegetables. It can also be mixed with other flour to make a substantial bread. It is pale gold in color and has more protein than wheat flour and is gluten free.

Chaat masala **/ Spice mixture for salads and kebabs:** This spice mixture has a little *amchoor*, a little salt, a little pepper, spices like cumin and always a little *kala namak* or black salt. Used on yogurt and fruit salads as well as on grilled meats, it has a spicy and slightly funky taste that is a signature flavor. (See recipe on page 5.)

Chawal da Atta **/ Rice flour:** This flour is ground from rice. Use it one part rice flour to four parts chickpea flour or all-purpose flour to add crispness to batter for fried foods.

Daal **/ Legumes/Beans:** The main source of protein in much of India. There are more than 60 varieties of beans and lentils that are found in the stores whole or hulled/split/washed (without seed coat), which makes a tremendous difference in the texture of a dish. Those with their hulls tend to need more water and cooking time and are firmer when cooked. Hulled lentils cook up "mushier," are good to thicken soup but unsuitable for lentil salads. Hulled lentils are also ground into flour, the most popular being chickpea flour (*besan*). *Chana daal* is a small chickpea and is yellow inside without its seed coat. The seed coat may be green if fresh, or very dark brown if dried. *Mahan dee daal* or *urad daal* is white on the inside and has a black seed coat. *Masoor daal* is the familiar flat brown lentil found in most grocery stores. Without its seed coat it is a vivid orangy pink, but Americans call them "red." *Moong daal* has a green seed coat and is yellow inside. It is fairly easy to distinguish washed *moong daal* from washed *chana daal* because *moong daal* is smaller and not as round. (See color photo insert.)

Dalcheenee / Cinnamon: The bark of the cassia tree is most often used in the west for sweets, but in Punjab it is only used to flavor savory dishes and ground into garam masala. I buy the sticks and grind them myself—much better aroma and flavor. Oil of cinnamon has been proven to kill all bacteria.

Dhania / Cilantro: The leaves of the coriander plant used extensively in Indian, Chinese, and Mexican food for flavor, and especially as a fresh garnish.

Dhania / Coriander seed: One of the "trinity" of spices used in almost all Punjabi food. It is a round, striated, brown crunchy seed that has a lemony flavor. Ground or crushed, it is especially useful to thicken wet curries. It is also used in the European tradition in pickling spice and to coat pastrami.

Garam masala: A mixture of ground spices used to bring aroma to a finished dish. These spices are supposed to bring heat to the body in Ayurvedic principles, therefore the name "*garam*" which means "heat" or "hot." If you toast and grind the spices yourself, you will notice a difference in the aroma. (See page 4 for the recipe.) You can also buy it ready-made at Indian markets.

Ghee / Clarified butter: Unsalted butter that has been slowly heated and strained of foam and milk solids. It is very valuable in India and is considered a panacea against an array of illnesses. (See page 7 for the recipe.)

Gulaab dee Arak / Rose flavor extract: An important flavoring for sweets and Moghul-inspired savory dishes. Only a few drops are usually needed.

Gurd / Brown sugar: Also called *jaggery* in Hindi, this sugar is made by boiling away the water in raw sugar cane juice, much like maple sugar is made. It is found in huge rock-like pieces, in large lumps, or in a more granulated form. The darker the color, the stronger the flavor. If it gets too dry to cut into pieces, put it into the microwave next to a small bowl of water and heat on half power for a minute. The brown sugar we get in the West—white sugar with some molasses added—is only an imitation of *gurd*.

Haldi / Turmeric: Another of the "trinity" of spices used in Punjabi cooking, mainly in its dry, powdered form. It has bright, yellow-orange color and is a rhizome of the ginger family, only smaller. Considered an antiseptic since Ayurvedic times, turmeric's active ingredient is curcumin, which recently has been shown to ease inflammation and may also prevent Alzheimer's disease.

Halva / Candy-like or thick "pudding": Several kinds of thick, cooked pudding-like desserts that can be made of many things, from wheat or seeds to root vegetables like carrots. Many times they contain nuts as well.

Harian Mirchan / Chile peppers: There are so many varieties of chile peppers available, but the ones most often used in Punjabi cooking are the long, green ones. The tip is usually less hot than the stem end, so take a little sample from each before deciding how much to use. The seeds and white "pith" running along the inside are even hotter. Be careful when discarding them—don't touch your eyes until you have thoroughly washed your hands with soap. I use "chile pepper" to denote a fresh, hot or mild pepper—your choice.

Hing / Asafoetida: A sulfurous, fetid smelling resin from a plant related to fennel. It is ground to a powder and used in savory dishes, many times to replace onion and garlic thought to have negative energies in Jain, Kashmiri Brahmin, and Taoist food culture. Warmed in oil, it has an onion flavor.

Ilaichi / Cardamom: This includes two important, but very different spices that are found in pods. The more familiar **green cardamom** is used in garam masala and savory dishes, but especially to flavor sweets and sweet dishes. Then there is the less familiar but larger pod of **black cardamom** (*buddi ilaichi*), used in only savory dishes and also in garam masala. It has a eucalyptus-like yet smoky scent.

Imlee (Imli) / Tamarind: Inside the long, locust bean-like pod is the brown, sweet-sour fruit. The process of obtaining the fruit is rather labor intensive, since the "bean" covering is paper-thin and the fruit is very sticky. You may purchase tamarind fresh or in a block form (which must be soaked in boiling water and strained) or in a jar of concentrate. There are dark, intensely flavored ones and lighter, fruitier types.

Kachri: A small pale fruit that dries into a papery, roundish husk, that when ground, adds body and a sweet-sour flavor, slightly more sweet and fragrant than dried green mango *(amchoor)* which could be used to replace it.

Kala namak / **Black salt:** A sulphurous mineral that comes in large, light purple-gray crystals that can be broken and then ground in a spice grinder. Or it can be found already ground. It is essential in all kinds of Indian salads and snacks called *chaats*.

Kari patta / **Curry leaves:** These can now be found in most produce sections of Indian markets in small packets. Attached to their stems, the leaves look much like small bay leaves. They are used mainly in South Indian dishes. They are usually lightly fried in oil or *ghee* and poured over a dish to impart a curry powder flavor to dishes after they have been cooked. Like bay leaves, they are not eaten.

Kesar / **Saffron:** The stigmas of a crocus, whole saffron threads, when lightly toasted and then crumbled and soaked in a little water or milk, produce a lovely yellow color and special aroma that makes the high price of this spice well worth it. It is the color of spirituality and is one of the colors of the Indian flag.

Kewrda / **Screw pine:** This is a heady, flowery scent that is used to flavor sweets and dishes of the Moghul lineage, like rich *biriyanis* or *roghani rotee*.

Khus khus / **White poppy seeds:** Punjabis never use black poppy seeds. The white seeds are ground into a paste and used to thicken meat preparations and sweet drinks.

Lal mirch / **Cayenne pepper:** A type of red chile pepper, it is usually used dried and ground. It is said to improve heart health and actually aid digestion. Capsaicin, the active ingredient that makes it hot, is soluble in fat, not water. So drink whole milk or yogurt to cool your mouth, not water.

Llong / **Cloves:** This dried bud adds an intense flavor to sweets in the west and savory dishes in Punjab and is used whole or ground. It is used sparingly in garam masala as well. Oil of clove will kill all known bacteria. No wonder it is used on an aching tooth!

Lussee or *Lassi* / **Milk-based drink:** A drink made with cold water mixed with buttermilk, yogurt, or milk. It may be sweet or savory.

Lusson / **Garlic:** Another of the "trinity" of aromatics found in Punjabi food. I like to use fresh garlic, but I know many cooks who use the jarred.

Magaz / **Melon seeds:** Small, flat and white, they are ground and used in drinks and to thicken sauces. You may substitute with pine nuts.

Methi / **Fenugreek:** This herb comes in three very different forms. The fresh dark green small leaves look something like large clover leaves. They are quite bitter and have been found to fight insulin resistance. The dried leaves are pungent and only a few pinches will flavor a curry. The seeds are squarish, yellow-orange, and have a butterscotchy aroma.

Papard or *Papadums* / **Lentil wafers:** Large or small wafer-like dry breads made of lentils, these can be plain or flavored with cumin seed, red or black pepper, or garlic. Purchase them from any Indian market. They are a great accompaniment to drinks or to rice. (See recipe on page 16.)

Rai / **Mustard seed:** Punjabis use the dark brown or black seed that has a little more flavor than the yellow seed. It is usually sautéed in hot oil until it "pops," most often as a first step in Punjabi recipes or a last step in South Indian recipes.

Sarson da tail / **Mustard oil:** There are three major uses for mustard oil in Punjab. One is for making pickles and, less often, for frying fish. The most common use is for a rub-down on the skin before bathing. So please check whether the mustard oil you buy is **edible**, because most are not! It has a strong flavor, so you may be wise to mix it with canola oil or try the mustard-flavored oils.

Saunf / **Fennel seed:** Used as a mouth freshener, digestif, and spice.

Sont / **Dried ground ginger:** This form of ginger is readily found in supermarkets in the U.S. It can be used to make a sweet chutney or sprinkled in a cup of *chai* or tea. It has been found to relieve seasickness better than prescriptions or placebos. (*See also Adrak* / Ginger root)

Sooji / **Farina** *or* **Semolina:** The coarser version of the familiar Cream of Wheat® cereal. It is used in halva as well as to give fried foods some crunch. In South India it is also made into a crepe-like savory pancake called a *ravi dosa,* as well as a savory pilaf-like preparation called *upma.*

Sowa / **Dill:** Seldom used in Punjabi cooking, but this herb may be found near the *cilantro* in the market and has a slightly sour/grassy flavor.

Tardka / **Finishing method:** Onions, garlic, ginger, and spices are fried in oil and then poured over a dish that has been boiling or simmering for additional flavor.

Tava / **Cast-iron griddle:** This is the slightly curved pan used for making breads. They come in many sizes. The huge ones used over open fires in the villages are called *lohs.* I use a Lodge™ cast-iron griddle with cast-iron handle made in the U.S., since it can be put in the oven or under the broiler as well.

Tej putter or *Patta* / **Bay leaf:** This leaf can be found dry or fresh in most supermarkets. It is used sparingly in curries and in garam masala. It is sometimes confused with the cassia leaf used more in South Indian cooking.

Zeera / **Cumin seeds:** Another of the "trinity" of spices used in Punjabi cooking (along with turmeric and coriander seeds). Actually there are two types. The first is the common white *zeera* that looks like caraway seed. The other is the black or *shah zeera* that is smaller, finer, and black in color. It has a smokier, more pungent flavor, and is more expensive.

GLOSSARY OF RELIGIOUS TERMINOLOGY

Akhand Paath: A continuous reading of the Sikh scriptures, the *Guru Granth Sahib*, over a forty-eight-hour period. The readings are usually done in two-hour relays by knowledgeable Sikhs who could be male or female, young or old. Others take turns day and night to listen. The host provides continuous food in the form of vegetarian meals, tea, and snacks for the readers and for the listeners. It usually culminates in a large gathering of friends and family.

Bhajan: Sacred hymns sung by both Hindus and Sikhs, usually accompanied by music on harmonium, sitar, flute, and/or the *tabla*, a small drum.

Gianni: Literally "knowledgeable one." In the past, one who had attained a certain level of interior knowledge of other spiritual planes. Now, a title for someone who has knowledge of Sikh scriptures and can lead a congregation.

Gurudwara / Sikh Temple: Literally "God's Door," the *gurudwara* is traditionally open in the four directions to symbolize that all people from all paths are welcome to worship God there. Sikhs believe that God is the same, though called by many different names in various religions, and that all people can find God. As a sign of respect before entering the main or *durbar* hall where the holy book is open, heads are covered and shoes removed.

Guru Granth Sahib: The book of inspired hymns of many saints of several castes including Muslims and Hindus as well as Sikhs. Unlike the Bible, it contains no history of a specific people or dogma, but is the songs of those in love with God.

Langar being distributed at the ashram founded by Yogi Bhajan in Espanola, New Mexico.

Langar: The free vegetarian meal that is eaten after a Sikh religious service anywhere, but especially in the temple called a *gurudwara*. It is distinguished from other meals eaten in India by the fact that all are welcome to eat together, no matter of what caste, religion, or social status. It is served by *sewadars* or volunteers to the people as they sit in rows on the floor. All eat the same food.

Namaaz/Azam: The call to prayer. In Islam, Muslims are required to kneel and pray facing the holy city of Mecca five times a day. The *muezzin* calls from the minaret high above the mosque in a plaintive reminder each time for those lucky enough to hear him.

Nitnem: The prayers that Sikhs recite every day that contain, in condensed form, an education in the spiritual life. Visit www.ranisrecipes.com and click on Nitnem and/or Links.

The holy book, the *Guru Granth Sahib*, is read at Dohdra on the anniversary of the founding of the Khalsa Brotherhood.

Panj Pyare: Refers to the five original men who offered their heads to the tenth teacher Guru Gobind Singh ji and who became the first baptized Sikhs, the order of the Khalsa. They were given a "uniform" of the five "k"s—to keep uncut hair (*kes*) with a comb (*kanga*) to keep it neat, to always cover themselves modestly with underwear (*kachera*), to wear a steel bracelet (*kada*), and to carry a short sword (*kirpan*) to defend the helpless.

Pir: Muslim saints. *Pirs* were revered by Hindus and Sikhs, as well as Muslims. For example, the *Pir*, Mian Mir, laid the foundation stone of the Golden Temple.

Pooja: The Hindu ritual of worship during which prayers, food, flowers, and incense are offered to the gods.

Qwallee: The ecstatic singing of hymns in the Sufi tradition, with accompanying music and rhythmic clapping that brings the singers and audience closer to God. It is a special form of religious music of the Punjabi Muslim community.

Sadh Sangat: The community that worships God together. Group prayer, and especially singing hymns in a group of like-minded souls, is said to be much more transformative than praying by oneself.

Sadharan Paath: A non-continuous reading of the *Guru Granth Sahib*. At the conclusion of the reading of the entire book, family and friends gather for a service.

Sewa: The act of helping the needy community, the poor, the sick, and the weak. It also includes serving, cooking, or cleaning with your own hands the *gurudwara* where one is most likely to find the *sadh sangat*. To wash or touch "the dust of the feet of the saints" is a privilege.

What will become sacred *prashaad* being made by our grandgirls Natasha (stirring), Grace, Sophia, Samantha, Lillie, Hannah, and Jessica Kaur.

Grandsons, twins Ethan and Jacob Singh, enjoy the sweet *kraa prashaad*.

"I have tasted all other flavors, but to my mind, the subtle Essence of the Lord is the sweetest of all!"

—*Guru Arjan Devji in the Guru Granth Sahib, page 100.*

ADDITIONAL READING

Books and Articles

"After Sixty Years, Will Pakistan Be Reborn?" by Mohsin Hamid, *New York Times* OP-ED (Aug. 15, 2007).

"Cooperation vs. Competition" by M.A. Nowak and K. Sigmund, *Financial Analysis* (vol. 56: 13-22, Jan. 2000).

"India's Internal Partition" by Ramachandra Guha, *New York Times* OP-ED (Aug. 15, 2007).

Sacred Nitnem translated by Harbans Singh Doabia: Singh Bros., Amritsar, 1976. The daily prayers of the Sikhs with humble and heartfelt commentary in the back. It has the *Gurmukhi* (Punjabi) script and a transliteration as well as English translation.

Sikhism: A Universal Message by Dr. Gurbakhsh Singh Gill, Sikh Study Circle DFW, Richardson, Texas, 1992.

South Asian Cooperation and the Role of the Punjabs by Trivadesh Singh Maini, Siddhartha Press, New Delhi, 2007.

The Bloodless Revolution: A Cultural History of Vegetarianism From 1600 to Modern Times by Tristram Stuart: W.W. Norton & Company, New York, 2007.

The Master Jewelers, edited by A. Kenneth Snowman: Thames and Hudson Ltd., London, 2002.

The Sikh Revolution by Jagjit Singh: Kendri Singh Sabha, New Delhi, 1984. A book about the new social and religious paradigm wrought by Sikhism in India.

Online Reading

www.harappa.com. An online resource for info on the ancient civilization of Punjab.

www.punjabonline.com/history. A resource for all things Punjabi, includes history.

www.Punjabilok.com. Punjabi culture, poetry, journalism.

www.sikhnet.com. The online network of Sikh Dharma International.

www.sikhtourism.com. Places of historical interest in India and Pakistan.

www.sikhitothemax.com. Read the entire Sikh scripture online in English, Gurmukhi (Punjabi), and in transliterated English.

Bhangra DVD

Dancing Bhangra with Ravi (Kaur Khalsa). Order online at HYPERLINK "http://www.sikhnet.com" www.sikhnet.com.

PURVEYORS OF INDIAN FOOD

There are now so many places all over the U.S. where one may purchase Indian food. I used several methods to find stores across the country but realized I would end up with a book of Indian grocers in addition to the cookbook.

If you are unsure of where to shop, there are several ways to find Indian grocery stores as well as Indian food shops. First, use the yellow pages of your phone book. If no grocers are listed, but a restaurant is, ask them where they shop.

If you have a computer or know someone who does, check out the following sources of information for your local area:

- www.local.com **type in Indian food or Indian grocer**
- www.sulekha.com **type in your city**
- www.thokalath.com **click on your state map and then Indian grocery store**
- Sometimes you are far from any sources. Then mail order may be the way to go.

Online Sources

Compare prices before you shop.

- www.indianfoodsco.com (To order 866-416-4165)
- www.kalustyans.com
- www.kamdarplaza.com
- www.patelbros.usa.com
- www.spicebarn.com

INDEX

PHOTO CREDITS

Photo Acknowledgements

Jacket: Tray from the "On the Farm" menu: Parmpal Singh Sidhu
Front Flap: *Samosas* with *masala cha* and *pudina chutney*: Parmpal Singh Sidhu
Back Flap: Author photo with permission of Gail J. Crafton of AC Photo Linwood, New Jersey
Back Jacket: Author at the Golden Temple, circa 1967: Parmpal Singh Sidhu

All black and white and color photos not specifically attributed below were taken by Parmpal Singh Sidhu or were the property of his mother, Jagdish Kaur Sidhu.

Other Photos, Courtesy of:

Sarah Bernstein and Eduardo Mencherini: pp. 3, 78.
Rajindra Kaur Brand: p. xvi on map—sign in Punjabi, Rock Garden of Chandigarh, rooftops and river. Also pp. 6, 25, 43, 86, 124,160, 167, 212 (*gurudwara*). Color – Snake Charmer With Mongoose, Village Girls and *Batna* Ceremony.
Victor Chen: p. 13.
Meghan Kaur Dhaliwal: pp. 2, 29, 36, 126, 141. Color – *Paraunthas* and Lotus Root.
Gurmeet Singh and Surinder Kaur Dhaliwal: pp.130, 135, 226 (upper).
Dr. Gurbakhsh Singh Gill: pp. xvi Map of The Land of Five Rivers from "Sikhism: A Universal Message," p. 68.
Jasbir Singh Kalouria: pp. xvi on map-princes, 68, 109, 132, 181 (both), 183.
Manjeet Kaur Tangri: p. 40. *sangeet*.
Navjot Singh Sandhu: p. 127.
Parvinder Singh of Sikhtourism.com: p. 179.

ALSO AVAILABLE FROM HIPPOCRENE . . .

The Kerala Kitchen
Lathika George

Since ancient times, seafarers and traders have been drawn by the lure of spices to Kerala, a verdant, tropical state on the Malabar Coast of South India. It is this legacy that *The Kerala Kitchen* brings us, through 150 delectable recipes and the unforgettable stories that accompany them. Featured here are such savory delights as *Meen Vevichathu* – fish curry cooked in a clay pot, *Parippu* – lentils with coconut milk, and *Thiyal* – shallots with tamarind and roasted coconut. Equally mouthwatering are an array of rice preparations and tempting desserts. Authentic and easy to prepare, these recipes are adapted for the American kitchen, and accompanied by a guide to spices, herbs, and equipment, as well as a glossary of food terms. Interwoven between these recipes, in the best tradition of the cookbook memoir, are tales of talking doves, toddy shops, traveling chefs, and killer coconuts. Full of beautiful photographs, charming illustrations, and lyrical memories of food and family.

238 pages • 16-page color photo insert • ISBN: 978-0-7818-1184-2 • $32.00 Hardcover

Healthy South Indian Cooking
Expanded Edition
Alamelu Vairavan and Dr. Patricia Marquardt

With the addition of fifty new easy-to-prepare dishes, *Healthy South Indian Cooking* is back, now totaling 250 recipes. In the famous Chettinad cooking tradition of southern India, these mostly vegetarian recipes allow home cooks to create such esoteric dishes as Potato-flled Dosas with Coconut Chutney; Pearl Onion and Tomato Sambhar; Chickpea and Bell Pepper Poriyal; and Eggplant Masala Curry. Rasams, breads, legumes and payasams are all featured here, as is the exceptional Chettinad Chicken Kolambu, South India's version of the popular vindaloo. Each of these low-fat, low-calorie recipes come with a complete nutritional analysis. Also included are sample menus and innovative suggestions for integrating South Indian dishes into traditional Western meals. A section on the varieties and methods of preparation for dals (a lentil dish that is a staple of this cuisine), a multilingual glossary of spices and ingredients, and 16 pages of color photographs make this book a clear and concise introduction to the healthy, delicious cooking of South India.

267 pages • 16 page color photo insert • ISBN: 0-7818-1189-9 • $32.00 Hardcover

Flavorful India
Priti Chitnis Gress

Located in northwestern India, Gujarat is known as the country's "Garden State," and is renowned for its vegetarian specialties. *Flavorful India* showcases the cuisine of Gujarat—from street foods like crunchy snack mix and vegetable fritters, to traditional home-cooked dishes that feature an abundance of locally available vegetables like okra, eggplant, bottle gourd, and many varieties of beans. Spicy dals, delicate flatbreads, and traditional sweets and beverages bring the Gujarati dining experience full circle. A chapter on the meat, poultry, and fish specialties that are enjoyed in the region is also included. This collection of authentic family recipes will introduce you to some of India's most flavorful, yet often overlooked, culinary offerings. The simple, delectable recipes are written for the home cook and adapted to the North American kitchen. An introduction to Gujarati culture, sections on spices, ingredients, and utensils, and charming line drawings by the author's father bring the flavors of India to life.

174 pages • ISBN: 0-7818-1207-0 • $14.95 Paperback

The Indian Spice Kitchen
Monisha Bharadwaj

A feast for the eyes as well as the mind, this is a comprehensive encyclopedia of the mouth-watering ingredients used in Indian cooking. The author shares the secrets of Indian cuisine and celebrates its variety and ingenuity. From asafetida to walnuts, each of 100 ingredients is explored giving useful advice about its appearance and taste, how it grows, how to store it and, of course, its culinary uses, complemented with over 200 classic Indian dishes.

240 pages • color photographs • ISBN: 0-7818-1143-0 • $29.50 Paperback

Taste of Nepal
Jyoti Pandey Pathak

Winner "Best Foreign Cuisine Cookbook": 2007 Gourmand World Cookbook Awards

One of the very few Nepali cookbooks on the market, *Taste of Nepal* is a thorough and comprehensive guide to this cuisine, featuring more than 350 authentic recipes, a section on well-known Nepali herbs and spices, menu planning, Nepalese kitchen equipment, and delightful illustrations. Instructions are clearly detailed and most ingredients are readily available in the United States. There is something for everyone in this book. For the most timid cook—Fried Rice (*Baasi-Bhaat Bhutuwa*) or Stir-Fried Chicken (*Kukhura Taareko*) are easily achievable. The adventurous home chef will be tempted to try Goat Curry (*Khasi-Boka ko Maasu*) and Sun-Dried Fish with Tomato Chutney (*Golbheda ra Sidra Maacha*).

470 pages • illustrated • ISBN: 0-7818-1121-X • $27.50 Hardcover

Exotic Tastes of Sri Lanka
Suharshini Seneviratne

The breathtaking island of Sri Lanka lies in the Indian Ocean, separated from southeastern India by a mere 30-mile chain of shoals. This proximity to India has had an inevitable effect on Sri Lanka's cuisine, as did the successive Portuguese, Dutch, and British occupations. However, over the centuries the majority of these dishes have been modified to suit the local palate. This book highlights the gamut of flavors of this cuisine, which runs from hot and spicy to comforting and mild.

288 pages • 9.5in x 6in • ISBN: 0-7818-0966-5 • $24.95 Hardcover

LANGUAGE:

Punjabi-English / English-Punjabi Dictionary
Dr. K. K. Goswami

This comprehensive bilingual dictionary has been compiled with the objective of facilitating communication between English and Punjabi speakers, and increasing the user's vocabulary in both languages. The dictionary includes over 25,000 total entries, providing multiple meanings, idiomatic usages, and colloquial expressions. Pronunciation is given in both languages, with phonetic transcription of Punjabi in roman script, and phonetic transliteration of English in Gurmukhi script.

• Over 25,000 entries
• Pronunciation for each entry
• Comprehensive translations
• Designed for both English and Punjabi speakers

782 pages • 7in x 4.5in • ISBN: 0-7818-0940-1 • $24.95 Paperback

HISTORY:

India: An Illustrated History
Prem Kishore and Anuradha Kishore Ganpati

India defies easy characterization and Indian history can be a lifelong study.ibrant history of India, with spirit and flavor intact. This volume succinctly recounts 4500 years of Indian history, from the earliest Indus valley settlements to the twentieth-century struggle against British imperial rule, and up to the challenges facing the country today. Sections on cultural traditions, regional cuisine, dress, and religion bring the varied facets of this nation to life.

234 pages • illustrations • ISBN: 0-7818-0944-4 • $14.95 Paperback

All prices are subject to change without prior notice. TO ORDER HIPPOCRENE TITLES: contact your local bookstore, call (718) 454-2366, visitwww.hippocrenebooks.com or write to: Hippocrene Books. 171 Madison Avenue. New York, NY 10016. Please enclose check or money order, adding $6.00 shipping (UPS) for the first book and $1.00 for each additional book.